What Is Mysticism?

Jon Mundy, Ph.D.

Listen, perhaps you catch a hint of
an ancient state not quite forgotten;
dim, perhaps and yet not altogether
unfamiliar, like a song whose name
is long forgotten, and the circumstances in
which you heard it completely unremembered.
Not the whole song has stayed with you,
but just a little wisp of melody attached not to
a person or a place or anything in particular.
But you remember, from just this little part,
how lovely was the song, how wonderful the setting
where you heard it, and how you loved those
who were there and listened with you.

A Course in Miracles

Royal Fireworks Press
Unionville, New York

Books and CDs by Jon Mundy, Ph.D.

— Books —

Missouri Mystic

Awaken to Your Own Call:

(A Comprehensive Introduction to *A Course in Miracles*)

Listening to Your Inner Guide

The Ten Laws of Happiness

For our Spanish Speaking Friends:

Descubriendo Un Curso de Milagros

(Discovering A Course in Miracles)

All books are available through

www.miraclesmagazine.org

www.rfwp.com

Amazon.com, Barnes & Nobles Stores

or BarnesandNobles.com

— CDs —

The Psychology and Metaphysics of A Course in Miracles

This is It: The Radically Simple Message of A Course in Miracles

Mysticism, Miracles and Metaphysics

(A five hour workshop)

Remembering to Laugh: The Healing Power of Humor

Including Standup Comedy with Dr. Baba Jon Mundane

The CDs are available only through:

www.miraclesmagazine.org

or tel: 845-496-9089

Thanks

I appreciate your feedback. Please visit www.miraclesmagazine.org.

Subject: Philosophy and Religion, the Psychology of Religion, Religious Studies, Spirituality, Inspiration, Mysticism

Published by:
Royal Fireworks Press
First Avenue, PO Box 700
Unionville, NY 10988-0399
(845) 726-4444
FAX: (845) 726-3824
email: mail@rfwp.com
website: rfwp.com

ISBN: 978-0-89824-677-3 Paperback

Printed and bound in the United States of America using vegetable-based inks on acid-free, recycled paper and environmentally-friendly cover coatings by the Royal Fireworks Printing Co. of Unionville, New York.

Section I — Introduction

What is Mysticism?

Acknowledgments

Thanks for opening this book. I hope you will read it through. The following individuals enrich my life and thus enrich this book.

My wife, Dolores, and daughter, Sarah, are the delights of my life. With these two beautiful women, I share my living, my learning, and my loving. My assistant, Fran Cosentino, helped in every stage of development. I am grateful for her editorial skills, diligence, and patience. I love people who love to edit, and that's Lynne Matous, Jean Weston, Judy Vaillancourt, Patrick Miller, Resta Burnham, Toni Creamer, Peggy Foster, and former assistant Irene Parcher. If you find any mistakes, it's not their fault!

Dedication—To My Teachers

It has been my good fortune to have worked and studied with several intriguing people. Thanks to Judith Skutch Whitson for her friendship of forty years and her husband, Wit, for their kind words and encouragement. For their ever-shining example, my thanks to Dr. Ken and Gloria Wapnick. Since 1975, Ken has consistently fostered my growth and understanding of *A Course in Miracles* by constantly challenging me to "take it deeper." I have not always followed his advice. Whenever I did, I discovered that he was right. Dr. Helen Schucman was my counselor for five years (1975–1980). I never paid her, and we did not have weekly sessions. She was, however, a wonderful guide and "mother hen," helping me sort through my feelings about the church and even that great enigma – women!

For their many writings and their inspiration, thanks to the mystics, masters, saints, and sages from all faiths and all ages. My thanks go out to the following teachers with whom I have had the good fortune to study. Each of them taught me something about mysticism. It is one thing to read someone's works; real learning occurs when we get to know the person.

Seminary

John B. Cobb, Jr., Ph.D. taught theology and Howard Clinebell, Ph.D. was my beloved professor of the psychology of religion when I did my masters.

Graduate School

Rev. John Johnson, Jr., Ph.D., an inspired man and Jungian analyst, was my doctoral supervisor. Hans Jonas, Ph.D., taught Gnosticism, and Aron Gurwitsch, Ph.D., and Hannah Arendt, Ph.D., taught phenomenology at the New School University in NYC. Joseph Campbell, Ph.D., taught hero mythology at the C.G. Jung Institute in NYC in 1973. It was my good fortune to be one of their students.

Extra Curricular

Rabbi Joseph Gelberman, Ph.D. (my spiritual father) and I met in 1972. We co-founded Interfaith Inc. in NYC in 1977 and The New Seminary in 1981.

Since 1972, Shanti Rica Josephs has been a spiritual companion and an ever-wise advisor.

Of the three "gurus" I spent time with in India, Osho was by far the funniest, intellectually the deepest, the most loving, and the easiest to get to know.

Stanley Kripner, Ph.D. did dream research in Brooklyn, NY, when I served a church there. We later traveled together to Prague, Moscow, and Leningrad looking into Russian parapsychological research.

I sponsored a retreat with John Lilly, M.D. in 1973 and he persuaded me to read Franklin Merrill-Wolff.

Thomas Hora, Ph.D. taught transpersonal psychology at Wainwright House in Rye, New York, during the late 1970's, and I was one of his students.

I studied Shamanism with Salvador Roquet, M.D. in Mexico and in New York from 1976–1979.

Itzak Bentov, Ph.D., author of *Stalking the Wild Pendulum*, led a workshop at my home in 1978. He died soon after in a fiery airplane crash.

Stan Grof, M.D. Ph.D's. books are fascinating. I sponsored workshops with Stan at Wainwright House in Rye, NY, and at my home in High Rock Spring.

Michael Harner, Ph.D. and I did a night-long shamanic workshop at High Rock Spring in 1978.

Rev. Diane Berke, Ph.D. and I co-founded Interfaith Fellowship in NYC in 1989.

Mehmet Oz, M.D., cardiothoracic surgeon in 1998 literally reached into my chest took my heart in his hands and helped heal it.

Robert Weltman, Ph.D., therapist and friend, has since the mid 1980s seen me through several difficult periods. I am very grateful.

Wayne Dyer, Ph.D., a lifetime subscriber to my little *Miracles* magazine, has endorsed two of my earlier books.

To You,

With Love,

Jon

I have no desire to work in a vacuum, and I appreciate your feedback.
You don't need to tell me about grammatical problems.
They are being sought out and corrected. On a substance level,
if there is any place you feel I've gone "off course," let me know.
If you know more about some particular area and feel it needs clarification—let me know.
Are there any redundancies? Anything I've left out?
Much of my learning comes from friends, so let me know! Thanks!
jon@miraclesmagazine.org.

Table of Contents

Section I — Introduction

Section II — The Nature of Reality

Section III — Six Great Illusions What is Metaphysics

Foreword
What is, *What is Mysticism?*

Although I do not possess a mystical consciousness,
there is something within me that responds
when I hear others talk about it.
William James, Ph.D.

Why pick up this book? Why read any further? Maybe you know something of the mystical. Maybe you have been there or are there. Maybe it's just a matter of remembering. Maybe you already know. Gurdjieff said it was important to have a sharply defined living question. We may think of this questioning as the development of a contemplative life that carries us ever deeper and more clearly to the truth. Everybody wants to know the truth.

What Is Mysticism? contains quotes from and/or stories about more than 200 different mystics. In most cases, the first time someone's idea is presented, that individual will be introduced along with a short bio. If a picture does not appear by a bio, I have not secured permission for its use. If a centered quotation appears with no name after it, it's from me.

The Most Romantic of Adventures

According to David Hay, author of *Something There: The Biology of the Human Spirit* (2006), the work of the Religious Experience Research Unit at Oxford University showed that in the years between 1990 and 2001, while churchgoing fell by 10 per cent, the number of people reporting mystical awareness increased by 60 percent. (See: www.religioustolerance.org) Something wonderful is happening! While freeing ourselves from traditional dogmas, we're opening ourselves to a more direct experience of God.

Evelyn Underhill spoke of mysticism as *the most romantic of adventures*. There is something so compelling about the mystical journey, something so unforgettable, that mystics often spend their lives clarifying the experience. The deeper they go, the lighter they become, the easier the peace. Inner light wants to shine. Vision wants to be shared. Talking about mysticism is like rolling strawberry shortcake around on the tongue. It's so delicious. It's like falling in love again and again. What is this wonderful experience people are talking about—to which we respond so deeply? *What Is Mysticism?* addresses and deepens this question.

Open at the Top

Ernest Holmes, the founder of Religious Science, said his philosophy was *open at the top*. He was always ready for clearer ways of seeing. Peter Abelard, a realist's mystic, said that whatever we know is only an approximation of reality. Every new observation brings us closer to reality. All of science is "provisional." That is, it changes when better solutions are found. I'm convinced that there is a truth which is unchanging. Like an airplane in the sky or a ship on the ocean, we must, however, continually adjust our setting ever more clearly toward that truth which brings us home. We are all looking for ever deeper clarity and contentment. *What Is Mysticism?* is not complete. It is however, a neo-genesis, and an introduction to mysticism. I'm circulating this first edition to get feedback and to make copies available for conferences, workshops and lectures, for subscribers to *Miracles* magazine, for study groups and folks in the New Thought Movement, Unity, Religious Science, Interfaith Churches, and more. While you're reading, I'm working on the next edition.

A good teacher clarifies his own ideas,
and strengthens them by teaching them.
A Course in Miracles

I would rather say that I am not enlightened and be wrong about that than to say that I am enlightened and to be wrong about that. Claiming enlightenment is a bit like skating on thin ice. Like a lot of folks, I have had the opportunity of seeing through "some" of the clouds. Like everyone on this planet, I'm still working my way home. I am now and have since the early 1960s been a student/teacher. Beyond that I make no claims.

A joy shared is a joy doubled.
Mark Twain (p. 162)

Some authors remain rather anonymously and/or authoritatively in the background. A journey is more interesting when it is shared, so I'm tagging along. When appropriate, I'll talk about personal experiences: how and why a particular mystic seems important, some insights, and some "fumbles" I've made along the way. I'll be pointing out some of the best sights on the mystical path and suggesting some silly games we might like to avoid. We're going on a seekers' journey. We're going to jump off a cliff and drift into nothing and everything. You'll see what I mean, or maybe you already know.

A Short Bio:

I grew up on a farm seven miles north of Mexico, Missouri from 1943 to 1961 as an only son with a younger sister, Ann. Our farm was near the middle of Missouri. Missouri is the middle state in the lower forty-eight, so I thought we lived in the middle of the world. You could stand in our front yard, look north, south, east or west, and see a bucolic view of land, fields, hills, and trees for miles. I was fortunate to have very loving parents and an extended family.

For over forty years, I simultaneously maintained two professions. I was a parish minister from 1961 to 2002, and since 1967, I've also been an adjunct university lecturer in philosophy and religion. During my college years (age 18–21); I was the student minister of three rural Missouri churches. I completed a master's in theology in 1967 and then spent the next twelve years working on a doctorate, while also teaching at the New School University in New York City and rotating through a teaching program of six different courses on the history of mysticism, covering different epochs. Since 1980 I've been teaching philosophy and religion courses at (in sequence) Mercy College, The State University of New York, and Marist College.

In the 1970s I did a backpack, guru-search trip through India, spending time with Sai Baba, Muktananda, and Osho (Rajneesh). Osho was the most interesting. When Osho (1931–1990, India) was handed a copy of *A Course in Miracles*, he looked through it and said, "Americans have to organize everything—even enlightenment." I'm a teacher and an organizer—thus this book.

For three years, 1976–1979, I worked with Dr. Salvador Roquet, a Mexican psychiatrist credited with banishing yellow fever from Mexico. Dr. Roquet took medicine to the natives of Mexico; and they in turn, ministered to him by introducing him to shamanism. He then combined the insights of Western psychiatry with shamanism. Now deceased, Dr. Roquet's work continues in the form of intensive therapy retreats. Salvador felt that traditional "talking" psychotherapy was slow and unproductive. His methodology was to awaken people from dreaming by introducing them to an experience of their own death (psychological, not physical). While working with Salvador in the jungles of Chiapas in Southern Mexico, I had a profound experience where I clearly saw seven things:

1. The world is as we make it.
   It is our construct—totally.
   We make up every aspect of the world.
   That is why (hold onto your hat!)—
   There is no world!
2. Time is relative. It can speed up.
   It can slow down. It can stop.
   In which case—(have you still got your hat on?)
   there is no time!
3. We are not bodies!
   Bodies are a temporal experience.
   In just a few decades, neither your body
   nor mine will exist, and it doesn't matter.
   And, it doesn't matter—now!
   Life does not begin with the birth of a body.
   Life does not end with the death of a body.
4. There is no duality. There are no opposites.
   There is only Oneness.
5. Neither you nor I exist in an individualistic
   (egocentric) way.
   Neither do we exist apart from God.
   This does not mean we don't exist.
6. All decision making must be turned over
   to God—the soon the better.
7. The script is written. There are no accidents! Or,
   as Albert Einstein said,
   "*God does not play dice with the universe.*"

Details of this experience can be found in *Missouri Mystic*. I never found what I was looking for in the traditional church. I did, however, meet a number of wonderful congregants, and I learned a great deal in my struggles with the church.

In 1977, Rabbi Joseph Gelberman (1912 – Present, USA), Swami Satchidananda (1914–2002, India, USA), and I founded Interfaith Inc. in New York City. We held "dialogues" one Sunday per month from 1977–1989. In 1981, Rabbi Gelberman, Father Giles Spoonhour, and I founded the New Seminary. Then, in 1989, Rev. Diane Berke and I founded Interfaith Fellowship with services in Cami Hall, across from Carnegie Hall in New York City. Thirteen years later, in January 2003, I became senior minister emeritus and retired. I am now an itinerate minister and a guest speaker at various churches throughout the year.

Being a university lecturer has been a continued blessing. If you want to know something—teach it. When I tell people I teach classes on mysticism, they often say, "What is Mysticism?" According to Gallup Polls, **one out of three Americans has had a mystical experience**. In my classes, it's more than two out of three. Actually, it's three out of three—some folks just don't remember the experience. **The best textbook on mysticism**, simply titled ***Mysticism***, was written by **Evelyn Underhill** in 1911, nearly 100 years ago. Evelyn's book is the Bible of Mysticism. *What Is Mysticism?* is a teacher's scrapbook and a legacy of written history in the form of essays, bios, photos, facts, figures, tables, statistics, poems, reflections, jokes, quotes, cartoons, and stories from all faiths, philosophies, and religious traditions.

A Few Heroes

Four of my earliest heroes were American renaissance men, scrap bookers, writers, and magazine and journal publishers: Benjamin Franklin, Thomas Jefferson, Mark Twain, and Elbert Hubbard. Our family farm was near Florida, Missouri, where Mark Twain was born. Although he is not thought of as a mystic, he was a great writer and humorist, as well as a brilliant theologian and social critic. At age sixteen, while directing cars at a county fair, I read Benjamin Franklin's autobiography and fell in love with this wonderful Renaissance man. I resolved then that I would one day create a little magazine like his *Poor Rich-*

ard's Almanac. That led to what is now *Miracles* magazine. www.miraclesmagazine.org.

Mystics enjoy meeting other mystics.

They do so freely and in a relaxed manner, being appreciative of whatever gifts their companions bring. Although a mystic might have any career, poets, writers, musicians, nature lovers, artists, and healers, ministers, philosophers, psychologists, and crafts people of all sorts are often mystics. Libraries are filled with mystical poetry, stories, philosophies and studies on mysticism. Although the memory of the mystical may fade, it is not easily forgotten.

Here are three more friends: Elbert Hubbard, Evelyn Underhill (a woman I would love to have known), and Father Pierre Teilhard de Chardin. In my early thirties, I stumbled upon one of Elbert Hubbard's scrapbooks in an antique store, and I became an immediate fan. His book was filled with wonderful quotes, poems, and short essays from the late nineteenth and early twentieth centuries. In one of his books, *Little Journeys*, he chronicled the lives of his heroes, Thomas Carlyle, Victor Hugo, William Wordsworth, William Makepeace Thackeray, William Shakespeare, and Walt Whitman.

Elbert Hubbard (1856–1915, USA) was a practical mystic and an American philosopher, theosophist, and Rosicrucian in the New Thought tradition. He wrote *A Message to Garcia* (the best selling book of 1901 and the 25th bestselling book of all time). He also founded the Roycroft Arts and Crafts movement in East Aurora, NY. The Roycrofter's produced hand-sewn books and mission-style furniture, now expensive antiques. Hubbard and his wife died in the sinking of the *Lusitania* on May 7, 1915, when it was torpedoed by a German submarine.

The narrow path of the mystic's climb begins where the philosopher's broad road leaves off.

Evelyn Underhill

Evelyn Underhill (1875–1941, England) was a mystic, novelist, pacifist, and metaphysical poet. To this day, her book, simply titled *Mysticism*, is the most widely read book on the subject. She describes her childhood mysticism as "abrupt experiences of the peaceful, undifferentiated plane of reality, like the 'still desert' of the mystic." Her beautifully written and clearly inspired books cover an immense amount of material and give special attention to women mystics. Perhaps the most brilliant researcher in the field, she devoted much of her life to the study of mysticism. She wrote over thirty books.

Since Evelyn, there have been several good books on mysticism and a great deal of research and writing in this field. In addition, we now have the insights of various scholars who have done psychological analysis of the mystical state. Last, but not least, are the testimonies of thousands of individuals who have mystical awareness. At each workshop and lecture, I hear the description of many magnificent, mystical moments, some of which you will read in this book.

Pierre Teilhard de Chardin (1881–1955, France). I wrote my master's thesis on Teilhard de Chardin and for many years thereafter taught classes on his work at the New School University. A French Jesuit paleontologist, he was present at the discovery of Peking man. He developed the idea of cosmic consciousness and questioned the notion of "original sin." He also popularized the idea of the noosphere as "a collective web or layer of consciousness that engulfs everything." An evolutionist, Teilhard de Chardin's books were condemned by his own Catholic Church. In 1962, the Church issued an edict saying his writings contained "serious errors" and were "offensive" to Catholic doctrine.

The Most Eminent and Most Revered Fathers of the Holy Office exhort all Ordinaries as well as the Superiors of Religious Institutes, Rectors of Seminaries and Presidents of Universities, to protect the minds, particularly of the youth, against the dangers presented by the works of Fr. Teilhard de Chardin

The edict produced a tremendous interest in Teilhard de Chardin. His work is now carried on by the American Teilhard Association.

[www.teilharddechardin.org].

No one becomes a mystic by reading a book. It doesn't hurt, however, and might help. Knowing about mysticism is not the same as *experiencing it* or *being a mystic*. With a little bit of luck, however, we might receive some inspiration to do the work needed to develop a contemplative life. If we're both fortunate, *What Is Mysticism?* will help to further our advancement on the spiritual path.

Mohammed said that a scholar who writes about mysticism without mystical awareness is like a donkey carrying a load of books. Mysticism is available to all. You might not know how close it is to you. Still, second-hand accounts don't suffice. Tell somebody who has never fallen in love what it's like to fall in love—you can try but you can't really explain it, precisely because it is an experience. Magnify falling in love again and again and again, and you may see something of the mystical. You get a glimmer of it, yet according to Taoism, the Tao that is described is not the Tao. How do you freeze the infinite? What follows, is a guide, a history, and an inspirational book. We must each walk the terrain for ourselves.

The finger pointing to the moon is not the moon.
Buddhist saying

All my life I sought for
God and when I found
Him I discovered that it
was He who was seeking me.
Meister Eckhart

Here is a Secret:
Seeking is unnecessary.
The first thing to learn
*is **not to seek**.*

When you seek you are window shopping.
J.G. Krishnamurti

It behooves us to become ignorant of this worldly wisdom; rather must we clutch at madness.
Rumi

Meet Dr. Baba Jon Mundane

Some years ago, I noticed an "altered ego" idiot following me around, every now and then trying to break through and talk to folks. He's a mad professor type who likes to tell stories. He often sees illogicality, irony, and the paradoxical nature of things. Just as he occasionally breaks through in various lectures, he's breaking though in this book. Whenever he speaks, you'll see a caricature of him beside a paragraph. My thanks go out to my friend and neighbor, Lori Frisbe, for drawing him out.

Chapter 1

The Mystic's Way

The Tug on the Heart

When birds are migrating to other lands, the instinct to migrate is strong. If a migratory bird is put into a cage, it will pace back and forth. It will beat its breast against the bars. It will do everything in its power to get out of the cage. If the same bird is put into a cage when it is not migration time, the bird will not try to break free. Throw it up into the air, and it won't fly far away. The tug at the heart is gone. Something tugs at the heart. We want to come Home to God. We want to fully be the Love we already are.

Every soul strives to rise above the mundane. Everyone hungers for heaven, for a space of timelessness beyond sometimes stressful, restless, and unsatisfying lives. We need a refuge from the rat race and the struggle for survival. Mysticism is the fulfillment of our deepest yearnings, past all the nonsense of the world—into a life of meaning.

What is Mysticism?

Comparative Mysticism

This book is a study in comparative mysticism. We're going to examine the most essential element in spirituality, the direct experience of God. The experiential "message" of mysticism reveals that in the center of our being we are one with God. It is a matter of remembering. This remembering requires the dismantling of the crusted-over masks of identity we've placed on reality. We did not create God. God created us. Still, we are in God, and He is in us.

I am the vine; you are the branches.

In the Elysian Mystery tradition of the ancient Greek world, an initiate was called a *myste*. This word in turn comes from *myein*, meaning "to close the lips and eyes." The *myste* were not to talk about the inner workings of their experiences. While *esoteric* does mean "secret or hidden," mystical knowledge is not hidden so much as it is not understood by non-mystics. Mysticism is not a secret. If a philosophical system has secrets and charges you money to learn those secrets, beware!

Two Manifestations of Mysticism

Mysticism is both an *experience* and an *ongoing developing awareness*. Jesus, Buddha, Mohammad, as well as all religious leaders give highest importance to the direct personal experience of truth.

1. **Mysticism is an experience.** There is no doubt about mystical awareness. While others may question the veracity of your experience, the mystic does not. Profound mystical experiences are transformative and life changing. Once you've opened the door to the mystical, you cannot shut it completely, and God's love will eventually flood your life.

George Fox (1624–1691, England), the founder of the Society of Friends (Quakers), said God could *only* be found experientially. We do not need the ideas of others or a book to learn about God. Opinions and beliefs can hinder more than help. "There is," Fox said, "something of the inward light in everyone, and anyone can make direct contact with God."

2. **Mysticism is a way of seeing, a process of being and becoming.** Mysticism is also a churning, turning, cooking kind of thing. Like pebbles rolling around in a tub of sand, we sometimes have to go through rough places in order to smooth things out. When the world is seen without the eyes of the ego, there is only purity—only wholeness. Even in the face of what may appear as evil, the mystic sees love.

Vast numbers of persons have mystical awareness. Many children have mystical experiences. Immediate spiritual intuition can come to anyone, regardless of religious training or spiritual inclinations. Having a mystical experience does not make someone a mystic. Mystical experiences are, however, doors and windows to a wider awareness. Such experiences simply signal a stage in the development of awareness.

Enlightenment must come little by little
Otherwise it would overwhelm.
Idries Shah

Indries Shah (1924–1996, India) was an author in the Sufi tradition. Most of his books were on psychology and spirituality. Over 15 million copies of his various books were sold in 16 different languages during his lifetime. His father was Afghan; his mother, Scottish; and he was educated in England.

Idries Shah's writings helped the Western world understand Sufism.

The essence of mysticism is that in the deepest part of your true being, in the very center of your own pure awareness, you are fundamentally one with Spirit, one with Godhead, one with the All, in a timeless, eternal and unchanging fashion.

Ken Wilbur

Ken Wilber, (1949 – Present, USA), an American Buddhist and a philosophical and psychological theorist, focuses his work on an "integral theory of consciousness" combining mysticism with science. He is interested in mapping perennial philosophy and mysticism with an account of cosmic evolution like that of Indian philosopher Sri Aurobindo. According to Wilbur, sentient beings in the world of form will ultimately realize their true identity as emptiness. Of special interest is his CD, *Kosmic Consciousness.*

Fifteen Definitions of Mysticism

Mysticism is a direct experience of God; falling in love with the Truth of our Divine Self; achieving conscious awareness of Ultimate Reality.

Mysticism is knowledge of the interconnectedness of all things.

Mysticism is the science and art of the spiritual life.

Mysticism is the science of self-evident Reality.

Mysticism is a personal experience during which one feels touched by higher or greater truth.

Mysticism is a transcending of the sense-world in order to experience Self.

Mysticism is knowing that the Source of information is the Self or Truth and not the self, or ego.

Mysticism is an experience of freedom from the ego.

Mysticism is about clearing the mind to access transcendence.

Mysticism is the inner pathway to the realization of the truths of God as immanent and transcendent.

Mysticism is being receptive instead of projective.

Mysticism is the awakening within the Self of divine reality.

Mysticism is the discipline of purifying perception and seeing through illusions, which means perceiving the world without the fetters of the ego.

Mysticism is the inner state of seekers who are carrying out the process of returning to their divine source in consciousness.

Mysticism is trust of the highest order; it is faith in an active and transformative "higher power" without a dogmatic belief in God.

Your vision will become clear only when you can look into your own heart. Who looks outside, dreams; who looks inside, awakens.

C.G. Jung

Carl Gustav Jung (1875–1961, Switzerland) was the founder of Analytical Psychology. Often mentioned along with Sigmund Freud with whom he initially collaborated. Jung was one of the first to bring an in-depth psychological exploration to the mystical experience. He was especially interested in studying dreams, archetypes, and mythology.

What Mysticism is Not

Mysticism is one of the most abused words in the English language. It has been claimed as an excuse for every kind of occultism, for diluted transcendentalism, vapid symbolism, religious or aesthetic sentimentality and bad metaphysics.

Evelyn Underhill

Mysticism is not vague. Some ideas or experiences are called mystical that are unclear. Mysticism is occasionally associated with *misty* because of the similar sound of the words. There is nothing misty, foggy or hazy about mysticism. It actually brings clarity to the mind.

Mysticism is not a mystery. While there is an etymological connection between *mysticism* and *mystery*, mysticism is not about secrets. To the uninitiated, any mystical path may appear mysterious—like an unfamiliar language. Mysticism is also, however, not something entirely within the realm of the intellect—not something comprehended with ordinary conceptualization alone.

Mysticism is not magic. A magic show has nothing to do with mysticism. Mysticism is not a display. Mysticism is not about using secret incantations or hocus-pocus of any kind. It's not about sorcery or the use of a ritual in order to get something. Evelyn Underhill says, "Magic wants to get. Mysticism wants to give." Despite what the billboards may say in Las Vegas, most magicians, or conjurers, are probably not mystics.

Outwardly (mystics) live a normal, straightforward existence, being good, kind and honest with everyone, without feeling the need to convert others to their own point of view.

John Davidson
(1944 – Present) English Scholar at Oxford

Mysticism is not about saving the world or other people's souls. There is no missionary movement in mysticism. To be part of a missionary movement, you must feel you are right and others are wrong. Mysticism is not interested in making anyone wrong. Mysticism involves changing our own mind to align with truth—which changes our relationships by making them more peaceful, which may change the world in a subtle and completely nonviolent way.

Mysticism is not an opinion; it is not a philosophy.
It has nothing in common with
the pursuit of occult knowledge.
Evelyn Underhill

Mysticism is not "occult." While mysticism may have some of the characteristics of parapsychological phenomena (including clairvoyance, clairaudience, distant vision, telepathic or precognitive abilities), mysticism is not about hearing voices, seeing visions, reading minds or walking on hot coals. On the other hand, practiced mystics have been known to develop any number of extraordinary powers of perception and intuition. In fact, it's inevitable that some such intuitive abilities will be developed. These abilities are the effects of mystical development, not the aim of it. Genuine mystical powers are not exhibited, promoted or sold.

Mysticism does not require retreat from the world. Mystics sometimes retreat from the outer world to develop a deeper awareness of inner reality. Becoming a mystic does not, however, require an escape from the so-called "real world." In fact, "practical mysticism" calls upon us to be highly present and aware of whatever is going on in the world without buying into the illusions of the world.

Mysticism is not concerned with the future or the past. Traditional religion places a major emphasis on the past—on sin, guilt, fear—and an emphasis on what life is going to be like after death. Will you get to go to heaven, or will it be hell instead? Mysticism is not concerned with time—its focus is on the eternal now.

Some Mysticism You Already Know

The Infinite Infant

Heaven lies all about us in our infancy.
William Wordsworth

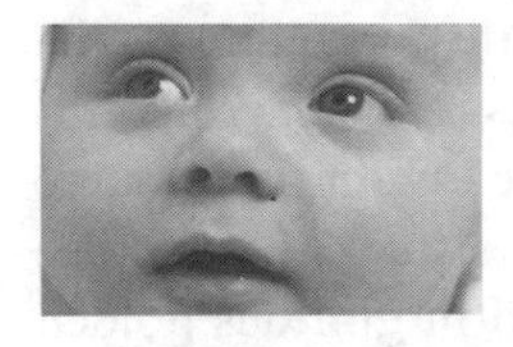

The *in* of both *infant* and *infinity* means "not"—infinity is "not-finite." An infant is someone who has not yet developed speech. We leave infancy for early childhood when we begin to talk. The infant merely sees and wonders. An infant's self-awareness isn't differentiated from the immediacy of mother and the environment. It is thus still a part of wholeness. Fear and shame are yet to be learned. The infant has no past and thus no guilt. An infant can "pee" or throw-up on us without embarrassment. We can look infants directly in the eyes, and they will look directly back without looking away. They have nothing to hide. Try that with some adults. Lovers can look longer into each other's eyes than most other people. Gurdjieff said that children are more at "essence" because they are not yet imprinted with automatic responses to input from the world.

The Wordless World

Words are the tools with which we create the world. Words are also forms of delimitation. Once we have a name for something, we will never again be able to look at it without labeling it. A "book" is now a "book" forever. This delimitation in form keeps us from seeing clearly. Thus, mathematics is a purer language. It is however, still a form. It is hard to remember when we were infants because there were no words to freeze and thus frame experiences. The wordless world is full of wonder.

Passivity, or "the ability to be totally receptive," is another quality of the mystic. Infancy is a time of passivity and of relative (though rapidly evaporating) innocence, as the outer world becomes progressively more real.

True Story Time

A family had a new baby boy and his sister, a girl of four years old. After the baby was born, the little girl asked her parents if she could be left alone with the baby for a little while. Concerned that she might be jealous of the baby and possibly even hurt him, the parents finally told the little girl that she could go into the nursery by herself. Their plan was to listen in on the monitor. The little girl went in, closed the door, walked up to the crib, looked in, and said, "Tell me about God, baby. I'm beginning to forget."

Early Childhood

Amazement and Imagination

Young children can literally be overwhelmed with sensations. Wonderful memories shine in the childhood of everyone. A few mystics, like Walt Whitman, never lost the marvel of childhood. Children laugh a lot more than adults. Every new discovery plunges them into jubilation. Children live in the wonderful world of imagination. Cartoon characters are real. Santa Clause is real. Fairies are real. Angels are real. The underground ant kingdom is a fascinating world unto itself. All kinds of things are possible. It is even possible to talk to God.

Some of the best descriptions of the mysticism of Childhood are found in the work of **Thomas Traherne, MA** (1636–1674, England) a poet/priest who describes the glories of both childhood and nature to inform the mind through beauty, and the ecstatic harmony of being a child in the natural world. He introduced a child's viewpoint unknown in the religious literature before this time. His poems, similar to William Blake and William Wordsworth, express an uncomplicated, simple love of God. Traherne influenced Thomas Merton, and C.S. Lewis called Traherne's writing the most beautiful books in English.

Ramakrishna (1836–1886, India) was an Indian mystic who, in order to support himself, became a temple priest. Having little interest in the material world, he would meditate for hours. His relatives, growing weary of his seeming madness, tried to restore him to sanity by betrothing him. Resisting domestication, Ramakrishna left the temple, discarded his possessions, and took a vow of poverty. He undertook the practices of Islam, Christianity, and various other sects, concluding that *the goal of all religions is the remembrance of God.*

As a boy, Ramakrishna would go into ecstasy at the simplest occurrence in nature. When, for example, he saw white cranes flying before the dark clouds of a thunderstorm, he was spellbound with wonder.

Children can become so engrossed in imagination and play that they lose awareness of the *outside* world. As a child, I enjoyed playing with the many animals on our farm and easily turned ordinary chores into play. The following one-sentence description of a mystical awareness comes from Leo Tolstoy in his book *Childhood, Boyhood and Youth*:

The chatter of the peasants, the tramp of the horses and the creaking of the carts, the merry whistle of quail, the hum of insects hovering in the air in motionless swarms, the smell of wormwood, straw and horse's sweat, the thousand different lights and shadows with which the burning sun flooded the light yellow stubble, the dark blue of the distant forest and the pale lilac of the clouds, the white gossamer threads which floated in the air or lay stretched across the stubble, all these things I saw, heard, and felt.

Leo Tolstoy (1828–1910, Russia) was a mystic, Christian anarchist (one who believes the only source of authority is God), vegetarian, moral thinker, and one of the greatest novelists of all time. He is best known for *War and Peace, Anna Karenina,* and *The Kingdom of God is Within You.* Along with Thoreau, he was a tremendous influence on Mahatma Gandhi and Martin Luther King, Jr. He thus in a quiet way transformed the world.

Mysticism and Nature, an Early Experience

Most all Missouri farm boys in the 1950s spent their free time hunting. If you didn't have to work, you got your gun and took off for the woods. Sometimes when you're hunting, you stop. You stand perfectly still; you watch and listen. It's called "freezing." You become motionless and soundless. If animals are not downwind from you and they cannot smell you, hear you or see you, they will begin to appear in the woods, sometimes walking right out in front of you. Squirrels, for example, can smell and hear well, but they have to get close before they can see you. While motionless, I once caught and took home a baby possum that walked right up to my boot. He got loose in the house and went to live in the dropped ceiling between the up- and downstairs. Mother was not happy!

One fine summer day in 1958 when I was fifteen, I was hunting in the woods on the back of our farm. It was a ten sort of a day, absolutely beautiful. Although it had rained the night before, now it was sunny, and it felt as if everything had been washed clean. All of the plants were a luxuriant, verdant green. Rotting logs covered with moss lay strewn about on large stones, and there were bushes covered with little white flowers. I could hear the water running over the rocks down on Salt Creek only a few yards away.

That day, while "freezing," I decided to play a game. I would disappear. I would just be eyes on the world—nothing more than that. I would be invisible—I wouldn't exist. No one would see me. As I played this "game," suddenly there was no person present, just a camera mindlessly recording a scene in the woods. There was no hunter hunting, no thinker thinking, no planner planning, no doer doing. There were just eyes seeing without "definition." There came then the most incredible sense of oneness.

Withdrawing the intention of needing anything to happen, I witnessed. The experience was simple, pure, unclouded—profound. It was what it was without question. Nothing mattered! Then came the question, "Who was the observer?" Or, "What was having this experience?" And then, "Who wanted to know?" Afterwards, I tried repeating this experience many times, but that "first time"—like the first time we fall in love—that was the best!

There is immediacy about farm life that quickens the mind and opens the doors of awareness. Weather permitting, I was always outdoors living life—with life. As the wheat came out of the hopper into the truck, I could see the straw and heads of wheat arrayed in glorious golden rainbow colors. When the alfalfa was cut and winnowed, its sweet smell filled the air. In the evening, I listened to the tree frogs, katydids, and crickets. On July nights, I stood mesmerized by the flicker of fireflies, the stars and occasional northern lights. Much of the time, the town of

Mexico smelled of soy beans being ground, a little like, though more pungent than, peanut butter.

The first twenty-one years of my life were spent bathed in the delightful smells, sights, and sounds of nature and farm life. Seeing God in nature is the mysticism of farmers, gardeners, campers, hikers, all lovers of nature, and all native people. It is Central Park that brings sanity to New York City, as do other parks in other cities. Henry David Thoreau went to the woods, he said, to live deliberately, to confront the essentials of life and not learn when it came time to die that he had not lived. Nature mysticism is the simplest, oldest, and commonest form of mysticism.

Falling in Love

Falling in love is probably the first experience we can all identify with as mystical. It doesn't matter with what or with whom we fall in love—another person, an animal, music, nature, a field of knowledge, craft, art or any activity. The soul longs to fall in love whenever possible.

When we fall in love, we are flooded with a deep, intense feeling of joy. We feel transported. There is a sense of emotional freedom, along with beautiful thoughts and images of our beloved. Our feet don't quite touch the ground. We are bathed in emotion. We can write poetry. One day my wife, Dolores, said to me, "You know, honey, you don't write me poetry anymore." She's right; I have not done so lately. What was it about that first year when I was falling in love with her? As my friend Tom Baker said: "I was like Hallmark on steroids." Falling in love is bigger than we are. The more we let it happen, the more it will happen. Then one day the ego kicks back in, and judgment begins. Now we look at our beloved and think things like, "This guy drinks every day; maybe he is an alcoholic. Why didn't I see that before?" Love is innocent and often blind.

Dreaming

Dreams are *altered state* experiences in which we temporarily abandon the rational mind. They are a way for the subconscious (whole) to communicate with the conscious (part). Dreams were, said Sigmund Freud, the Royal Road to the Unconscious. According to Carl Jung, wholeness results from establishing a working relationship with the unconscious levels of the psyche. If information arising from the unconscious is attended to, it can move us toward greater equilibrium, health, creativity and a sense of well being. Although most dreams are ego-oriented (replaying surface desires and anxieties), when we look at them, we gain access to a larger world. The dream is telling us something. Below the surface dreams there are guidance dreams.

Transformative Dreams

A man comes rushing into his psychiatrist's office, apologizing for being late because he overslept. "But I had an incredible breakthrough dream," the man says breathlessly. "I was talking with my mother and she suddenly turned into you! That's when I woke up, got dressed, grabbed a Coke and a donut and rushed to your office." And, the psychiatrist says, "A Coke and a donut! You call that breakfast?"

Though many dreams are "surface dreams" concerned with daily anxieties or problem-solving, deeper guidance dreams are even more symbolic or metaphorical. What is the meaning behind the dream? If we listen and watch carefully enough, we can hear the Voice of God speaking in our dreams. Dreams can also introduce us to our shadows. Even though we may not always like what we see, spiritual growth occurs as we willingly look at the dark side. It is in doing so that we overcome its power over us. Yet other dreams tap deep, archetypal levels of awareness. [See: *Dreams: God's Forgotten Language* by John A. Sanford]

Lucid Dreams

An especially heightened state of dreaming is called "lucidity," in which we become aware that we are dreaming, and we are able to act consciously within the dream. Lucid induction techniques have been known for centuries in Tibetan dream yoga. Lucidity delivers heightened sensations and experiences, involving flying, spinning or erotic content. Groundbreaking work in the study of lucid dreams was done by researcher Dr. Stephen La Berge of The Lucidity Institute [www.lucidity.com].

Active Imagination—Certain conditions and techniques can increase the occurrence and richness of dreams. Active Imagination provides a portal between everyday awareness and the dreaming state by bringing alertness to the dream. As we look at the dream, the dream "comes back" to look at us. The marriage of inner and outer worlds provides aliveness, meaning, insight, and excitement—making the dream a mystical experience.

[See: www.bodysoulandspirit.net]

Despair and Depression

We fall into depression and despair as the result of the failure of our egos. Thank God for failure and the jolt that wakes us up. Although this path is not fun, it is the one most frequently traveled. Learning to invite and accept spiritual surrender transforms the *dark night of the soul* from punishment to—*a saving grace*.

Living "in the Now"

Sometime mysticism comes unbidden—when, for example, we achieve a *runner's high* or "fall" into the flow and lose ourselves in creative work, writing, painting, making love or listening to music. Time can be superseded. Living in the now exemplifies a transitory suspension of ego-driven awareness. Beyond these experiences, there are higher and higher, deeper and deeper states achieved through the disciplined observance of a chosen path.

Mini Mystical Experiences

What the unawake person sees in brief glimpses
few are far between, the awakened person
sees at all times and in all things.
Jed Mc Kenna in *Spiritual Warfare*

Mini brief encounters with the mystical provide a *taste* of truth without *full* revelation. These experiences are usually transient, or fleeting, and commonly take several forms:

Insight is literally in-sight, seeing inside. Insight is "suddenly seeing something that was already there." The mystic's way of "seeing" may consist in abrupt insights. St. Hildegard said that each of her great revelations was received "in an instant," and St. Brigid of Sweden reported that an entire book was given to her in a "flash."

St. Bridget of Sweden (1303 –1373), was a mystic and founder of the Bridgettine Order. As a child, she had frequent visions. She married and had eight children, including St. Catherine of Sweden. After the death of her husband she devoted herself exclusively to the mystical life. In 1999, Pope John Paul II chose Bridget as a patron Saint of Europe.

Since time is an invention of consciousness and has no objective reality, it takes no time for someone with such awareness to receive revelation. Mystical intuition thus sometimes takes the form of, and is often described as, an ***epiphany***—a sudden realization or comprehension of the essence or meaning of something. It's as though one has found the last "piece of the puzzle" and now sees the whole picture.

The only real valuable thing is intuition.
Albert Einstein

Intuition is a direct form of knowledge. While insight is an affair of the head, intuition is a *gut-heart* experience. Intuition is fast, automatic, natural, and not available for introspection. It is also frequently emotionally charged. As we come to live a "natural" life, intuition also develops "naturally." Intuition brings us to an awareness of truth. Often it's a *feeling* leading to an understanding of why certain events are occurring or the deeper nature of our own or another's motives. Sometimes intuition is a "hunch," or a guess with an enigmatic gravity—we may not be sure how we came to this knowledge, but we feel sure it will prove true in essence.

Whilst the doors of the temple stand open, night and
day, before every man, the oracles of this truth cease
never, it is guarded by one stern condition,
this, namely; it is an intuition.
Ralph Waldo Emerson

Freud said that the unconscious knows everything; it contains all the information about the mind. But the unconscious is not readily available to us; it's not part of our everyday awareness. Not knowing where intuitive information comes from signifies that it derives from the greater collective and thus does not involve linear thinking. Both insight and intuition enable us to make many connections all at once, as does a complex computer. Intuition is powerful and wise, but sometimes risky, especially when we *overfeel*—when we first fall in love, for example—or *underthink*, we may ignore the possible consequences of our actions.

Déjà vu is a French expression meaning "already seen." It is a first-hand experience of timelessness, or the simultaneity of experience. Such a mini-mystical moment can also provide insight into the unity or oneness of all things.

A **holy instant** (comparable to the experience called *Kensho* in Japanese) is a moment of "brief enlightenment" when the whole of reality is perceived clearly. A holy instant is a moment outside of time in which we chose Spirit instead of the ego. Such moments may be accompanied by "bright light" experiences and sometimes an overwhelming sensation of universal love. In these experiences, the individual has an *absolute conviction* that awakening has occurred and often feels he or she has been "blessed." Some new knowledge or understanding is gained in such an experience. Still, most of these experiences, while potentially life-changing, are not enough to make someone a mystic. Only in rare instances do they produce a permanent state of awareness of essence or enlightenment. Most often, they signal a step along the way. Mysticism is not fully realized until we live a deliberate, disciplined, contemplative life.

People come to me and say,
"There was a great light during the meditation,
but I lost it again. Infinite light was there, but it
disappeared again. There was immense bliss, but now
it is gone." Now they are searching for it again
and cannot find it. A glimpse means you had come
close. But glimpses are bound to be lost.
Meditation can, at the most, give only a glimpse.
Do not stop there; do not get stuck looking for that

same glimpse again and again. The only purpose of meditation is that one gets a glimpse.
Then one has to go ahead, into Samadhi, into enlightenment, so that one becomes the very flower.
In meditation is a glimpse; Samadhi is being it.
Osho

Osho or **Bhagwan Shree Rajneesh** (1931–1990, India) Of the three teachers I spent time with in India, Osho was the most interesting. A former professor of philosophy, when I met him in 1971, he was giving daily lectures in Mumbai. He gave me the name *Nitam*. I still enjoy listening to his lectures on CD. I never, however, became an active disciple (sanyasan). He said the greatest values in life are awareness, love, meditation, and laughter. According to Osho, enlightenment is natural. The ego, however, is distracted from enlightenment by emotional ties to societal expectations, personal fears and inhibitions. Since he disapproved of organized religion and the institution of priesthood, not surprisingly, he was not liked by the establishment.

Mysticism According to the Students of Mysticism

With the exception of American Transcendental and German Idealistic philosophers, general interest in "the science of mysticism" did not begin until the latter part of the nineteenth century. The beginning of the twentieth century saw a flowering of interest in mysticism because of the newly developing field of psychology. At the same time, Catholic scholars were interesting themselves in the experiences of the famous mystical saints of their past.

Ralph Waldo Emerson (1803–1880, USA) is thought by many to be the greatest of the American Transcendentalists. The natural world according to Emerson is coursed through with the immanent flow of a deity, *a world soul.* The ego is "nothingness." He first expressed the philosophy of *Transcendentalism* in his 1836 essay, *Nature*. After leaving the church, Emerson made a living as a popular lecturer in New England and New York. In the few instances when he was not able to make his appearances, Frederick Douglass took his place. He was a friend of Nathaniel Hawthorne and Henry David Thoreau. The land on which Thoreau built his cabin on Walden Pond belonged to Emerson.

Richard M. Bucke (1837–1902, Canada) was the superintendent of two of Canada's asylums for the insane. In 1901, one year before he died, he published his great book, *Cosmic Consciousness*. He described Cosmic Consciousness as a transpersonal awareness of the universal mind and oneness with it. Mystical or cosmic consciousness is, he says, "primarily an awareness of the life and order of the universe." An individual who attains Cosmic Consciousness is "Enlightened." Such a person is aware of immortality as something he or she "already" has; thus, there is nothing to be attained. Bucke's friendship with the celebrated poet Walt Whitman was the subject of a National Film Board of Canada co-production, *Beautiful Dreamers*, the story of a mystic who was truly alive and in love with life. (Look for the DVD; it's well worth watching.)

Seven Characteristics of Mysticism According to Richard M. Bucke

1. An intuitive, non-intellectual, ineffable understanding.
2. An elevated moral awareness and an inability to hurt others.
3. A freedom from a sense of sin, guilt, and fear.
4. An awareness of immortality.
5. Freedom from a fear of death.
6. A definite peak experience and a moment of transformation.
7. An intellectual illumination or revelation.

William James (1842–1910, USA) was a philosopher and pragmatist who taught the first class in psychology as a separate science (from philosophy) at Harvard in 1885. He wrote *Principles of Psychology*, one of the first textbooks in the field. He said that "New Thought" was "the religion of healthy-mindedness" and the only original American contribution to a systematic philosophy. In 1902, James wrote *Varieties of Religious Experience*, a classic in the field of Psychology of Religion.

Four Characteristic of Mysticism According to William James

1. **Ineffability:** Indescribable, beyond our capacity to fully express in words.

2. **Passivity:** It's out of our hands and seems to happen to or through us (you) without our direction.
3. **Transience:** Time stops or the mystical experience seems to happen outside of time.
4. **A "Noetic" quality:** We come to "know" something profound.

Four Characteristics of Mysticism According to Evelyn Underhill

1. **Mysticism is practical, not theoretical.** It is something the whole self does—not just the intellect.
2. **It is entirely a spiritual activity.** It is in no way concerned with adding to, exploring, re-arranging, or improving anything in the visible universe.
3. **The business and method of mysticism is love.** It draws the whole being homeward, always under the guidance of the heart.
4. **Mysticism entails a definite psychological experience** arrived at by arduous psychological and spiritual progress.

Rudolf Otto (1869–1937, Germany) was a professor of systematic theology at the University of Marburg. In his book, *The Idea of the Holy*, Otto coins the word numinous to define the mystical. *Numinous* comes from a Latin word *numen* meaning "a non-rational, non-sensory experience or feeling whose primary and immediate object is outside the self." Otto says that mysticism has three components designated by the Latin: *mysterium, tremendum* and *fascinans.*

As ***mysterium***, the numinous is "wholly other" and entirely different from anything we experience in ordinary life. It evokes a reaction of silence and leaves us speechless. As *mysterium tremendum*, the experience provokes terror because it presents itself as overwhelming. As *mysterium fascinans*, it produces a state of mercy and grace. Otto describes mysticism as follows:

> *...an ineffable experience which grips or stirs the human mind. The feeling of it may at times come sweeping like a gentle tide, pervading the mind with a tranquil mood of deepest worship. It may pass over into a more established and lasting attitude of the soul, continuing, as it were, thrillingly vibrant and resonant, until at last it dies away and the soul resumes its "profane," non-religious mood of everyday experience. It may burst in sudden eruption from the depths of the soul with spasms and convulsions, or lead to the strongest excitements, to intoxicated frenzy, to transport, and to ecstasy.*

Five Characteristics of a Mystical Experience According to Rudolf Otto

1. The element of "awe" fullness.
2. The element of over poweringness.
3. The element of energy or urgency.
4. The element of the "Wholly Other."
5. The element of fascination.

The most beautiful and profound emotion we can experience is the mystical. He to whom this emotion is a stranger, who can no longer wonder and stand rapt in awe, is as good as dead. To know that what is impenetrable to us really exists, manifesting itself as the highest wisdom and the most radiant beauty, which our dull faculties can comprehend only in their primitive forms—this knowledge, this feeling, is at the center of true religion.

Albert Einstein

Albert Einstein (1879–1955, Germany) I love Einstein. He is a true mystic. He saw into another dimension and then tried to tell us about it. He is widely considered one of the greatest, if not the greatest, physicists of all time His mysticism is similar to Jnana (Knowledge) Yoga, the *amour intellectualis* of Schopenhauer, and the "divine love" of Flemish mystic Ruysbroeck (1200-1256). Born a Jew, Einstein was respectful of all religions. In addition to his brilliant mind, he had a great heart. *"Anyone,"* he once wrote to the Royal Society of London, *"who finds a thought which brings him closer to Nature's eternal secrets partakes of a great grace."* Amen.

Mircea Eliade (1907–1986, Romania, USA) makes the next major contributor to the study of mysticism. Influenced by Rudolf Otto, he was editor-in-chief of Macmillan's *Encyclopedia of Religion* and for thirty years, Director of History of Religions at the University of Chicago. He wrote extensively on what he called the "eternal return" (the belief that religious behavior, as a participation in sacred events, restores mythic time). He saw mysticism as central to genuine religion. His best book is *Cosmos and History: The Myth of the Eternal Return*, 1954. The perception of time as linear is different from sacred time, which is cyclical.

John Davidson (1944 – Present, England) of Oxford England is another bright and shining light. In his book, *The Gospel of Jesus*, he notes the following characteristics of mysticism.

Four Characteristics of Mysticism According to John Davidson

1. **Mystics speak with the certainty of personal experience.** They do not need to "justify" their experience. It is not an intellectual position.
2. **The experience is of the soul and mind**, not of the body.
3. **There is a feeling of inner joy or bliss.**
4. **The ultimate consummation of the experience is union with God.**

Now let's combine concepts from Bucke, James, Underhill, Einstein, Otto, Eliade, Maslow, Wilbur, Davidson, and others. I've also added a few of my own suggestions.

Sixteen Characteristics of Mysticism Mysticism is:

1. **An Experience of God.**
2. **A Personal Soul Experience.** It is not just intellectual, emotional or sensory. It usually occurs in solitude.
3. **A Definite Peak Experience**, including personal transformation, energy, fascination.
4. **Ineffable**—words are inadequate.
5. **A Noetic Quality, Illumination or Revelation**, including an awareness of immortality and freedom from fear of death.
6. **It is Simple and yet Profound.**
7. **Transcendental.** It happens outside of, or it transcends, time.
8. **Passive** (obedient). There is a release of all control and the will is given over to God
9. **Practical, Not Theoretical**, involves action, such as "forgiving." It is something the whole self does, not just the intellect.
10. **Not Interested in Changing, Adding to, Rearranging, Improving or Fixing Others.** Despite this, mysticism often has a profoundly positive effect on others.
11. **Monistic**, meaning there is no other—All is one.
12. **Oceanic**, meaning a blending and melting into whatever is.
13. **Freedom** from sin, guilt, and fear.
14. **Awe-fullness, Wonder, Joy, and Bliss**
15. **Enlightenment**
16. **Love is All There Is**

We'll examine each of these characteristics in the following pages.

Mysticism as Perennial Philosophy

Whether the flower of mysticism blooms in India or in China, in Persia or on the Rhine, its fruit is one.

Rudolf Otto

The phrase *perennial* (meaning "persistent" or "enduring") *philosophy* was coined by Gottfried Wilhelm Leibniz. Perennial philosophy is also called *universal* because it shows up in all cultures from Asia to Africa, from Europe to the Americas. The perennialist view holds that at the core of truth we are looking at one phenomenon with many different expressions in many different times. According to perennial philosophy, people in many cultures and eras have experienced and recorded comparable perceptions about the nature of the self, reality, the world, and the purpose of existence.

Gottfried Wilhelm Leibniz (1646–1716, Germany) was a polymath, Deist and metaphysician with an incredible intellect. (Deists believe that reason, rather than dogma, should provide the foundation for belief in God.) Leibniz discovered calculus independent of Newton. According to Leibniz, a world "containing free will is better than a world in which free will does not exist." Thus, a perfect God allows for imperfection.

Aldous Huxley (1894–1963, England) was one of my first heroes in the early 1960s. In 1966–1967, I met and worked with his second wife, Laura. He popularized the word perennial in his book *The Perennial Philosophy*. He wrote *Brave New World* and *The Doors of Perception*. A true mystic and a seasoned meditator, he was a student of Vedanta. (He died the same day as John F. Kennedy.) In *Perennial Philosophy*, Huxley says, "Mysticism is the one unifying principle in all religion."

Mystics in every religion speak the same tongue and teach the same truth.

Swami Vivekananda

Swami Vivekananda (1862–1902, India), the main disciple of Ramakrishna was one of the most important leaders of Hinduism during the 19th century. He is one of the first to bring Hinduism to the West. At the World's Parliament of Religions in Chicago, in 1893, he opened his speech with this line, "Sisters and Brothers of America." The audience clapped for two minutes, and the speech catapulted him to fame with lectures all over the US. A street in downtown Chicago is named Swami Vivekananda Way.

We find in comparative mysticism that the medieval German mystics Eckhart and Tauler agree in essence in their descriptions of mysticism with the Indian sage Shankara and the *Upanishads*. Two cultures, centuries apart, that may never have heard of each other, tell of the same experience. The empty nothingness of pure awareness as described by Christian mystics is almost indistinguishable from the Void of the Mahayana Buddhists. The truth is inevitably the same in every soul, culture, and tradition.

Mysticism is universal. Mysticism is the height of religion, as it includes all attempts to reach the beyond within. Regardless of how they are practiced in the mainstream, each of the great world religions receives their most sublime interpretations from the mystics. Lao Tzu, Buddha, Jesus, Nanak, Mahavira, and the other founders of the various religious traditions were not institution builders. They were mystics and teachers.

The Main Points of Perennial Philosophy According to Ken Wilbur

1. Spirit exists.
2. Spirit is found within.
3. Most of us don't realize this Spirit within because we live in a world of duality, sin, and illusion.
4. There is a way out of illusion.
5. If we follow the path to its conclusion, there is a direct experience of Enlightenment and Liberation.
6. This marks the end of suffering.
7. Then follows social action, mercy, and compassion for all sentient beings.— From *Grace and Grit*

[More information at www.religioperennis.org]

Mysticism, Traditional Religion, Rules, Regulations, and Freedom

The word *religion* comes from the Latin *religio* and means "to constrain, to restrain or to tie back." It also means "the observance of a rule." Before a holy order like the Franciscans or the Dominicans could be established, a set of rules had to be written for members to follow. Mysticism doesn't have any rules. Mysticism is free. Mystics follow God's laws naturally because they want to, not because they are "required" to do so by an external authority. There is no outside force for the mystic. God works within. The moment that rules, laws, and required ways of living come into play; religion moves away from mysticism. Organized religions emphasize belief, rather than intuition and revelation. It then gets lost in doctrine. Traditional religion splinters into subgroups and aberrant belief systems that become dualistic and divisive.

Orthodoxy means not thinking,
not needing to think.
Orthodoxy is unconsciousness.
George Orwell, (1909–1950, England)
in his book *1984*

As William James and Kent Wilber point out, mystical awareness may come to anyone, regardless of religious training or inclinations. Mysticism transcends beliefs precisely because it is an experience. When mystics tell us of their experiences, they are not repeating a belief or something they read in a book. Inevitably in this world, the mystical illuminations of the founders of the worlds' various religions are formalized into laws, dogmas, creeds, and regulations to which the faithful must subscribe. Otherwise, they are not considered faithful, and they can then be ostracized, excommunicated, and even, crucified!

Once there is a church, a denomination, a hierarchy, and a system of controls, there is someone on the top, someone in the middle, and someone on the bottom and thus there arise ego games about who gets to be on top and who has to remain on the bottom. Harriett Martineau (1802-1876, England), a Unitarian, prolific writer, and philosopher, describes the church as a chain of command that easily becomes a system of oppression, repression, and despotism.

Religions pass away, but God remains.
Victor Hugo

Victor Hugo (1802–1885, France) was a novelist, poet, playwright, human rights campaigner, and a leading exponent of the Romantic Movement in France. He is best remembered for *Les Miserables* and *The Hunchback of Notre Dame.* A non-practicing Catholic, he settled into a *Rationalist Deism.* He had an antipathy towards the Catholic Church because of the arrogance and wealth of the Church and its indifference to the poor. His books were consistently on the Pope's list of "forbidden books." He believed Catholic dogma was outdated and dying. He remained a deeply religious man who strongly believed in the power of prayer. Christianity he said would one day disappear, but people would still believe in "God, Soul, and the Power."

Mysticism is Devoid of Politics

There are thousands of different religions, some more divisive than unifying and some even willing to go to war to prove the superiority of their way to peace. Mysticism is devoid of politics. Mysticism has no hierarchy, no creeds, laws or dogmas. It has no required ways of believing and worshipping. It has no buildings, priests, ministers or reverends, though a priest, minister or reverend may very well be a mystic. While mysticism has no rules, a mystic nevertheless knows that there are certain basic laws of the universe. When life is lived in accordance with these laws (God's laws), not the ego's, things work out fine. When life is lived in conflict with these laws, it takes a little longer.

I know a man who saw God
so clearly that he lost all religion.
Aegidius of Assisi (? – 1262, Italy)
A disciple of St. Francis of Assisi

Organized religion has a built-in system of controls. As such, it easily can obscure the truth by presenting some individual's version of the truth. Several of the founding fathers of the United States, including Benjamin Franklin, Roger Williams, Thomas Paine and Thomas Jefferson, insisted on the separation of church and state. Jefferson swore "eternal hostility" toward every form of tyranny over the mind of man including organized religion, for he saw how prejudicial it could be and how easily it distorted reality. "I am," he said, "of a sect by myself as far as I know."

John Tyler, the 10th President of the United States, wrote, "No religious establishment by law exists among us. The conscience is left free from all restraint and each is permitted to worship his Maker after his own judgment." Abraham Lincoln, perhaps our most spiritual president, never joined a church. He once confided to a friend that his religious code was the same as an old man he knew in Indiana, who said, *"When I does good, I feels good, and when I does bad, I feels bad, I reckon that's my religion."*

Nothing is more dreaded than the national
government meddling with religion.
John Adams, 2nd President of the USA

Thomas Paine (1737–1809, USA) was an intellectual, revolutionary, deist, and pamphleteer who helped foment the American Revolution with his best-selling book *Common Sense*. His book, *The Age of Reason* advocated deism and took issue with the traditional church.

I do not believe in the creed professed by the
Jewish Church, by the Roman Church, by the Greek
Church, by the Turkish Church, by the Protestant
Church, nor by any church that I know of.
My own mind is my own church.
Thomas Paine

A 2005 *Newsweek* Beliefnet Poll found more Americans, especially those younger than 60, describing themselves as "spiritual but not religious." According to the article, "We are looking for transcendence in the midst of the mundane." An American Religious Identification Survey released in 2001 by the Graduate Center of the City University of New York found that the number of Americans who follow no organized religion increased from 8 percent in 1990 to 14 percent in 2001. During the same period, the number of Americans who identify themselves as Christian shrank from 86 percent to 76 percent—a reduction of ten percent in just ten years!

Religion is a fruitless effort to mark a pathway on
the shifting sands of the desert. The infinite, cannot
be trapped, described or noted. We are one with the
infinite even as we pretend that we are not.
Anthony de Mello

Anthony de Mello, (1931–1987, India) was a Jesuit priest and psychotherapist who became well known for his books on spirituality, including *Contact with God* and *The Song of the Bird*. In 1998 his writings were condemned by the Catholic Church because they were interfaith in tone and not strictly Christian. *"In order to protect the good of the Christian faithful, this Congregation declares that Father Anthony de Mello's writings are incompatible with the Catholic faith and can cause grave harm."* The Papers of Condemnation were issued by the then Cardinal Ratzinger, now Pope Benedict XVI. [See www.demello.org]

The Rise of a New Spirituality

Christianity as a religion of certainty and control is
dying. The signs of that death are present in the
emptiness of the churches of Europe, in the decline of
candidates for the priesthood in the Roman Catholic
Church, in the increasing obsession about issues of
sexuality that bedevil church leaders, and in the
rising secularization of our society.
Bishop John Shelby Spong

John Shelby Spong (1931 – Present, USA) is the retired Bishop of the Episcopal Diocese of Newark, New Jersey. He is an author, lecturer, theologian, and biblical scholar. He calls for a basic rethinking of Christian belief, away from the ideas of Heaven and Hell as reward and punishment. He is also a proponent of feminism, gay rights, and racial equality.

In the midst of spiritual growth outside the church, pathfinders like Bishop John Shelby Spong are trying to reform the church from within. As philosopher Ken Wilbur points out, the new awareness that is dawning is more a matter of transformation than reformation or translation. It's not about changing our denomination. It's about changing our mind. It's about becoming wholly new.

You don't change the old by resisting it.
You change the old by making it obsolete
through superior methodology.
Buckminster Fuller

Buckminster "Bucky" Fuller (1895–1983, USA) was an American visionary, designer, architect, poet, author, and inventor best known for the creation of the geodesic dome.

The growing interest in non-church-based spirituality and the esoteric is seen in the popularity of *The Da Vinci Code*, the *Jesus Papers*, and the *Harry Potter* books. Interest in these books reflects the desire we have to find some hidden spiritual revelations rooted in the mystical. Mysticism is about revealing to the mind something that *appears* to be hidden. The quest for the "Holy Grail" is not, however, about material objects or sacred bloodlines. In fact, the quest transcends this world altogether. The "Holy Grail" is Revelation and Enlightenment!

We stand at the beginning of the twenty-first century looking for a new way of "seeing" that is the oldest way there is. There is a new awareness gaining a foothold on planet Earth. According to David Hawkins, the collective awareness level of mankind is moving upward. As D. Patrick Miller expresses it in his monograph *A Different Kind of Miracle*, "Rather than feeling the evangelicals' need to persuade others to adhere to a traditional vision of absolute truth, the new spiritualists are bent on experiencing *mystical truths* by their own direct experience."

My belief is that the truth is a truth
until you organize it, and then it becomes a lie.
I don't think that Jesus was teaching Christianity,
Jesus was teaching kindness, love, concern, and
peace. What I tell people is don't be Christian,
be Christ-like. Don't be Buddhist, be Buddha-like.
Wayne Dyer

Dr. Wayne W. Dyer (1940 – Present, USA) is a popular self-help advocate, author, lecturer, and friend. His 1976 book *Your Erroneous Zones* is one of the best-selling books of all time. He has become progressively interested in spirituality as seen in his referencing *The Tao Te Ching*, *A Course in Miracles*, and other spiritual traditions.

The City of No Gate

Mysticism is completely free and open to anyone at anytime. You join this invisible, non-dues-paying club by *realizing* that you already are one. No other qualifications are needed. You may be male or female; nine or ninety; black, white, brown or polka dotted. There is no pledge you have to make, no oath to take, and nothing to sign. You don't even have to make weekly contributions!

The creative impulse in the world, so far as we are
aware of it, appears upon ultimate analysis to be free
and original, not bound and mechanical.
Evelyn Underhill

Mysticism is non-church, non-denominational, non-hierarchical spirituality. While a mystic may be a part of a specific religion, mysticism transcends doctrinal perspectives. Mystics engage in independent studies with a guide, perhaps a book or a teacher, and the companionship of a few other students. I once asked students in a class I was teaching on *The History of Mysticism* what they noticed as common traits of the mystics. One student said, "Most all of them were single." This is true for many, though certainly not all mystics. All "structures," all forms, even the seemingly solid ones pass away when a greater truth is realized. According to Danish Theologian Soren Kierkegaard, institutional religion subverts and sabotages the individual's awareness and the experience of truth. The mystic steps away from illusion, rather than becoming immersed in it.

Soren Kierkegaard (1813 –1855, Denmark) achieved recognition as the first existentialist philosopher. He was also a humorist, psychologist, and poet. Champion of the "individual thinker," he believed that the rituals of the Danish Lutheran Church were futile customs. He experienced an unrequited love relationship with the beautiful Regina Olsen. Though she married another man, she was buried next to Kierkegaard. At Kierkegaard's funeral, his nephew Henrik Lund protested the hypocrisy of Kierkegaard being buried by the church when he had himself so thoroughly denounced the church. For his tombstone, Kierkegaard wanted only his name and dates and the words, "The Individual Thinker."

Truth, being limitless, unconditioned,
unapproachable by any path whatsoever,
cannot be organized; nor should any organization
be formed to lead or coerce people along a
particular path. The moment you follow someone you
cease to follow Truth. I am concerning myself with
only one essential thing: to set man free. I desire to
free him from all cages, from all fears, and not to
found religions, new sects, nor to establish new
theories and new philosophy. My only concern is to
set men absolutely, unconditionally free.
J. Krishnamurti

J. Krishnamurti (1895–1986, India) was born in India but spent most of his life in the United States. His primary teaching is the pursuit of freedom from the ego. For sixty years he traveled the world, speaking about self-knowledge. His teaching was interfaith in perspective, transcending man-made limitations of religion, nationality, ideology, and sectarian thinking. George Bernard Shaw said Krishnamurti was the most beautiful human being he ever saw. Krishnamurti and Aldous Huxley were friends. Huxley wrote the foreword to Krishnamurti's book *The First and Last Freedom.* Krishnamurti was also friends with and influenced the works of Joseph Campbell. He was considered a great teacher by Ramana Maharshi, Anandamayi Ma, and Osho. He would not accept disciples, as he said, *"People use the guru as a crutch."* Refusing to play the role of a guru, he urged his listeners to be a light unto themselves. A spiritual teacher who disavowed rituals and dogma, Krishnamurti claimed that liberation is available, here—now.

One contemporary Western document has a strongly mystical perspective. *A Course in Miracles* is a program of spiritual psychology that, through *revelation* and *forgiveness*, enables the reader to release fear and achieve inner peace. It encourages a significantly different way of "seeing" from the ordinary framework of the ego. The Course was scribed (written down) by Dr. Helen Schucman, a New York City psychologist, between the years 1965–1972. Helen never thought of herself as the author of the Course. I met Helen and her co-worker Dr. Bill Thetford in 1973. Along with Dr. Kenneth Wapnick, they introduced me to the Course in April 1975. Since I knew Helen personally, I can assure you there was no way that Helen, herself (as wonderful as she was), could have written the Course. The message of the Course is so beautiful, so clear—it is in fact impeccable.

Picking a Path

You can pick no path at all as Krishnamurti and Wei Wu Wei (Terrance Gray) suggest, or you can find another path that works for you. *A Course in Miracles* is one of many thousands of paths, and there is nothing that says you have to do it. The New Thought Movement, Unity, Religious Science, Christian mysticism, Buddhism, Bahai, Sufism, The Kabbalah, Vedanta, yoga, and meditation are a few of the many helpful paths. What the path looks like is less important than whether you "work" it, so it can "work" you. It's often best to work within the mystical branch of the tradition in which you were born. What the Course has is simplicity with sophistication. It is a manual for the awakening of mystic vision without dogma, rituals, and the fetters of traditional religion.

Mysticism is the prosecution of a spiritual and
intangible quest; the finding of a "way out" of
illusion or a "way back" to absolute truth.
It is an intimate personal adventure.
Evelyn Underhill

Religion	Symbol	Founder	Century it Began	Country of Origin	Name of Holy Book	No. of People	% of the World	Increase/ Decrease/ Stable
Christianity	✝	Jesus, Peter & Paul	1st Century	Israel	New Testament	2 billion	33%	—
Islam	☪	Muhammad	7th Century AD	Saudi Arabia	Koran	1.3 billion	21%	+
Hinduism	ॐ		C. 1500 BC maybe earlier	India	Vedas Upanishads Bhagavad Gita	1 billion	15%	+
Buddhism		Buddha	6th Century BC	India	Tripitaka Sutras	376 million	6%	+
Taoism	☯	Lao-Tzu	6th Century BC	China	Tao-Te-Ching	20 million	0.31%	—
Judaism	✡	Abraham 2000 BC Moses 1, 200 BC	Around 1500 BC	Israel	Torah	14 million	0.22%	—
Sikhism	☬	Kabir Nanik	1400s AD	Pakistan	Grantah	23 million	0.36%	+
Confucianism		Confucius	6th Century BC	China	Analects	6 million	0.02%	—
Jainism		Mahavira	6th Century BC	India	Agama Sutras	4.2 million	0.01%	+
Shinto	⛩		6th Century BC	Japan	Nigorgi	4 million	0.01%	+ (after years of decline)
Zoroastrianism or Parses		Zoroaster	9th Century BC	Persia Iran	Avesta	2.6 million	0.01%	+
Tribal or Shamanistic				All over the world		300 million	6%	—
New Religions			20th & 21st Century	All over the world		130 million	3%	+
Non Religions				All over the world		1.1 billion	16%	Fastest Growing

The Great Commandment According to All Religions

Do not condemn your brother until you have walked a mile in his moccasins. ~ Native American
Do naught to others which if done to thee would cause thee pain. ~ Hinduism
Hurt not others with that which pains thyself. ~ Buddhism
What you don't want done to yourself don't do to others. ~ Confucianism
Regard your neighbor's gain as your own gain and regard your neighbor's loss as your own loss. ~ Taoism
We should regard all creatures as we regard our own self, and should refrain from inflicting upon others such injury as would appear undesirable to us if inflicted upon ourselves. ~ Jainism
Do not do unto others all that which is not well for oneself. ~ Zoroastrianism
What is hateful to yourself, don't do to your fellow man. ~ Judaism
Whatsoever ye would that men should do to you, do ye even so to them. ~ Christianity
Treat others as thou would be treated thyself. ~Sikhism

Chapter 2

Mysticism as a Journey

The Quest

According to mysticism, we are strangers in this world, *seekers* on a journey back home to God. Mystics often described different *stages* or *levels* of development. The journey is described in steps, degrees, and stations. We see it in Jacob's ladder extending to heaven (Genesis 28:12), St. Bonaventure's "pilgrimage of the soul," and Walter Hilton's "ladder to perfection." *A Course in Miracles* speaks of a "ladder of separation," down which we have descended into illusion. There is also a ladder home to God, whereby we undo all of our previous errors.

Life has to be lived forward
but it can only be understood backward.
Soren Kierkegaard

Levels or stages are more clearly understood when we look back over the path we followed. Different mystics describe different stages. Studying the various stages you inevitably begin to see similarities in different paths. This is very instructive. Purgation, cleaning house, coming to greater clarity, for example, is always near the beginning of any path.

Different mystics describe differing number of stages. The pathway home is individualized. As we each go through our own stages in different times, at different rates in different ages. We experience physical growth in our youth, we experience increasing spiritual growth as we grow older. Some people are very clear about being on a mystical path. Others may have no or little awareness of any spiritual path until something happens which forces them to take a closer look.

Gregory of Nyssa (335–394, Greece), a Christian bishop and saint who argued for the infinity of God, speaks of three stages of spiritual development:

1. Initial darkness or ignorance.
2. Spiritual Illumination
3. A darkness of the mind in contemplation of the God who cannot be comprehended with the intellect.

It is through not-knowing and not-seeing that God can be seen. This notion is extremely influential in both Western and Eastern mystical writings. We find it again in Pseudo-Dionysius and later in the anonymous 14th century work, *The Cloud of Unknowing*.

The Sufis speak of three stages in the mystical journey:

1. **The Journey to God:** when we awaken enough to realize we are "in exile."
2. **The Journey in God:** Begins after the ego has been through some annihilating experiences.
3. **The Journey Through God:** God takes the lead. This requires an advanced degree of surrender, which is difficult to achieve but the result is a life of inspiration and happiness unknown to those who know life as a daily routine of struggling to earn money, raise children, and find respectability in the world.

Saint Teresa of Avila (1515–1582, Spain) was an important person of the Catholic Reformation and a famous Spanish mystic, writer and a monastic reformer. According to Teresa God dwells in the soul and the soul travels within herself to unite with God. She is recognized as one of only three female Doctors of the Catholic Church, along with St. Catherine of Siena, and St. Therese of Lisieux. St. Teresa describes in her autobiography four stages of the ascent of the soul to Heaven.

1. **The Hearts Devotion**, or and the withdrawal of the soul from external things along with recognition of one's own mistakes.
2. **The Devotion of Peace**, where the human will is lost in God by virtue of a charismatic, supernatural state given by God. Though memory, reason, and imagination are still distracted by the world, there is a growing sense of quietude and inner peace.
3. **The Devotion of Union** is an ecstatic state and an absorption in God. Though reason is given over to God, memory and imagination are still left to ramble. This state is characterized by a blissful peace, a sweet slumber of the higher soul's faculties, and a conscious rapture in the love of God.

4. **The Devotion of Ecstasy** is a passive state, in which the awareness of being in the body disappears. Sense activity ceases; memory and imagination are also absorbed in God. Body and spirit are then in the throes of a sweet, happy pain.

Evelyn Underhill describes five stages.

1. **Awakening** – one begins to have awareness of divine reality.
2. **Purgation** – This involves some self-discipline and is characterized by an awareness of one's own finiteness.
3. **Illumination** – often reached by artists and visionaries and seen by some as a final stage.
4. **The dark night of the soul.** This stage is marked by complete purification and involves confusion, helplessness, stagnation of the will, and a sense of the withdrawal of God's presence. It is a period culminating in final surrender to divine will.
5. **Union with the object of love:** One Reality, God.

One of the courses I taught at the New School University in the 1970s covered the work of G. I. Gurdjieff and his student P.D. Ouspensky. In 1976 I met Tom Forman, one of Ouspensky's students and held sessions with Tom as the teacher at my home in High Rock Springs in Katonah, New York, and in New York City.

G.I. Gurdjieff (1866–1949, Greek-Armenian) was a mystic and spiritual teacher known for his *Fourth Way.* He established a school for spiritual growth called The Institute for the Harmonious Development of Man. Perhaps his best book is *Life is Real Only Then, When I Am.* His complete set of books is entitled *All and Everything.*

Gurdjieff describes 4 stages of consciousness.

1. **Slumber Sleep**, a passive state, a place of dreams' unconsciousness awareness—something is there.
2. **The Ordinary "Waking"** state, in which we spend our ambulatory life—day dreaming.
3. **Self-Remembering or Self-Consciousness.** This is a place of self honest appraisal without defensiveness or the need to retreat from the world. Here attention to self is constantly refined. One becomes increasingly compassionate, non-judgmental, and nearly unblinking. It is a way of being present to oneself that excludes daydreaming. It is a rising above the *automatic* self.
4. **Objective Consciousness or Enlightenment** where things are seen unfiltered with out our interpretation. Objective Consciousness is indescribable, ineffable. As with the other states, it must be developed in order to be maintained.

In *The Path to No Self,* Bernadette Roberts describes six stages in the mystic journey: beginning in a "Unitive" state; progressing to a permanent, irreversible transcendence of the ego; and *ending* in an abiding awareness of God.

Bernadette Roberts (1931 – Present, USA) has been called a post-Christian mystic. A devout Catholic, as a child, she had a number of mystical experiences in nature. When she was eighteen, she entered the Carmelite order. When a Mother Superior asked her about her prayer life, she said, "I do nothing; there is just silence." The Mother Superior thought Bernadette should be thinking about something like Jesus suffering on the cross. By thinking of nothing, she had unwittingly opened herself to the devil. Bernadette left the order, married, and raised four children. She understood mysticism to be a contemplative *journey* beyond self.

Mythology, Mysticism and Meaning

A myth is an image in terms of which
we try to make sense of the world.
Alan Watts

Alan Watts (1915–1973, USA) carried out the pursuit of the mystical from the mid 1930s though the early 70s. He is known as an interpreter of Zen Buddhism in particular and Indian and Chinese philosophy in general. He wrote over twenty books and numerous articles on mysticism.

To understand the meaning of a myth, we engage in demythologizing. To **demythologize** is to understand the basic story behind the story: what the story is saying on an anthropological, psychological, social, and moral level. A myth does not have to be "true" in the literal sense of the word in order for the story to have its impact on the human psyche.

The Adventure of the hero
is the adventure of being alive.
Joseph Campbell, Ph.D.

The twentieth century's greatest "mythologist", **Dr. Joseph Campbell** (1904–1984, USA), based much of his work on the teaching of Dr. Carl Jung. Campbell served as consultant to George

Lucas in the production of the first *Star Wars* Trilogy of the 1970s. *Star Wars* contained almost all of the elements of a hero myth.

Individuation – Finding the Self

Carl Jung, more than anyone, explored the realms of the "collective unconscious." While Freud explored the unconscious, Jung looked deeper into the collective unconscious found in dreams, myths, fairy tales, esoteric sciences, and alchemy, together with other hermetic and occult disciplines. He described spiritual growth as the "Process of Individuation." This process is the gradual integration and unification of the Self. Individuation is a "coming to terms of the inborn germ of wholeness with the outer acts of fate." It is through individuation that we give form to the characteristics that express who we are. The spiritual pathway is thus for each of us highly individualized; therefore, each mystic's story has a unique expression—in time.

There is more to life than going through the daily routine. Mysticism opens the door to this other, spiritual part of life. Although mysticism can be seen as a journey, it is not like taking a train to a given destination. Mysticism "is" the journey. The development of mystical awareness is similar to a flower developing from a seed. The flower already possesses its beauty while still in the seed. It just has to be drawn out.

Whoever is willing the Fates will lead.
The unwilling they will drag along.
Old Roman saying

Mystics are aware of an active, inner process of realization "cooking away" inside. They have a sense of *kismet*, an awareness of a deep inner fate. The seekers proceed and regress, proceed and regress again. Something is gained when we move forward; something is gained when we retreat. Whether we are aware of the spiritual process or not, it is still there. The more we are aware of the process, the more we make a living connection with it, and the richer life becomes. The less aware we are of an inner life, the more we experience feelings of anxiety and dread. We sense that life either has no meaning or, if it does, we're missing out on it. Many seem caught in the illusions of "Maya," unable to find a way out. The spiritual journey is one of discovery. The task is to find ourselves: to discover why we came here and what our destiny is—then to fulfill it. Life becomes and is meaningful as we give in to the urge toward creative Self-realization and Self-expression.

Reality as a Parable

Then the disciples went up to Him and asked, "Why do you talk to them in parables?" "Because," He replied, "the mysteries of the Kingdom of Heaven are revealed to you, but they are not revealed to them. The reason I talk to them in parables is that they look without seeing and listen without hearing or understanding." In all this, Jesus spoke to the crowd in parables; indeed, He would never speak to them except in parables.
Matthew 13: 10, 11, 13 and 34

Jewish philosophy consisted more of stories than philosophical reflection. Matthew says that Jesus never spoke to people directly, but *always* chose to teach through stories. A myth is a metaphor for the experience of life. We cannot see the ineffable straight on, so some type of translation, or symbolism, is necessary. In mystical literature, that translator is the myth, the metaphor, the tale, the dream—the story. His parable of the prodigal son is a typical hero myth, providing a vivid image that lingers in the mind. Theologian Rudolph Bultmann said the parables of Jesus are stories about *the other side* told in terms of *this side*. The story plants a seed in consciousness, and like music, the theme remains after the story is told. Without parables, the teachings of Jesus would sound like those of many philosophers: profound but unengaging. The meaning of his messages is understood on a deeper level because of the illustrative quality of the teachings. Thus, imagery provides the hint of something more. It is possible to hear more in poetry or music or see more in surrealism than in an essay or realistic art.

Jesus life is a parable, a description of a pathway to the Kingdom. At an early age, he was sure of his destiny. Tormented, crucified, and given every reason to be angry, Jesus, like any true mystic, remained faithful to his clear perception of God's call. From Bethlehem to Golgotha, his is the story of a hero. It is also your story and mine. It belongs to each of us, unique and divine. What matters most is not the Gospel according to Matthew, Mark, Luke or John but the Gospel according to you.

The Hymn of the Pearl

Imbedded in the *Gospel of Thomas* is a beautiful, complete Gnostic myth describing the exile and redemption of the soul. The text is known as the "Hymn of the Pearl." The following is a shortened, paraphrased version of this myth.

A young man dwells in a marvelous, rich kingdom. His parents send him on a mission with provisions "great yet light" so that he can carry them. Before he leaves, he removes his Robe of Glory and splendid mantle. In his heart is inscribed a message concerning his destiny: He is to obtain a pearl lying in the middle of a sea encircled by a snorting serpent.

Making his way out of the kingdom, he is accompanied by two royal envoys. The way is dangerous and hard, and he is young. A stranger in the new world, he disguises himself to look like those around him. He keeps to himself till he recognizes another "anointed one," with whom he develops a mutual trust. His friend tries to warn him about the "unclean" ones who, when they see that he is not a countryman, will ingratiate themselves with him. But the young journeyer falls prey to the unclean ones, who cunningly mix drink and give him their meat so that he becomes unaware of his mission. He forgets that he is a king's son; he forgets the pearl.

His parents learn of all that befalls their son and write a letter that calls him to awaken, rise out of sleep, break free of his bondage, and remember his destiny. The letter comes in the form of an eagle, which "becomes wholly speech." At its voice, he awakens, embraces the letter, breaks its seal, and recalls in his heart the words of the letter.

He remembers that he is a king's son, a "freeborn soul." He remembers the pearl and the snorting serpent. Going to the serpent, he charms it to sleep by repeating to it his Father's name. Seizing the pearl, he repairs for home, leaving behind his "impure garments." The voice of the letter now guides him with its light, discourages his fears, and with its light draws him homeward. He had forgotten the "Robe of Glory" he had left behind in his youth. Seeing it again, it becomes a mirror image of himself. "I saw it in all of me, and saw me all in it." Clothed in his robe, he ascends to the gates of salutation and adores the splendor of his Father, who had sent him on the mission and whose command he has now fulfilled.

Pilgrim's Progress

Another wonderful mystic journey is told by John Bunyan in *Pilgrim's Progress*, published in 1664. After the parables of Jesus, it is the most famous Christian allegory. Bunyan wrote the work while in prison for "preaching without a license." Required reading in schools in the nineteenth century, it was second in sales only to the Bible until the twentieth century. *Pilgrim's Progress* is the story of a hero named Christian who goes off in search of the celestial city (Heaven). He is carrying on his back a number of burdens, and he must go through a series of experiences: "The Slough of Despond," "The Valley of Humiliation," and even "The Valley of the Shadow of Death." As he goes through the various experiences, his burdens are lifted from him until he arrives at the Celestial City completely naked (unburdened).

The Search

Jesus said, "The world is a place of transition, full of examples: be pilgrims therein, and take warning by the traces of those that have gone before."

From Christ in Islam

From the most primitive mythological traditions to sophisticated twentieth-century societies, there are stories of heroes and heroines who go off in search of a greater destiny than sleeping, eating, earning a living, raising a family, and dying. Symbolic of each of us, the hero leaves home and ventures into a strange land, encounters difficulties and falls prey to a variety of forces and illusions. Here the hero also meets a guide who provides tools to help in a journey that involves some *task* or specific *function*.

Guides and Companions

Accepting a calling, we soon receive unexpected help. The life of Jesus is full of protective guides—angels and wise men appeared at his birth. In myths, there often appears a caring figure or figures—an old man or woman, a medicine man, hermit, shepherd, escort, shaman, smithy, ferryman, pilot or other similar figure. Moses speaks directly to God. Cinderella has her fairy godmother; King Arthur has Merlin; Luke of *Star Wars* has Obi-wan Kenobi and Yoda. Castaneda encounters Don Juan; Dorothy has the Good Witch. The hero of *The Celestine Prophecy* encounters Dobson, Will, and Father Carl. The guide is encountered when the hero is alone—off in the desert, on the mountaintop or sitting in his room.

In today's world, the guide might be an older friend, an uncle, therapist, coach, teacher, mentor, minister or guru. Gail Sheehy notes in her book, *Pathfinders* that most people who become pathfinders have at least one strong role model who influenced them, someone who exerted a forward pull and offered guidance. A *polestar*, or guide, is a friend and counselor, one or two generations older, who endorses the seeker's quest and helps him or her toward realization. Children who have absent or undependable parents gravitate naturally towards other figures—perhaps a grandparent or a great aunt or uncle—who can function as a polestar.

The Inner Guide

Jesus tells the disciples that it is to their advantage that he is going away—for if he does not go away, the Comforter, the Holy Spirit, cannot come to them. In *Star Wars*, Obi-wan Kenobi becomes more powerful after he leaves his body. Mystics develop an "inner dialogue" with spirit. Bernadette Roberts calls it a "*Unitive Life*." The mystic tunes in to what Native Americans call "The Great Man in the Heart" or what the Christians call the "Holy Spirit," or the mentor within. With practice we can learn to differentiate between the anxious voice of the ego and the "still, small voice" of God. The question is not "Is there really a voice?" The question is *"Why don't I do what He asks me to do, so that I can hear his voice even better?"*

> *There is not in the world a life more sweet and delightful, than that of a continual conversation with God. Only those who comprehend it can practice and experience it.*
>
> Brother Lawrence

Brother Lawrence (1611–1691, France), a lay brother of the Carmelites, is famous for his *Practice of the Presence of God.* (See www.PracticeGodsPresence.com).

Companions join us on the journey: brothers, sisters, husbands, wives, partners and friends. While the guide is usually a generation or two older, a companion is about the same age and also in search of their destiny. We reach the Kingdom holding on one side the hand of someone who helped us and on the other side, the hand of someone whom we have helped. *Christian* of *Pilgrim's Progress* has a companion called "Faithful," who plays a dual role as a guide. In the Babylonian tradition, *Gilgamesh* has *Enkidu*, who is an enemy until they get into a wrestling match that neither is able to win. Exhausted, they begin to talk, and each finds out that the "other guy" is not so bad after all.

Moses has his brother, *Aaron*. When Moses himself is unable to speak, his brother Aaron gives voice to that which Moses cannot utter. *Jesus'* companion is *John the Baptist*, the first to pronounce him "the Christ." The disciples are also companions, although their roles are more that of students. *St. John of the Cross* has *St. Teresa of Avila* as guide and companion. *Dorothy* of *The Wizard of Oz* has the *Tin Man*, the *Lion*, and the *Scarecrow*, each of whom has certain important qualities needed in their search. *Luke Skywalker* of the *Star Wars* series has *Han Solo*, *Princess Leia*, and *Chewbacca*.

Tools: The Word

The guide often gives a tool to help throughout the journey. In Catholicism these various tools are sometimes call "attributes." It might be knowledge, motivation, patience, psychic ability or some kind of useful object. The guide, the companion, and the tool may all be one and the same thing. The Word is the most common of all tools and guides. It is often in the form of a book: the *Bible*, the *Upanishads* or other scripture. Moses is given the *Ten Commandments*; Mohammed gets the *Koran*; in *The Celestine Prophecy*, the tool is an ancient manuscript. When Helen Schucman handed me *A Course in Miracles* and said, "I think you are supposed to teach this," I knew that something very important had just happened.

Useful objects can be almost anything: a paint brush, a pencil, a fishing pole, a chisel, a hammer, a surveying device, a ball and a bat, a surf board, a musical instrument, a camera or a computer. Objects can carry both practical and symbolic value; King Arthur of *Camelot* receives *Excalibur*, a magical sword. Obi-wan Kenobi gives Luke a laser sword. The amulet is an ancient Egyptian symbol of power. Other talismans include the cross, a crystal or a medal (such as those worn by many Catholics). Still, there is no magical power in physical objects; the power is in the mind.

Money has played a role in mysticism since its invention. Wise men brought Jesus gold, frankincense, and myrrh. With money, we can either further ourselves along the path or misuse its power. With money, we can buy a book or a tool that helps us or our companions along the way. Money can either enrich or poison our relationships. [For an engaging history of how money has influenced mysticism and religious history, see philosopher Jacob Needleman's *Money and the Meaning of Life*.]

Familiars are guides of a special sort: animals, dolls, puppets, teddy bears or cartoon characters, imaginary companions, or symbolic entities invented by our imaginations. Animals instinctively know some things of a spiritual nature that humans do not. Every animal, for example, knows how to be still—how to shut down or quiet the mind. Many people are not even aware of the possibility of being still. Dogs can sense the distress of their masters when their masters feel bad or ill, and they will try to cheer them up. Animals can teach us a great deal about living life free of judgment and worry.

In mythology, it is often the familiar or animal spirit guide that saves the day. In *Peter Pan*, *Tinkerbelle* is a companion and guide. For *Pinocchio* there is *Jiminy Cricket*, who sings "When you wish upon a star" and "Always let your conscience be your guide." *Dorothy* in *The Wizard of Oz* has her dog *Toto* who pulls apart the curtain hiding the Wizard. In *Star Wars* there are two droids, *R2-D2* and *C-3PO*. They each have unique personalities. It is *R2-D2* that breaks into the computer bank of the Empire and "saves the day." Animals are familiars in *Cinderella* and *Beauty and the Beast*. My first familiar was my black cloth doll, Joe, who I thought was alive until I was nine, when I had an unfortunate epiphany that, in fact, he was not alive—although, of course, he is still very alive to this day. He now sits on my desk, and occasionally I turn to him and say, "What do you think of that Joe?"

I have lived with five Zen Masters, all of them cats.
Eckhart Tolle

The Enemy Within

Along the mystic path, we may meet what appear to be evil forces. Moses must deal with Pharaoh; Jesus has the Romans, the Pharisees, and the Sadducees. Dorothy of *The Wizard of Oz* encounters the Wicked Witch, and Cinderella must deal with her evil step-sisters. There comes a point on the journey when you cannot go back. (You are not in Kansas anymore). You must go forward and fulfill your destiny. Yet the distractions are many and so our hero may fall into an addiction, a dark night of the soul. Something has to happen to awaken the hero. Maybe the guide will be able to help, maybe a companion can assist. Most likely there will be some sort of crash and burn. For mystic heroes like Martin Luther, Gandhi or Martin Luther King, Jr., the opponent is *the establishment*, the old system, the traditional and tyrannical ways of doing things. But the most stealthy and difficult opponent is always one's own little self, the ego, the fear-driven part of the self which has temporarily taken over as director of our lives. Thus it is for Christian (of *Pilgrim's Progress*) or Castaneda, and so it is for you or me.

There is a scene in *Star Wars* where Luke Skywalker (being trained by Yoda) feels a call to explore something lurking within a dream like darkness. Yoda tells Luke that he will not need to take his laser sword, but he does anyway. In the dark, he encounters Darth Vader. They battle and Luke cuts off Darth Vader's head—only to discover, when the head rolls off onto the ground and the mask opens, that the face looking up at him is his own.

Completing the Mission

Gilgamesh and Enkidu must save their city. Moses must lead his people to the Promised Land. Jesus came to tell us about the Kingdom of Heaven. King Arthur must find the Holy Grail, and Dorothy must find her way home. The mystic is called to live the ordinary life in an extraordinary way, to imbue all activities and relationships with aliveness, richness, and purpose. Mysticism is an *inner* journey of transformation through which our highest potential may be fulfilled. All the great mystic journeys of literature are symbolic of this path of transformation. The heroic journey is often a dream, as it is for Dorothy in *The Wizard of Oz*. We wake up only to find that we never left home. For the hero, destiny summons and awaits a response. The more the call is acknowledged, the less we seem to have anything to do with it. The more strongly the call is felt, the more fate seems to step in, reducing the sense of life's randomness. As with Luke Skywalker in *Star Wars*, the task may seem Herculean, but incredible things happen when the call is accepted. Destiny unfolds.

Hero Mythology Chart

Hero	From	Guide	Other Guides	Primary Companion	Other Companion	Familiar(s)	Tool(s)	Task	Opponent
Gilgamesh	Ancient Babylon	Shamash	Anu	Enkidu				Save the City	Humbaba
Moses	Ancient Israel	God		Aaron			Staff	Lead People Out of Egypt	Pharaoh
Jesus	Christianity	God	Wise Men Simon Anna	John The Baptist	Disciples		Money Incense Oil Bread/Wine	Tell About Heaven	Pharisees Sadducees
King Arthur	Ancient England	Merlin		Lancelot	Knights of the Roundtable		Sword Excaliber	Find the Holy Grail	
Christian	*Pilgrim's Progress*	Faithful		Faithful			Staff	Find Entrance to Heaven	Himself
Castaneda	Mexico	Don Juan	Don Genaro			Cows and other Spirits	Writing Words	Self Discovery	Himself
Dorothy	*The Wizard of Oz*	Good Witch		Tin Man Lion Scare Crow		Toto	Red Slippers	Find Way Back Home	Wicked Witch
Luke Skywalker	*Star Wars*	Obi-Wan Kenobi	Yoda	Solo Princess Leia	Princess Leia	R2D2 C3PO	Laser Sword	Fight Evil Forces	Darth Vader
Cinderella	*Cinderella*	Fairy Godmother				Horse Mice	Glass Slipper	Marry the Prince	Wicked Sisters
Robin Hood	England			Little John Maid Marian	The Merry Men		Bow and Arrow		The Sheriff of Nottingham
Simba	*The Lion King*	Rafiki	Zazu	Timon Pumbaa	Nala			Accept his position as King	Scar

Section II — The Nature of Reality

Chapter 3

The Problem of the Ego

Four Zen students decided to go into a week of meditation together. The first couple of hours went by in complete silence before one of them suddenly said:

"I wonder if I remembered to turn off the stove."

The second student replied, *"You fool, you have spoken, and we had agreed not to speak."*

Then the third student said, *"Who are you to talk? You too have spoken."*

To which the fourth student said, *"I am the only one who has not spoken."*

The ego is that which defines, interprets, projects, judges, and analyzes. It is that which is *always* making up the world. I am always making up the world. You are always making up the world. We are always making up the world. There is a sense in which we can't help doing it.

In the West at least, we are nearly all busy polishing our mirrors or perfecting the hansom-cab, as I have termed it, instead of understanding that neither the polisher nor mirror, perfector nor cab, has ever or could ever exist.

Wei Wu Wei in *Ask the Awakened*

Wei Wu Wei, (Terence Gray), (1895–1986, England), was a Taoist philosopher.

Origins of the ego

Although we've not always had the term "ego" to describe the part of the mind that blocks awareness of the mystical, mystics have always talked about what gets in the way of true perception. In Jesus' day and for many centuries afterward, the word "devil" was used to describe that which is other than one's highest self.

We did not have a clear psychology of the ego until the work of **Sigmund Freud** (1856–1939, Austria). While Freud popularized the use of the term "ego," the word had been around for a long time, its origin being in the Latin word for "I am." It is Freud who explains ego defense mechanisms, and he tells us how they work. Freud's model of the mind reduces the scope of reason. Reasoning he says, occurs in the ego, but the ego is only a small part of the whole. The mind also contains hidden irrational motives outside of our conscious control. This fact calls into question our ability to act purely on the basis of reason, since the unconscious "drives" our life.

The importance of the ego in philosophy wasn't clear until the birth of modern philosophy in the sixteenth century. Even then, it wasn't until the eighteenth century that the role of the ego as the determiner of reality was more clearly understood.

The role of the ego was presented by **Immanuel Kant** (1724–1804, Germany) in his theory of *Transcendental Idealism.* Kant never traveled more than 100 miles from his hometown in Königsberg, the capital of East Prussia. He was so precise in his movements that people said they could set their clock in accordance with the time he passed their houses on his daily walk. Kant defined the Enlightenment as an age fashioned by the motto "Dare to know," meaning to think free of external influence. Kant asserted that no one could really know if there is a God and an afterlife. But, then again, no one could really know that there was not a God and an afterlife. To know God, some other element beside reason would be required. We perceive and know things as they appear to us, not as they are in and of themselves. The mind surrounds things with space and time. The world as we know it is not an objective fact apart from us. For example, we see only one or two walls of a house at any one time. The mind gathers up our sense impressions and mentally builds a complete house.

Philosopher **J.G. Fichte** (1762–1814, Germany) wrote *The Guide to the Blessed Life.* He insisted that a study of the ego should be fundamental to philosophy and to the then newly emerging field of psychology. Fichte pointed out that human understanding of the world is not derived from experiential knowledge; rather the observed world is the creation of the ego. For Fichte the world is "absolute ego." Fichte's first work, *Attempt at a Critique of All Revelation*, investigates the connections between divine revelation and Kant's philosophy.

Later, **Arthur Schopenhauer** (1788–1860, Germany) wrote a book called *The World as Will and Idea*. A student of Plato, Kant, and Fichte, Schopenhauer was one of the first Western philosophers to take an interest in Eastern thought. His work is thus also based on Vedanta. He was astounded to discover that some of the central doctrines of Hinduism and Buddhism coincided with conclusions that he and Kant had reached through an entirely different route. The world, he said, "is my representation." The world, says Schopenhauer, is ultimately in itself nothing. Only through denial of the ego's irrational will (insanity) can one obtain wisdom.

From Kierkegaard onward, a form of mysticism appeared in Western civilization as Existentialism, a philosophy in which individual human beings are understood as having full responsibility for creating or discovering meaning in their lives. According to Existentialism (and similar to Buddhism), we should not have mental preconceptions about the meaning of experiences but know our experiences with such immediacy that we no longer project our understanding of reality onto others.

How did the ego get started?

The Garden of Eden, or the pre-separation condition, was a state of mind in which nothing was needed. When Adam listened to the "lies of the serpent," all he heard was untruth.

A Course in Miracles

Demythologizing Adam and Eve

The ego really never got started because it does not exist, and what does not exist could not have a beginning. Still it "seems" like there is this "thing" that demands our attention. Perpetuating the "myth" of the ego keeps the "dream" alive. The real question is not how did the ego get started; the real question is why do we perpetuate it? Why can't we stop it?

The most fundamental myth of the Western World explains the origin and persistence of the ego through the story of Adam and Eve. *Adam* (meaning "man") and *Eve* (meaning "woman") are created in a state of pure innocence, un-self-consciousness. Then something happens. Adam apparently does what he was asked not to do. The Bible says that his "eyes were opened and he was able to distinguish good and evil." (Genesis 3:7) The moment we have good and evil, we have duality. We have self and other, good and bad, pretty and ugly, all of which require judgment to discern and differentiate. In terms of the myth at hand, judgment is symbolized by the Serpent. The word *Satan* means *the great separator*. There is no mention of an apple in the book of Genesis. I have often joked that the fabled apple was probably a mushroom. Foraging around for food, primitive man may well have bitten into something that suddenly changed everything, facilitating the creation of a dualistic self-consciousness.

If we have judgment, we have separation. We do not have the whole; we do not have vastness; we do not have the infinite. Instead, we have the concrete, the physical, the material, and the limited. Don Juan in the Carlos Castaneda material says we are *nagual* (unconscious, irrational) at birth and for a short time thereafter. Then we become *tonal* (conscious, rational, egoistic), and we begin to distinguish "differences," or "pairs."

Adam was but human—this explains it all.
He did not want the apple for the apple's sake;
he wanted it only because it was forbidden.
The mistake was in not forbidding the serpent;
then he would have eaten the serpent.

Mark Twain

Animal and Human Consciousness

Although animals think, they do not think about thinking; that is, they don't have *self-reflection*. Not only do we humans think, we also think about thinking. Self-reflective thought creates a divided mind. It creates a sense of separation, a sense of isolation, angst, anxiety, and hell. After Adam bites into "the fruit of the knowledge of good and evil," he runs and hides in the bushes. According to the Bible, God goes looking for Adam ("in the cool of the day"). God finds Adam hiding in the bushes, and He says, "Why are you hiding?" Adam says, "Because I was naked." And God says, "Who told you [that] you were naked?" (Genesis 3:11) How did Adam get naked? "Naked" means that he has been exposed, and now he feels shame. The first experience of guilt—dirty, stinky, awful guilt—has entered the mind.

Ego Defense Mechanisms

Let's leave Adam in the bushes for a moment and talk about modern psychology. Freud delineated the different aspects of ego defenses and told us how the ego works. Thanks to Freud and Jung and the other founders of modern depth psychology, we now have more clarity than ever about the structure, origin, and evolution of the mechanism of the ego. We've all experienced the workings of the ego firsthand. We all have a pretty good idea how it works. We know a lot about what ego defenses are, but we don't know how to stop them from running our lives.

Mystics pursue a variety of ways to stop the ego. Being always on either the offense or the defense, our egos are well protected. Attack and defense make the ego real. The fiercer our defenses, the more real attack seems. The more intensely we experience attack, the greater our defenses. It is a two edged sword. To deny is to hold in, to hide or to repress. To project is to hurl outward like a "projectile" so that we blame others for the problems we find in the world and in ourselves.

Denial: The simplest form of denial is lying. What is the first thing that Adam does after "his eyes are opened" and he is able to distinguish between "good and evil"? He hides in the bushes. Lying is a form of hiding. The first person you probably lied to (which produced an experience of guilt and separation) was your mother. It probably happened a little bit like this: Mother walked into your room, saw a mess you made, and said, "What happened here?" And you said: "I don't know!"

Projection: Let's get Adam out of the bushes. God presses Adam to tell Him a little more about what has happened. Adam goes to his second line of defense and comes up with Eve. (What other choice did he have?) "Eve gave me the apple and I did eat thereof." God goes to Eve and says, "Look Eve, what happened?" Eve immediately goes to the second line of defense and says, "The serpent did beguile me, and I did eat thereof." And thus began the habit of finding someone to blame for our flaws, mistakes, and simple misunderstandings.

Resisting the ego only nourishes it. The desire to have the ego annihilated keeps the ego alive.
Ramesh Balsekar

Ramesh Balsekar (1919 – Present, India) is a former C.E.O. of the Bank of India and teacher of Advaita Vedanta (non-dualism). He has been influenced by Ramana Maharshi and Wei, Wu Wei. His basic philosophy is that *"Consciousness is all that exists."* According to Ramesh, analyzing, conceptualizing, and introspecting are a waste of time. Enlightenment is an empty, receptive mind. Our task is to "wake up." We have already achieved what we are trying to realize. His books are *Consciousness Speaks* and *Who Cares?*

Denial and projection strengthen the ego. Mysticism provides another way of looking at things. However strongly we identify with the ego, it is not our "true Self." Self is united with, or a part of, God outside of the realm of the ego.

It is a mistake to set up the ego as one's enemy to be conquered. It is more profitable to merely adopt it as a pet and melt it away with compassion.
Dr. David Hawkins

Sin, Guilt, and Fear: The Playground of the Ego

The ego is the belief in the reality of a separated or false self, made as a substitute for the Self that God created. The ego's nucleus centers around three basic ideas on which it builds its system of defense—namely, the belief in *sin*, *guilt*, and *fear*. To understand the interweaving of sin, guilt, and fear is to understand the structure of the ego. According to Eastern mystical philosophy, the most basic law in the universe is the law of cause and effect. What "goes around, comes around." As we give, so do we receive. As we forgive, so are we forgiven. Sometimes cause and effect are obvious; sometimes we don't see the correlations between events until they are well past. Sometimes we never know what caused what. I was listening to a fifteen-year-old girl talking about a near-death experience she had, and all she could say was: "Everything we do at every single second has its effect. It's all connected." Here was a young American teenager who knew nothing of the Eastern doctrine of karma, but she had experienced an insight into the working of the universe.

According to mystics, both good
and bad actions bear fruit.
The law of cause and effect is always satisfied.
It is a law of strict justice and judgment,
functioning automatically just as surely as
a rubber ball thrown against a wall will rebound.
John Davidson

According to the Chinese philosopher **Xunzi (Hsun Tzu**, c. 300–215 B.C.E.), human nature is basically evil. Similarly, from the Christian, Jewish, and Islamic points of view, humankind's fundamental nature is evil, and it must be held in check. This belief is like saying that we are guilty until proven innocent. From the mystic's point of view we have simply forgotten our originally divine nature and therefore make choices that result in pain to ourselves and others.

What is Sin?

One Sunday a man went to church without his wife. When he returned home, she asked him what the preacher talked about. He said, "Sin." "Well," said the wife, "what did he have to say about it?" "He's against it," said the husband. Billy Sunday, the famous baseball evangelist who fought a vigorous war against sin from the Gay Nineties through the time of the Great Depression, once said:

I'm against sin.
I'll kick it as long as I've got a boot, and I'll fight it as long as I've got a fist. I'll butt it as long as I've got a head and I'll bite it as long as I've got a tooth. When I'm old and fistless and footless and toothless, I'll gum it to death.

The belief in sin is the central concept in the ego's thought system. The belief in guilt and fear evolve from this concept. According to traditional Christianity, sin is quite real. Tell a fundamentalist there is no sin, and he will tell you there is plenty of sin—all you have to do is to look around you. Tell someone else there is no sin, and he or she will say that you can then do whatever you want without consequences. The belief in sin is sacrosanct to the ego's thought system.

Error or Truth

I have a book containing illustrations for use in sermons by Christian ministers. It defines sin as "that abominable thing that God hates." Could God call something abominable? Can God hate if God is Love? From the mystic's perspective, sin is the belief that we are separated from God. Once we believe we have committed this "sin" of separation, we naturally feel guilty. To identify with the ego is to feel guilty and then fear that we will be punished for our sins. Error should not be confused with sin. Error can be corrected, and the wrong made right. Sin calls for punishment. Error calls for correction. The belief that punishment is correction is insane. In our usual thinking about sin, we do not think of it as error. We think of it as some deed that cannot be corrected.

Story Time

A young woman went to see her priest. "Father," she said, "you must forgive me for I have sinned." "My goodness," said the priest, "what is your sin?" "Well," she said, "I have committed the sin of vanity." "How is that, dear?" asked the priest. "Everyday I go and stand in front of the mirror and say, you are so beautiful. You are absolutely gorgeous." "Oh my goodness," said the priest, "That is not a sin. It's just a mistake."

Saying that sin is an error in thinking or perception doesn't mean that we can justify inappropriate, deleterious or hurtful behavior. It simply says that such behavior is the outgrowth of a false belief about our own identity. The word *sin* (*amartia*), as Jesus uses it in the New Testament, means "missing the mark," or "missing the point." If we sin, we miss being centered in God. We are then egocentric, rather than God-centered.

The Forgiveness of Sin

A Sunday school teacher had just concluded her lesson and wanted to make sure she had made her point. Thinking that someone would say "repent," she asked, "Can anyone tell me what you must do before you can obtain forgiveness of sin?" There was an interval of silence, and then from the back of the room, a small boy spoke up. "First," he said, "first, you must sin." This story is a little like the one about the young boy who was explaining basic Christian theology to his younger sister: "You see, it was Jesus' job to die for our sins—it's our job to sin." To say there is no sin does not mean that we can do whatever we want in the world without consequence.

Men are not punished for their sins, but by them.
Elbert Hubbard

A mystic is someone who has stopped projecting fear and attack and now extends (through acceptance) only love. A mystic would not want to hurt someone else, knowing that to hurt a part of the whole is to hurt oneself. The mystic simply chooses to no longer perpetuate error. From the mystic's point of view, our reality is not that of a frightened, vulnerable, mortal, separated self. According to the mystic, we are a part of God, a "Thought in the Mind of God." This is not arrogance. It does not mean that we are God.

According to mysticism, in so far as we are not enlightened, we have forgotten who we are. We have misidentified ourselves as abandoned, unloved, unlovable, alone, and vulnerable. We have mistaken one another for enemies and thus justified unloving treatment of each other. There is no guilt in Heaven—by definition there could not be—for Heaven is perfection. While there is no guilt in Heaven, there is no one in this world who has not struggled, or is not now struggling, with guilt. Each of us can think of things about which we feel guilty. We have all lied. We have been thoughtless and condemning of others. There are times in our lives when each of us has been selfish, pushy, arrogant, and rude. We have lost our tempers, cheated at a game in school or on our taxes. Guilt is not a fun place to visit. Though there is no such thing as eternal hell, the experience of guilt in the now moment is hellish, and the experience keeps us from knowing heaven.

What Is Guilt?

Guilt is anything you did
and fear others to know about.
Muhammad

Guilt is the experience of having separated ourselves from God. Guilt is a basic feeling of the "wrongness" of our being. It manifests as self-hatred and as feelings of inferiority, incompleteness, failure, apathy, despair, depression, and loneliness. It is always disruptive. It is never a fun place to visit.

Guilt is the psychological experience of this belief
in sin and can be defined as the total of all our
negative thoughts, feelings
and beliefs about ourselves.
Dr. Ken Wapnick, *Awaken from the Dream*

The ego lives within the sore spots in our psychological systems, and those sore spots can be labeled "guilt." Much of our guilt is unconscious. Like an iceberg with most of its mass beneath the water, our guilt is hidden. Freud said that we need to make the unconscious conscious. We each need to look at the dark sides of our own natures and then accept responsibility for this darkness in order to dispel its energy and seeming power over us. To deflate the ego, we look at the dark side, and then we (1) do not deny it; (2) do not repress it; and (3) do not project it onto others. For the mystic, there is no enemy—either in us or in another. The process of looking at our own selfish, separated selves is often the real dark night of the soul. Yet, the acceptance of responsibility brings us great freedom, for we are then no longer controlled by darkness.

The ego needs "enemies" to strengthen the sense of
separateness on which its identity depends.
Eckhart Tolle

We need enemies so we can project our guilt. We thus accuse others of things we are afraid to look at in ourselves. We might find fault with people who have trouble controlling their weight when we have trouble controlling our own. Or, we might project our hate onto homosexuals, fearing such tendencies within ourselves.

I am not using the word evil. It is more
helpful to call it unconsciousness or insanity.
Eckhart Tolle

Fear and Punishment

The basic source of guilt is the belief that we have done something against God. We thus believe we will be punished. This belief makes us fearful. We associate guilt with the need for punishment. Thinking we are going to be punished for our sins, we become even more afraid. Adam and Eve hide because they fear God will punish them for their transgression, even though God had never been anything but loving toward them. This lie is the basic dynamic of the ego. Believing it is guilty, the ego projects guilt as anger. Projecting fear and guilt onto God transforms our experience of a loving, caring Father into a view of God as wrathful and punitive. Consequently, we read in the Old Testament "'Vengeance is mine,' sayeth the Lord, 'I will visit the sins of the fathers unto the third and fourth generation'" and "The wicked shall perish." I once heard a televangelist say that there must be a hell and sinners must go there—otherwise "it just wouldn't be fair."

When we are anxious and needing help, we turn not to God, but the ego. The ego, fearing God, makes God's Love inaccessible. This reinforces and increases our experience of separation, sin, guilt, and fear. Freedom, abundance, wholeness, and eternity are impossible ideas for a mind filled with guilt and fear.

Time and Guilt

There are two time traps, the past and future. Guilt is experienced in relationship to the past. Infants and very young children have no guilt because they do not have a past. Young children would just as soon run around naked as to have a wet cloth wrapped around their middle. In an episode from *America's Funniest Home Movies*, a father has a young child sitting on his shoulders with his legs straddling his father's neck and his hands grasping his father's head. With a look of total innocence, the child regurgitates on top of his father's head. We must be "taught" guilt. Guilt keeps us from the present by making us hostage to the past. Forgiveness of ourselves lies in the acceptance of the fact that we could never have had a different past. It was what it was, and the best thing we can do is to release it and leave it where it belongs, namely in the past.

Correction—Overcoming Guilt

Just as the father never condemned the prodigal son, never sent him away or punished him, God has not condemned us. Still, belief in separation keeps us living in "*the far country*" of misery, pain, guilt, and fear.

1. The Ego's Plan

The ego's plan for dealing with guilt is to make us *expiate* or *pay* for our sins through punishment. When people go to prison for a period of time, we then says that they have "paid" their debt to society. If, however, there has been no change in the mind of the individual in question—nothing has changed.

From 1982 to 1990, I worked as a teacher for Mercy College inside Sing Sing prison. Near the gate to the entrance of Sing Sing, there is a sign saying: "Sing Sing, New York State Correctional Institution." Sing Sing is not a place of corrections. Sing Sing is a place of punishment. If we do not know how to correct ourselves, how can we know now to correct others? Not knowing what else to do, we lock up people who do not know how to behave in society. The ego's plan is to make guilt real. We must then "atone" for our sins. Try as we might, however, we do not get rid of guilt by ritual practice, fasting, sacrifices or "paying" for our sins with time or money.

2. The Mystic's Plan

The correction for guilt is neither to deny nor project it. Rather, our task lies in the acceptance of responsibility. Awakening is readjustment to what is, instead of what we have been making up. We then realize another, better way. We can then make choices in line with Spirit, instead of ego. We undo guilt by forgiving ourselves for having made a faulty choice. We then realize that we can now choose once again. Mysticism calls upon us to exchange our perceptions of sin and guilt for the perceptions of error and innocence. Having forgiven ourselves, we then move forward in greater truth.

You Are Not Guilty

One day, in 1975, I went to see Dr. Helen Schucman. I was struggling with guilt over breaking off a relationship, which had caused the woman in question to also enter into a great deal of pain. In fact, the woman became very upset and started acting out inappropriately. Toward the end of our session, Helen reached out, lightly touched my knee, and said, "You know you're not guilty." I told Helen that I was sorry, but she was wrong. She did not understand what I was talking about. I was guilty! I had hurt someone. There was no denying it. Yet on a deeper level, I understood what Helen meant. In the truth of who we are as Sons and Daughters of God, we cannot be guilty. In truth we are not ego beings who do things that hurt other people. It is important now that we understand three basic ideas.

1. Projection Makes Perception

Projection makes perception.
The world you see is what you gave it,
nothing more than that.
But though it is no more than that,
it is not less. Therefore, to you it is important.
It is the witness to your state of mind,
the outside picture of an inward condition.
As a man thinketh, so does he perceive.
Therefore, seek not to change the world,
but choose to change your mind about the world.
Perception is a result and not a cause.

A Course in Miracles

The sentence "As a man thinketh so does he perceive" is from Proverbs 23:7. Jesus repeats it in the Gospels. The ego is dominant until its illusory quality is recognized. Until we see it for what it is, it will continue to edit our perception. Thus, the ego sorts, accepts, rejects, and combines and then produces a "concept" of the world. Most people see the world in line with the standard brand version of reality. The mystics recognize the game of the ego and then choose not to play.

Evelyn Underhill says that the mind is like a blackboard or slate. The white scratches upon it, which the ordinary man calls specifics (and the scientists call facts), are relative and conventionalized symbols. As Underhill expresses it, "We have no reason to suppose that matter, space, and time are necessarily parts of reality. Probability points rather to their being the pencil and paper with which we sketch."

Eyes and ears are bad witnesses
to those who have barbarian souls, and even those
whose souls are civilized tend to see and hear all
things through a temperament.

Heraclites

Heraclites (540–480 B.C., Greece) is a deist and the first philosopher to create a rational philosophical system. He influences Socrates and Plato, and he is one of the most quoted pre-Socratic philosophers. He said, "The Logos (which means "thought" or "idea") is the manifest power of God." As a manifestation of the Logos, man can therefore discover the Logos (God, Spirit) within himself.

We do not see things as they are.
We see things as we are.

The Talmud

2. Perception is a Choice

Perception is a choice of what you want yourself to
be; the world you want to live in, and the state in
which you think your mind will be content and
satisfied. It chooses where you think
your safety lies. At your decision,
it reveals yourself to you as you would have you be.
And always is it faithful to your purpose.

A Course in Miracles

A young man went to a psychiatrist. The psychiatrist empathetically listened to his patient and then offered his insight. "It appears to me you have trouble making decisions. Would you agree?" The young man thought about it for a moment and responded, "Well, yes and no."

The power of decisions is your one remaining freedom.
As prisoner of this world you can decide to see it right.
What you made of it is not its reality,
for its reality is only what you give it.
A Course in Miracles

We are every moment at choice. How we live this moment determines the next moment and the next. We have free will. We can get caught in the nonsense of the ego. We can let the world of illusion go. We can let illusion be what it is without thinking that we have to fix it. Not having to "fix it" doesn't mean not paying attention to the world. It just means not being caught up in the world. The ego's world is insane, and the ego is in charge in this world. It always has been. Occasionally, the truth breaks through. The voice for God is always there—it's always immediately available to each of us. Mystics are "listeners." In every second, says Meister Eckhart, there is a little spark—a tiny flicker of the remembrance of God.

Meister Eckhart (1260–1326, Germany), a Dominican, is often regarded as the greatest of the Medieval Christian mystics. He embraced the Neo-Platonist view that the world is an emanation from an ultimate, indivisible being with whom the soul is capable of being reunited. He held senior ecclesiastical and teaching posts all over Europe. Charged with heresy by the Inquisition, he died before he could be burned at the stake. He is consequently "Meister" Eckhart, not Saint Eckhart.

3. True Perception or Knowledge: The Acquisition of True Perception

There is such a thing as true perception. It corrects the ego's misperceptions of separation by reflecting true unity. True perception is the complete opposite of the way we see the world through the ego's glasses. When we change our vision from the ego's perspective to that of Spirit's, we behold a wholly sinless world. As we see a sinless world, the love God feels for us becomes us. Correct perception sees innocence, sinlessness, and freedom. In the Don Juan/Carlos Castaneda series, very often when the word "see" or "seeing" is used, it's in italics—meaning that we are not talking about "seeing" with the body's eyes. Our body's eyes see only form. They see form because they are made of form and are made to see form. The body's eyes alone cannot see past form, nor can they by-pass error and go to truth.

When I fell in love with Judy Femmer, my high school sweetheart, I looked at her and thought she could do no wrong. She wouldn't even have known how. She was just virtue, purity, and innocence. A similar thing happened many years later when I fell in love with my wife, Dolores. When the heart opens in love, we see truly. When we are in love, we are happy about the way we see things. When we fall out of love, we are unhappy about the way we see things. Innocence has been lost.

Perfect vision does not see sin.
It cannot see what is not there.

Innocence is Truth. Nothing but truth exists, and the mystic sees truth and perfection—even behind the mask of ego and separateness. Only what we create with God has existence. Truth is all that the innocent see because they see with God-like vision. We have true vision, or true perception, when our hearts are pure. Any impurity, selfishness, judgment, complaint or attack makes our vision fuzzy. The *innocent of eye* do not see problems. Mysticism surpasses the illusions of the ego. The ego needs to be "de-energized." Until it is, it will continue to revise, rework, manage, and manipulate the world it sees. We can always change our minds about the mind.

When the ego is silent, life goes on effortlessly. At any moment of any day, the real us that we are—our true selves—that little spark can choose which direction we will go. If in doubt about a decision, ask: "Will this bring peace of mind, or will it take away my peace of mind?" The decision is right when it brings peace. Repeatedly choose peace, and peace will come.

If the cause of the world you see
is attack thoughts, you must learn
that it is these thoughts which you do not want.
There is no point in lamenting the world.
There is no point in trying to change the world.
It is incapable of change
because it is merely an effect.
But there is indeed a point in changing
your thoughts about the world.
Here you are changing the cause.
The effect will change automatically.
From Lesson 23 of *A Course in Miracles*

Chapter 4

Stopping the World

Skepticism, Cynicism, and Mysticism

Men become civilized, not in proportion to their willingness to believe, but in proportion to their readiness to doubt.

H. L. Mencken

Known as the "Sage of Baltimore," **H. L. Mencken** (1880–1956, USA) was a satirist, social critic, skeptic, and freethinker and one of the most influential American writers of the early twentieth century.

Great doubt results in great enlightenment,
small doubt results in small enlightenment,
no doubt results in no enlightenment.

Zen Saying

Skepticism is the first step
on the road to philosophy.

Denis Diderot

Denis Diderot (1713–1784, France) was a philosopher, writer, and editor-in-chief of the 17 Volume *Encyclopedie,* the first encyclopedia. He did not like organized religion, and organized religion did not like him.

If you have not by nature a critical mind
your staying here is useless.

G.I. Gurdjieff

Skeptics question traditional or commonly accepted ideas and social norms that serve a ritualistic or habituated pattern, rather than a practical purpose. Cynics take things deeper and question whether it is possible to get to the truth. Cynics are less objective than skeptics. Not only do they read bitter lessons from the past but they are also doubtful of the future. Healthy skepticism is absolutely essential in the face of the incredulous.

Story Time: Who Cares?

Every month a young disciple faithfully sent his master an account of his progress toward enlightenment. In the first month he wrote: *"I feel an expansion of consciousness and experience my oneness with the universe."* The master glanced at the note and threw it away. The following month, the disciple reported: *"I have finally discovered that the Divine is present in all things."*

The master seemed disappointed. The third month the disciple's words enthusiastically exclaimed: *"The mystery of the One has been revealed to my wondering gaze."* The master shook his head and threw the letter away. The next letter said: *"No one is born, no one lives, and no one dies, for the ego is not."* The master threw his hands up in utter despair. A month passed by, then two, then five months—and finally a whole year without another letter. The master thought it was time to remind his disciple of his duty to keep him informed of his spiritual progress. Then the disciple wrote back: *"Who cares?"* When the master read those words, a look of satisfaction spread over his face.

I Don't Give a Damn: The Great Disillusionment

In order to come to mysticism, we must first be disillusioned with the standard brand version of reality. In order to be "dis-illusioned," we must be living with an illusion. Something dramatic needs to happen in order to make us question the assumptions we've been living with. On May 7, 2001, a tumor the size of a lemon, along with 18 inches of colon, was removed from my insides. The next morning, I was lying in bed in a somewhat soporific state. I opened my eyes and saw the oncologist standing at the foot of my bed. His first words were words you never want to hear: "Mr. Mundy, I have to tell you that the cancer has spread." The following morning, I awoke at 4 a.m. I was wide awake and knew I would not be going back to sleep. This is the way I described the experience in *Missouri Mystic*:

> *Lying there in the dark, I became empty in a way I'd not been empty before. I don't mean to sound crude, but I took a deep breath, sighed, and then said, "I don't give a damn! Whatever will be will be. I entered a place of no will, no energy, no feeling—nothing. I was so nothing. I wondered, "What is it that thinks, talks, and walks?" I became empty of desire and anger, and I understood, in a way in which I had previously only understood intellectually, what the Buddha meant when he said that the loss of desire is the key to enlightenment. I achieved by this profound "letting go," some sort of objectivity.*

Disenchantment

Almost dying is character building. It brings clarity about what's important and what's not, and it gives us a deep sense of the preciousness of life. Gurdjieff urged his students to keep their deaths in mind, as a means of self-observation. For the mystic, the outside world—as constructed by the ego—is one gigantic case of multiple personality disorder. Disillusionment, or giving up on the world, is an important prelude to mysticism. Being trapped in the world, we can't see that it's not real until we question the conventional and habitual patterns handed to us through societal standards, religion, politics, the media, our families, and ourselves.

Mark Twain (Samuel Clemens) (1835–1910, USA) and **Frederick Wilhelm Nietzsche** (1844–1900, Germany) were contemporaries and two of the most quoted writers of all time. Neither of them thought much of the church, society or humanity as a whole.

Mark Twain saw the follies of "The Gilded Age" and "The Gay Nineties"—the post Civil War reconstruction era of 1870 to 1900—which saw a rapid rise of super-rich capitalists and of the American upper class's opulent self-indulgence.

Civilization is a limitless multiplication
of unnecessary necessities.
Mark Twain

Though his profound skepticism kept him from deep mysticism, Mark Twain spoke from the heart, an important mystical trait. He also had the gift of seeing the divine within the ordinary, as in, "A soap bubble is the most beautiful thing and the most exquisite in nature." What if he had known about DNA, mysticism, and fractals? His penultimate work, Mysterious Stranger, was not published until 1916, six years after his death. In the book, he exposes the hypocrisy of organized religion. He saw it as immoral, oppressive, and self-serving. In his last work *Letters from the Earth*, written the year before he died, he also proves himself a brilliant theologian, way ahead of his time. Had the work been published in his lifetime, he would have come under attack from the church. It was not published until 1962 after the death of his daughter Clara, who consistently blocked its release.

The experience of consciousness
free of concepts is freedom.
Frederick Nietzsche

Like Meister Eckhart, Nietzsche was prepared to empty his mind of all concepts and beliefs, even the idea of God. Sometimes it's necessary to throw God out in order to let God in. Nietzsche's honesty and open mindedness are deeply admirable. His thought was always evolving, and every time he suffered through a psychological crisis, his philosophy went deeper as well.

Cynicism is the only form
in which base souls approach honesty.
Frederick Nietzsche

Nietzsche is often associated with Nihilism, a philosophy that rejects the world around us, resulting in apathy toward life. In fact, however, Nietzsche opposed Nihilism and describes it as a poisoning of the human soul and "a will to nothing."

The Mystic Finds a Better World

Like the skeptic, the cynic or the nihilist, the mystic questions the nature of reality. Unlike the nihilist, the mystic finds a better world. The mystic finds God's World. Though he did not think of himself as a mystic, Nietzsche's thought brought philosophy closer to the truth and thus closer to mysticism. Many a mystic has appreciated his depth.

After coming into contact with a religious man,
I always feel I must wash my hands.
Frederick Nietzsche

Do not allow yourselves to be deceived.
Great minds are skeptical.
Frederick Nietzsche

While Twain and Nietzsche were both saying much the same thing at the same time, there were some significant differences in their lives. Twain was nine years older and lived ten years longer. He was a family man, Nietzsche was not. Twain was not formally educated. Nietzsche was.

The First Thing That Has to Happen: Getting to "Stop"

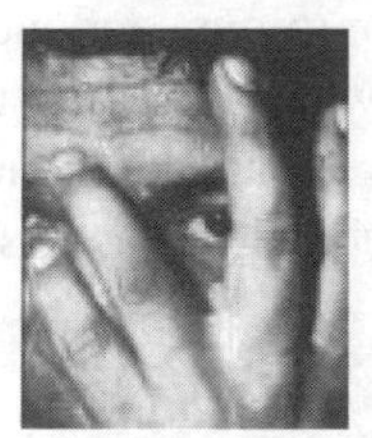

Carlos Castaneda (1925–1991, Brazil, USA) wrote twelve books on the teachings of Don Juan, a Mexican shaman. Carlos Castaneda allowed only this one picture to be taken of him for the cover of *Time* magazine. Several of his books made it to the *New York* Times bestseller list. From the 70s to the 90s, his books were a tremendous influence on thousands of active seekers for truth.

Our task is to *see*, rather than to *perceive*. Don Juan instructed Castaneda in the art of "stopping the world," the first step in learning to *see* without judgment. True mystics do not project anything onto the world. They give the world the freedom to be what it is. Mysticism is "just" seeing—seeing without projection, contamination or corruption. It is seeing without ego involvement—or *pure* seeing—the way the pure in heart see. We maintain our view of the world with inner dialogue. Our perception of the world changes when we stop the inner dialogue. If we insist on holding to our inner dialogues, a standard brand version of reality renders us blind to seeing purely.

Don't seek the truth. Cease to cherish opinions.
Zen Saying

Do you know the difference between a crow and a raven? Crows have four long feathers called pinions that come out of the ends of their wings. Ravens on the other hand have five of these feathers, so the difference is just a matter of a pinion. Opinions are just opinions. Opinions are not the truth. Likes and dislikes are not the truth. They are ways we "make up" the world and try to make everything "concrete." Notice the desire to be right, which signals an ego-vested interest in an opinion, a like or dislike. Mysticism *sees* without adding anything to the picture.

Look at a cup, for example. Do you see a cup, or are you merely reviewing your past experiences of picking up a cup, being thirsty, drinking from a cup, feeling the rim of the cup against your lips, having breakfast and so on. Are not your aesthetic reactions to the cup, too, based on past experiences? How else would you know whether or not this kind of cup will break if you drop it? What do you know about this cup except what you learned in the past? You would have no idea what this cup is, except for your past learning. Do you, then, really see it?
From Lesson 7 of *A Course in Miracles*

In order to have mystical awareness there is something which must happen first. **First, we must stop thinking!** Our minds are so busy with thoughts, opinions, and judgments it is difficult to see. To be truly aware, we must stop all of the ego machinations and maneuvering. Blindness is based on prejudice and fear. Spirit sees through eyes of love free of contamination.

If you could get out of your not self light,
you could be illumined.
If you could stop anxiously cogitating,
you could give yourself a chance to be cogitated.
Aldous Huxley

Imagine what it would be like if we loved everything our eyes fell upon. Instead, we judge things almost instantly. To see what is true is to be deceived no longer by the ego.

Stop all your doing. Stop all your beliefs, all your searching, all your excuses, and see for yourself what already is always here. Don't move. Be still.
Gangaji

Gangaji (1942 – Present, USA), formerly Antoinette Robertson Varner, is an American-born spiritual teacher dedicated to sharing the mystical path through direct self-inquiry, as taught by Ramana Maharshi. Gangaji travels the world, holding gatherings and retreats.

The ego talks, chatters, prattles, and babbles. The constant "chatter" inside our minds keeps us from seeing and hearing clearly. When I was serving as minister of Interfaith Fellowship in New York City, I would sometimes get to church early and go to a corner coffee shop to look over my notes. The coffee shop had a U-shaped counter. One day, I noticed a homeless man sitting across from me with a cup of coffee in front of him, talking to himself. There were few people around at the time. He was talking so loudly that if I leaned forward and listened carefully, I could hear what he was saying. Most people keep their thoughts to themselves. For some street people, however, the thought goes all the way to the tongue and finds utterance through the mouth. I could not make out everything he was saying but realized that he was practicing a speech he was going to give to a judge or a brother or someone else. It was clear that he was building a case and defending himself. Did you ever build a case for yourself or practice a speech while driving somewhere in your car? The mind gets so full of this "stuff" that it's impossible to see what is going on in the greater scheme of things.

The purpose of meditation is to quiet the mind or at least to slow the pace of internal chatter, and if we're lucky, maybe even stop the mind-talk. If we can disengage from the constant inner babble and projection of our beliefs and prejudices, then we might be able to really see something.

What Produces a Mystical Experience?

Sir Alister Hardy (1896–1985, England) was Professor of Zoology at Oxford and author of *The Living Stream* and *The Divine Flame*, books on the evolution of religion. In 1969 he founded the Religious Experience Research Center to investigate the nature of mysticism. The Center has since received a grant for the computerization of its archives. Originally located at Oxford University, the Religious Research Center is now located at the University of Wales. It sponsors lectures, publishes journals, and has a distance learning program as well as on-site presentations. [You can add a description of your own mystical experience by going to www.lamp.ac.uk/aht/]

Hardy's contribution to the scientific study of religion is reviewed in David Hay's book, *Something There: The Biology of the Human Spirit*. Hardy's organization has studied over 5,000 descriptions of mystical experiences. He asked each respondent what had triggered the experience and what the experience looked like. The following results are given in terms of average number of mentions per 1,000 experiences. (Bold type denotes *seemingly* negative experiences.)

Major Stimulations to a Mystical Experience

1. Depression and Despair	**183**
2. Meditation & Contemplation	136
3. Natural beauty	123
4. Participation in worship	111
5. Literature, drama, film	82
6. Illness	**80**
7. Music	56
8. Crises in personal relations	**37**
9. Grief: the death of a loved one	**28**
10. Sacred places	26
11. Visual arts	24
12. Creative work	20
13. The prospect of death	**15**
14. Silence, solitude	15
15. Anesthetic drugs	11
16. Physical activity	10
17. Relaxation	10
18. Childbirth	9
19. Happiness	7
20. Psychedelic drugs	7
21. Sexual relations	4

Four Ways of Getting to "Stop"

I see four ways to stop the busyness of the ego-mind and thus come to mystical awareness:

1. **Crash and Burn**
   (The Dark Night of the Soul)
   This method includes all of the various ways listed in bold above, a divorce or bankruptcy, the loss of a love one or the prospect of our own death. These are real "stoppers."
2. **Contemplation and Meditation**
   What is the purpose of meditation, if it is not to stop the mind and provide freedom from incessant worrying and the mental working through of problems? We'll explore this process in the next chapter.
3. **Relaxation: It Just Happens!** (Or does it?)
   Various experiences can bring on a dropping or temporarily stopping of the inner chatter of the mind. These experiences include participation in solo sports (running, skiing, skating, bicycling), listening to music, group singing, creative work or just becoming very relaxed.
4. **Working on Ourselves**
   This method entails deliberately engaging in spiritual discipline with the dropping off of unhealthy addictions and the purposeful practicing of spiritual exercises. We'll explore this process in chapter 17.

The Gate of Sorrow
The Path Most Frequently Chosen: Crash and Burn—Despair, Depression and Surrender

Sometimes the emergence of the mystical consciousness is gradual, unmarked by any definite crisis. The self slides gently, almost imperceptibly, from the old universe to the new. The records of mysticism, however, suggest that this is exceptional: that travail is the normal accompaniment of birth.

Evelyn Underhill

At the top of Hardy's list is despair and depression. Obviously, despair and depression are not mystical states. Despair and depression can lead us, however, to a mystical state when we let the experience take us all the way to the bottom of the pit. We call this experience "Crash and Burn." According to the Buddha, the most common path to enlightenment is slow and gradual and takes place predominantly through suffering. Mystical awareness thus can come as the result of, for example, a heart attack, an unexpected calamity, a bankruptcy, divorce, illness, crisis in personal relations, the death of a loved one or the prospect of one's own death. Surviving near death is almost always enlightening.

The most frequent entryway to the sacred is our own suffering and dissatisfaction . . . alcoholic or abusive parents, grave family illness, loss of a loved relative, or cold absentee parents and warring family members all recur in many of these stories.

Jack Kornfield, in *After the Ecstasy, the Laundry*

One of the best known stories of depression followed by crash and burn and a resultant mystical experience is the story of **Bill Wilson** (1896–1971, USA) the co-founder along with **Dr. Bob Smith** (1879–1950, USA) of Alcoholics Anonymous. In 1934, Wilson was struggling with alcoholism. One night lying in bed filled with despair he cried out, "I'll do anything! Anything at all! If there be a God, let Him show Himself!" Then, a bright light appeared, and feelings of ecstasy and serenity came over him. He never drank again. In 1938, he wrote a book, called "the big book" in Alcoholics Anonymous. It included the list of suggested activities for spiritual growth called the Twelve Steps. For the rest of his life, he continued to be interested in mysticism and psychotropic drugs as means for inducing spiritual change.

It is by going down into the abyss
that we recover the treasures of life.
When you stumble, there lies your treasure.
Joseph Campbell

Only conscious suffering makes any sense.
Gurdjieff

Crash and burn is not a consciously chosen path to enlightenment. Were we fully aware, we would not choose despair and depression as a path to awakening. We have to learn how to bring the dark to the light. Not doing so, we continue to do dumb unconscious things.

Suffering is the first step in enlightenment.
The Dalai Lama

The next step after having crashed and burned is to take responsibility. The mystics who seem the most authentic come to truth as a result of falling apart, hitting bottom or "losing everything." We rarely come to truth through rites, ritual, customs, and traditions.

Despair, the result of hitting the bottom, is 25 times more likely to produce a mystical experience than is happiness.

The time will come when your mind will
suddenly come to a stop like an old rat
who finds himself in a cul-de-sac.
Yun-man (Buddhist)

Story Time: Emptying the Cup

A Zen master received a visit from a professor who wanted to learn about Zen. The master poured his guest a cup of tea and kept on pouring when the cup was already overflowing. The professor saw it and finally could no longer keep quiet. "The cup is over-flowing; you can't pour any more into it!" The master replied, "Like this cup, you are overflowing with your ideas. How am I to teach you Zen when you don't have an empty cup?"

The ego has a tenacious hold on the psyche, and it will not let go easily. The ego, however, has a built in "implode." At some point it will collapse. All false systems are doomed. Communism, for example, failed because as practiced it was an "untrue" system. With a theoretical ideal of bringing about a more prosperous, peaceful, and harmonious world, dictatorial communist regimes had believed it necessary to first take the lives of over 50 million people. The denial of individual freedom and the use of totalitarian means in an attempt to practice the communist system was an affront to the human spirit. Any philosophical system that isn't love-based isn't truth-based and will not prevail. When all else fails, we are given an opportunity to wake up as the ego implodes.

For many of us, letting go will not take place without a "dark night of the soul," which is something that is not in our power to prevent. It is an emptiness that often takes the form of a deep depression. The feelings are numb and there is no light anywhere. According to St. John of the Cross, whoever will hold out—so that the depression does not lead to suicide, but to the loss of the greedy self—will arrive at a "new comprehension of God in God." The "I" then experiences its deepest ground; not from the vantage point of the "I" itself, but from the other side of the ground—which is God."
Bruno Borchert in *Mysticism: Its History and Challenge*

In order to get out of the quagmire of despair and depression we must first admit that we are not happy. For despair and depression to lead to awakening, we must go all the way with the experience. We can't be on our way to bottoming out. We can't be in a state of high nervous anxiety. We've got to go all the way and actually hit bottom. When all ego strategies fail in the face of overwhelming misfortunes, we are given the opportunity to wake up.

If I were to make a religion, this would be a basic thing in it: That anybody who becomes enlightened first will have to go through a nervous breakdown, only then will we have a breakthrough.
Osho

The mystical experience occurs when we let go of control. Crash and burn stops the wandering mind and forces us into the present. Once we surrender, once we turn everything over to a power higher than the ego-mind, something remarkable happens: the experience of grace. Love floods into our awareness when we stop choosing the ego. Then, despite the seeming severity of our situation, we are okay. Everything is taken care of, even if we don't understand how it's happening. We can then *rest* in the arms of God, rather than trying to manipulate our experience.

We usually come to crash and burn as a result of having first tried a number of things that proved unsatisfactory. Pick an illusion: politics, fame, power, authority, drugs, alcohol or wealth. One will serve as well (or poorly) as another; an illusion is an illusion. Eventually, all illusory paths lead to despair and then a final surrender.

The soul is not empty, so long as the desire for sensible things remains. The absence of this desire for things produces emptiness and liberty of soul; even when there is an abundance of possessions.

St. John of the Cross

St. John of the Cross (1541–1591, Spain) belongs to the Spanish School of mystics, along with his teacher Teresa of Avila. Known for his deep love for God, he was among the first to subject mystical experience to intellectual (psychological) analysis. Suffering, he said, is "epistemology." We learn through suffering. His famous book is the *Dark Night of the Soul.*

Tolerance for pain may be high, but it is not without limit. Eventually everyone begins to recognize, however dimly, that there must be a better way. As this recognition becomes more firmly established, it becomes a turning point.

A Course in Miracles

What is the Wanting Creature?

If we hit bottom and give up, we might see how we were blinded by our own projections. Buddha said that the loss of desire is the key to enlightenment. When we need something, we are coming from weakness. When we *need* nothing, we are present in the moment. Spirit has no needs. There is a story about a man who is praying to God. He says, "Dear God, I want peace." And God responds, "When you get rid of the 'I' and the 'want,' you will have peace." The first question is, what is the wanting creature? What is it that needs anything? What if there were no "wanting creature"? What would you have then? Ramana Maharshi said, "As each thought arises, one must be watchful to whom is this thought occurring?" When asked a spiritual question he often said, "Who wants to know?" Thus he said to all his disciples, "Learn first who you are."

Ramana Maharshi (1879–1950, India). In 1896 when Ramana Maharshi was 17 years old, he suddenly felt he was going to die. In fact, he thought he had died. Even though he thought he had "died," there was still awareness transcending the body. His ego was then lost in a deluge of Self-awareness. His teachings about Self-Enquiry represent the Path of Knowledge. The teachings are Advaita or non-dualistic. He did not publicize himself as a guru; he never appointed any successors, and he never claimed to have any disciples.

An Anonymous Crash and Burn Mystical Experience

A therapist friend told me the following true story about one of her clients. A man in deep despair raised a gun to his head, and realizing he is going to be dead in a few seconds, he decided to give his mind a little rest before he died. He decided to temporarily lay aside his anger and judgments and just relax for a moment before he pulled the trigger. And then he thought, "Wait a minute..." He put the gun down. Free for the first time from his attack thoughts, he found himself in a state of bliss.

The death of a friend or loved one often brings a "stopping of the world," especially when the death is sudden and unexpected. Grief can be a profound eye opener. The growing awareness of our own death as we face a serious or terminal illness also often heightens our sensitivity to higher realms of experience.

Lester Levinson is a good example of a mystic who awoke through "crash and burn." A physicist and engineer who lived in New York City during the 1950s and 60s, Levinson attained a high degree of success. His life revolved around being a businessman and a New York City playboy. In 1952, he had a second heart attack. He suffered from jaundice, kidney stones, migraine headaches, and a perforated ulcer. As open-heart surgery was not yet being performed, Levinson's doctors told him that unless he wanted a third and probably fatal heart attack, he should not even move. This caused Levinson to undertake a serious assessment of his life. He began walking the streets of New York City late at night. Walking and walking, over a three-month period, he succeeded in releasing each of his blocks to an awareness of love's presence. His health problems disappeared, and he became enormously happy. He lived to the age of 84 and spent the rest of his life teaching others what he called The Sedona Method. It consists of asking someone a series of questions that lead to the awareness of what that person is truly feeling in the moment. This awareness then can result in the letting go of any painful or unwanted feelings.

In his deep, personal evaluation, Lester asked himself what he really wanted. The answer was "happiness." The next step was to ask what made him happy. He realized that when he was the recipient of love he was happy. Then he had a further revelation: *He was the happiest of all whenever he was loving.* Lester's discovery is not new. A 1999 study by social psychologists concluded that the happiest people are those who spend time giving their love away.

Another story of a "hitting bottom" leading to "waking up" is that of contemporary teacher **Byron Katie** (1942 – Present, USA). In her thirties, a businesswoman and mother living in a little town in the desert of southern California, she became severely depressed. For over a decade she lived with paranoia, rage, self-loathing, and thoughts of suicide. One morning in February 1986, in a mental health treatment facility, she experienced a life-changing spiritual awakening that she calls "waking up to reality."

I discovered that when I believed my thoughts,
I suffered, but that when I didn't believe them,
I didn't suffer, and that this is true for every human being. Freedom is as simple as that.
I found that suffering is optional. I found a joy within me that has never disappeared, not for a single moment. That joy is in everyone, always.

Yet, another contemporary example of crash-and-burn leading to a mystical experience is the story of **Eckhart Tolle** (1948 – Present, Germany, Canada). This is how he describes his experience in the beginning of his book *The Power of Now*:

> *I cannot live with myself any longer. This was the thought that kept repeating itself in my mind. Then suddenly I became aware of what a peculiar thought it was. "Am I one or two? If I cannot live with myself, there must be two of me, the 'I' and the 'self' that 'I' cannot live with. Maybe," I thought, "only one of them is real." I was so stunned by this strange realization that* ***my mind stopped***.

Tolle goes on to describe himself being drawn into a deep void until he lost awareness. After he awoke, the whole world had about it, he said, a spotless freshness, and he found himself in a state of bliss which lasted for days.

One lesson that is taught in myths is that at the bottom of the abyss comes the voice of salvation.
The blackest moment is the moment when the real message of transformation is going to come.
At the darkest moment there is the light.

Joseph Campbell

If we go all the way with crash and burn and hit bottom, we might then do something significant: We might give up. We need to say, "I give up" or "Who cares?" or "I don't give a damn." If we give up entirely, we must then say a very sincere one-word prayer. It is sometimes necessary to send up a *"flare" prayer*. We must mean this prayer. The prayer is *"Help!"*

We are always on the anvil;
by trials God is shaping us for higher things.

Henry Ward Beecher

What is so wonderful about hitting bottom is that it enables us to move beyond the intellect, which is never going to figure out the route to a mystical awareness. A musician told me a story about being out of work for two years because he had been an alcoholic. He was invited by a friend to play in a band in a large hotel. Newly sober and afraid he might not do a good job, he prayed for help and heard: *Just remember the first note—and have fun!*

The only way out is to be submissive, to accept our helplessness and to recognize the peace of soul—
the way it can be found—is our greatest ally.

Bernadette Roberts

If we truly mean that we need help and we are willing to surrender our own attempts to figure things out, a miraculous thing happens. It's called grace. God steps in. God can't help us when we're trying to control things. We have free will. We can muck things up as much as we want to. Or, we can follow God's lead and enjoy life.

When you are in the dark, listen,
and God will give you a
very precious message.

Oswald Chambers

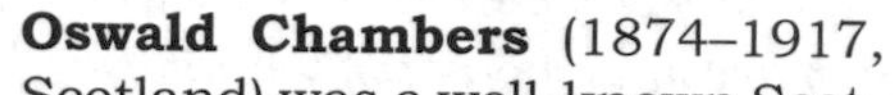
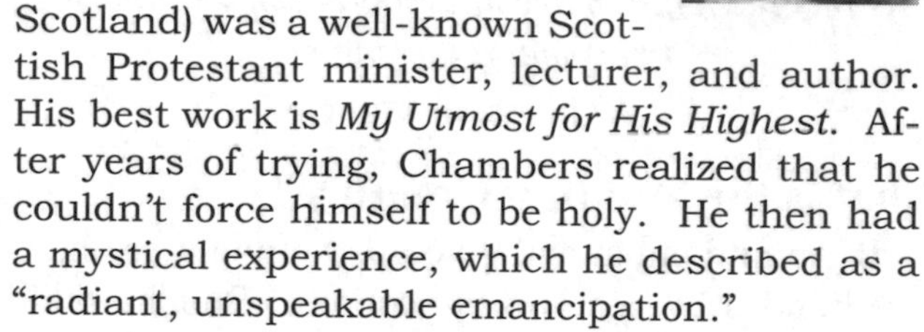

Oswald Chambers (1874–1917, Scotland) was a well-known Scottish Protestant minister, lecturer, and author. His best work is *My Utmost for His Highest*. After years of trying, Chambers realized that he couldn't force himself to be holy. He then had a mystical experience, which he described as a "radiant, unspeakable emancipation."

In the dark night of the soul,
bright flows the river of God.

St. John of the Cross

Don't Do Crash and Burn!

Crashing and burning is not fun. Crash and burn can waken us, but the price is high. We can go through repeated episodes of loss and despair before truly surrendering—after which some kind of spiritual path or discipline becomes necessary. Crash and burn is not a conscious choice; we fall into great loss and despair when the strategies of the ego take us there. While no one wants to hit bottom, it is inevitable that each of us will encounter difficulties with relationships, finances, health issues, and the other challenges of life.

We handle such difficulties more easily when we allow them to transform us. Sometimes the only way to find out what is going on is to have the rug pulled out from under us. Whenever this happens—pay attention! Life has giving us one of its lessons. We can respond responsibly, or we can project. We can blame others, or we can ask ourselves—what did I do to bring this into my life? What lesson can I learn from this experience, and how can I keep this same thing from happening again?

Chapter 5

Meditation, Contemplation, Prayer, Play and Creativity

The pure truth of Atman, which is buried
under Maya and the effects of Maya,
can be reached by meditation, contemplation
and other spiritual disciplines such as
a knower of Brahman may prescribe.
Shankara

The second most common way of coming to mystical awareness is through meditation, contemplation, and prayer—through getting really quiet and listening. Osho defined meditation as a state of watchfulness that has no ego fulfillment in it. Meditation happens when we are in a state of not-doing.

Far from idleness being the root of all evil,
It is rather the only true good.
Soren Kierkegaard

The *intention* of meditation and contemplation is liberation. Crash and burn brings us to stop. Meditation brings us to stop. If we cannot stop the mind, at least we can get it into neutral, to a place of detachment. In meditation we observe the mind and our thoughts without attachment to them. The mind, however, only really stops when it is no longer narcissistically engaged. Once we stop "making up the world," we have clearer perception. Meditation and contemplation are means of sharpening the mind, a process of developing a lifestyle where one's whole life becomes a *living* meditation.

When one's mind becomes stilled, intelligence is
experienced separate from appearances.
Heraclites

"Be still and know" describes a central feature of the effort to directly comprehend reality. Each of the world's religious faiths has a monastic branch. The purpose of the monastery is to step away from the world, to go into a "cloistered" situation where talking is minimal. Not talking makes room for inner reflection. Some of our most devoted mystics have been monks and nuns who stepped away from the world and went inside to find ultimate reality.

Awakening & Awareness

A new awareness and an opening to a larger perspective are necessary initial steps in the development of mystical awareness. The final stage reached by a teacher of God is complete open-mindedness. In essence, we are working our way to seeing things as God does. At first, we see things in a new light. This new perspective, or method of seeing, may be brought on in many ways, but it must be right there in the beginning. Then with the new awareness there comes a letting go, a cleansing, and a relinquishment of the old. What good is the old when its worthlessness is seen plainly?

Purgation

Miracles are everyone's right,
but purification is necessary first.
Principle No. 7 of the 50 Miracles Principles
of *A Course in Miracles*

Once we have experienced some revelation, some kind of awakening, then we must be done with the old. The negative habits that were hurting us must be laid aside. After a few weeks of being sober, folks who join AA (Alcoholics Anonymous) often report a new clarity of awareness they had not realized they'd been lacking. According to Evelyn Underhill, no mystic can omit the initial stage of purgation. There must be a putting aside of the old in order for the new to be born. Sometimes, though not always, this purgation includes a catharsis, a confession, and a "getting it off one's chest." The fifth step in the suggested twelve steps in AA is to admit to God, ourselves, and to another human being the nature of our misperceptions. This helps prevent (but not necessarily), a falling back into the same patterns of behavior.

If you don't wash out the stone and sand, how can
you pick out the gold? Carefully seek the heart of
heaven and earth with firm determination.
Suddenly, you will see the original thing!
Liu I-Ming (Taoist)

Having built up a number of defenses against the truth, we should not be surprised to find that when we get quiet it's not unusual for us to become aware of the blocks we have placed between ourselves and enlightenment. Now we need a willingness to look at our own darkness. In his book on *Vipassana Meditation*, William Hart writes, "The meditator undergoes a process analogous to the surgical operation, to lancing a pus-filled wound." As Thomas

Merton says of his early experiences, "...my soul (was) broken up with contrition, but broken and clean, painful but sanitized, like a lanced abscess."

Those who awaken as a result of "crash and burn" undergo a profound purification. Not realizing they have brought this purification on themselves, they often believe it has come from the outside. The mystic seeker, however, undergoes the process consciously. Eliminating negatives, false ideas, and limiting prejudices, the conscious seekers uncover the ongoing, dynamic truth of spirit. There may be a literal "letting go" of things and "thingness." Desiring clarity and freedom, the soul now divests itself of unnecessary attachments. At this point, people may give up on their old traditional religions. They may let go of the political fight, the climb up the corporate ladder, the unhappy marriage or an addiction to a drug or alcohol—whatever may be blocking awareness. Understanding the non-reality of the material world, people are more capable of participating in the world without entanglements.

It is in deep solitude that I find the gentleness with which I can truly love my brothers. The more solitary I am the more affection I have for them. Solitude and silence teach me to love my brothers for what they are, not for what they say.
Thomas Merton.

One of the clearest of the twentieth century mystics, **Thomas Merton** (1915–1968, USA) was an American Trappist monk who wrote his masters thesis on the mystic William Blake. Merton's first book, *The Seven Story Mountain* (his autobiography), was on the *New York Times* bestseller list for several weeks in 1949. He was known for his interfaith interests and his stand on nonviolence and the Vietnam War. Merton had ongoing struggles with the church and his abbot concerning not being allowed to go out of the monastery. He was accidentally electrocuted by a fan when stepping out of a bathtub on Christmas day 1968.

Something equivalent to the solitude of the wilderness is an essential part of mystical education.
Evelyn Underhill

Before he began his ministry, Jesus spent forty days and forty nights in the wilderness, where he was tempted by the devil (the ego). Then the Bible says, "After that he began to preach." (Matthew 4:17) There was no ministry until after his awakening while alone in the dessert. Buddha was alone under the Bodhi tree when he experienced his enlightenment. Again, there was no teaching until after

Jesus in the Wilderness by Ivan Kramskoi

the experience of awakening. Buddha then found his previous disciples and gave his famous "Sermon at the Deer Park at Benares." Mohammed was sitting alone in a cave when he heard "recite" and received the Koran. Zoroaster was alone in the mountains when he received his revelation, as was Moses when he saw the burning bush.

St. Catherine of Siena (1347–1380, Italy) spent three years in hermit-like seclusion in a little room, which can be seen to this day. Within her own small house, entirely cut off from the life of her family, she found, she said, the desert and solitude in the midst of people.

Fasting as Purgation

Fasting is sometimes regarded as a necessary preparation for visionary experiences. Catherine of Siena said she had no need for food, as she found nourishment from the abundance of grace she received. Fasting for prolonged periods of time produces a change in blood chemistry as surely as does the ingestion of a psychotropic drug. Fasting is part of the puberty rights of the Sioux Indians; in fact it is a part of the training of mystics all over the world. The Greek medical scholar Galen said dreams produced by fasting are clearer. "The overstuffed body cannot see," says Don Juan of the Castaneda series. Revelation comes to Moses, Elijah, and Daniel after long periods of fasting. The Koran stresses fasting, as does the Old Testament. Fasting heightens mental clarity, removes unnecessary weight and toxic waste, helps retain energy, enhances inherent wisdom, and sharpens the senses. Fasting is not, however, a required step in the development of a contemplative life, and no one should do an extended fast without supervision. The main purpose of spiritual fasting is to clarify the mind, not the body, although clarifying the body may help to clarify the mind. [For more information on fasting go to www.fasting.com]

Solitude and Silence

Profound silence is more beneficial than words. Words after all are just words, all of which are projections.

Time away from the world is necessary. Solitude provides time to work, think or rest without being distracted. A number of *hermits* (from the Greek word *eremos* meaning "desert-dweller") lived in seclusion during the first centuries of the Christian Church. Before there were monasteries, individual hermits lived in caves. Seclusion makes it easier to concentrate, maintain mindfulness, and remain absorbed inwardly. While mystics often spend time alone, they can also be highly "connected" because, having no blocks to awareness of love's presence, they love everything. Therefore, paradoxically, solitary mystics are the most connected individuals.

Retraining the mind to think with spirit, instead of ego, is like body-building for someone who has been sick and weak: daily, gentle workouts are helpful. If possible, begin and end the day free from distractions and noise. It's best not to wake up with an alarm clock, especially a radio alarm. Avoid immediately turning on the television or the computer, as doing so jolts consciousness back to the external world. Go where it is easy to be silent and perhaps read something inspirational, like the lessons of *A Course in Miracles* or *The Daily Word* from Unity. Quiet time in the morning can infuse the entire day with energy and purpose. The early morning hours may also be a good time for writing. My favorite time for writing is in the morning, before my family gets up, before the phone begins to ring, before anything. Most importantly, after I awaken, first there is a movement from dreaming to a place of simplicity.

Morning is when I am awake
and there is a dawn in me.
Henry David Thoreau

Henry David Thoreau (1817–1862, USA), transcendentalist, deist, author of *Walden*, and student of Ralph Waldo Emerson. Thoreau is one of my favorites as I know he is for many. He was a deeply religious man who was never interested in institutional religion. He was fourteen years younger than his friend and neighbor Ralph Waldo Emerson. Although Thoreau was Emerson's student, he was also Emerson's counterpart; but Thoreau was more of a rebel—a classical anti-establishment person. The search for reality begins, says Thoreau, with simplification. He believed that being free of the encumbering thoughts of others and dispelling with superfluities and distractions leads to clarity of vision and spiritual insight.

Still, still with Thee, when purple morning breaketh,
When the bird waketh, and the shadows flee,
Fairer than morning, lovelier than daylight dawns
the sweet consciousness, I am one with Thee.
Harriet Beecher Stowe

Harriet Elizabeth Beecher Stowe (1811–1896, USA) was an abolitionist and author of *Uncle Tom's Cabin*, which brought to light the brutality of slavery. Upon meeting Harriet, Abraham Lincoln is reported to have said, "So you're the little woman who wrote the book that started this great war." She is said to have had a vision of "Uncle Tom's death" and was moved to tears. She later wrote *How to Live in Christ*. Her mother was the sister of the famous Brooklyn preacher Henry Ward Beecher. Her house in Hartford, Connecticut, is next to Mark Twain's home and can be visited to this day.

Contemplation as Conversation with God

It is present everywhere.
There is nothing it does not contain.
However only those who have previously
planted wisdom - seeds will be able
to continuously see it.
Zen Master Dogen

We can think of contemplation as an ongoing dialogue, or communication, with God. The more awake we are, the more actively we can engage in this conversation. Contemplation is a focusing of thoughts. It involves deliberate attention and a conscious stilling of the ego-mind so that deeper thoughts can arise. In this sense, contemplation is not a stopping of the mind, as much as it is a looking quietly into the mind. Contemplation involves a simple regard for what is. It is *loving sight*. Mathematicians, artists, writers, musicians, or any people who focus attention away from themselves to enlarge their awareness, engage in contemplation. Through contemplation, artists become great artists. Through contemplation, Einstein became both a great mathematician and a great mystic.

Meditation depends upon the strength of mind.
It must be unceasing
even when one is engaged in work.
Ramana Maharshi

Mystic, Robert Adams, says he was awakened at the age of fourteen while studying for a mathematics exam. According to Evelyn Underhill, all artists are of necessity contemplative. She calls it being "innocent of eye," and she describes three forms of contemplation:

- ***Contemplation of the natural world of becoming***—witnessing the natural world in whatever form presents itself to the eye, be it an ant or the Alps.
- ***Contemplation of the metaphysical world of being***—witnessing without the bodily senses, being engaged in any "attachment," or awareness, without evaluation.
- ***Contemplation on Divine Reality***—in this stage, the first two are combined into one, and there is a dying away of one's own will so that Absolute Love is experienced.

In order to develop a deeper awareness of the inner life, it's good to have some quiet time every day, even if it's just for a few minutes. It's also good to have a couple of hours or more every week for solitude. Sunday afternoon is a good time. Just observe without judgment—be "innocent of eye." Go for a walk in a cemetery or a park or find a trail. Discover why some people want to ride a motorcycle across the desert. Go for a bike ride, go fishing, play music, paint, write, read, do some journaling or just sit. Do not talk and don't watch television! The main thing is not to be projective. Be receptive—listen. Become involved in silence and the natural world.

Spend some time alone every day.
The Dalai Lama

Once a year, more frequently if possible, get away from the *normal* environment and everyday life. Thoreau headed for the woods. Thomas Merton went to a monastery. The mystic is not interested in going someplace where there are lots of people; where you spend lots of money, eat lots of food, and drink intoxicants. For "relaxation" Americans often go to Disneyland and Las Vegas. The point is to retreat *from* the world of the superficial, not deeper into it. Take a hike in the woods or mountains. Go to a yoga center or a Zen retreat center. In the Hindu tradition, older people take longer and more frequent retreats—they become forest dwellers, spending time in contemplation of liberation in peaceful preparation for the transition from life to life.

Relaxation: It Just Happens—Or Does It?

The mind must disengage from the ego to see the mystical. Crash and burn may take us there, but meditation and contemplation will take us there more reliably. We can utilize several of Sir Alister Hardy's ways of coming to a mystical experience, or we may think of a method of *relaxation* where for some reason we just "let go." This letting go often involves an unexpected "state of grace." Such experiences tend to happen in nature or in what we think of as sacred places, especially when we are alone. These moments can come while we are listening to music, reading or watching a film during an especially touching or powerful moment. They also can come when we are engaged in creative acts that require the repetitive use of the hands without thinking (like playing a musical instrument, knitting, crocheting, and painting) or hard labor (like smithing, gardening, and brick laying).

Everyone should find some suitable time,
day or night, to sink into his depths, each according
to his own fashion. Not everyone is able to engage in
contemplative prayer.
Johannes Tauler

Johannes Tauler (1300–1361, Germany) was a Dominican and Rhineland mystic influenced by Eckhart and Mechthild of Magdeburg. He stressed the inner person, rather than outer works. His writings were popular in Protestant circles during the Reformation and later Romanticism. He was part of the community that produced the *Theologia Germanica.*

A friend in his sixties tells a story about taking a walk among the giant Sequoia trees in Washington State with his four-year-old grandson and a puppy. The child was completely lost in play with the puppy, and the puppy was lost in sniffing out all of the wonderful smells of the forest. My friend sat down at the foot of a huge Sequoia tree, laid his back against the trunk, and just watched the boy and the dog in play. The moment, he said, was absolutely perfect. He felt like he was in Heaven. He had no major cares or concerns. Suddenly a deep sense of the interconnectedness of all things came over him, and he found himself in a state of bliss. Then the boy fell and started to cry; my friend jumped up. The world was back, and he was back in it.

Solitary sports like running, hiking, rock climbing, biking, sailing, flying, soaring, gliding, and fishing provide time for inner reflection and revelation. When I was growing up as a kid on the farm in Missouri, on Sunday mornings my mother Milly, my sister, Ann, and I would go to church, and Dad would go fishing. We had a pond on the back of our farm, which he kept stocked with fresh water bass. Daddy couldn't say. "You guys go to church. I'm going off by myself in the back pasture to meditate."

He had to have a reason to go off by himself, so he took along a fishing pole.

Many men go fishing, all of their lives,
without realizing – it's not fish they are after.
Henry David Thoreau

Athletes and artists often talk about getting into the flow when they just let go, lose track of time, and then enter into a deep place of peace, like "the runner's high." An international triathlon winner told me he won a triathlon event when an inner voice told him he did not need to stop and rest as the others were. His legs went into automatic pilot and kept moving. He transcended the pain and found a place of peace.

In the Shower: You're alone, (probably). No one is likely to walk in. Your eyes are closed. The water is washing your body. You are literally being baptized. The mind is not yet cluttered with the activity of the day, and there is a growing awakening and awareness. My friend John Nagy got the title for his book *Ours Is The Voice for God* while in the shower. A woman going to see her doctor that day about a possible hysterectomy received guidance in the shower to "take in a urine specimen," which she did, and they found out she was pregnant.

Driving: Dr. John Lilly called driving "the American mode of meditation." According to *Scientific American Mind Magazine* of June/July 2007, although driving a car initially requires concentration, it becomes second nature: the hands and feet do it intuitively. During my early 20s, when I had a motorcycle, a favorite modes of meditation was riding through the open desert in Southern California. One place in the desert had a series of small hills, like a roller coaster, that were tremendous fun for riding a motorcycle. Now, driving home at night from New York City, I will not turn on the radio or a CD because with awareness and listening only to the sound of the tires on the pavement, I am free to meditate on the way home.

In 1964, I took the Aurelia, a student ship, to Europe. Since there was no place to go to meditate, I stood for long periods on the deck looking out at the pewter sea, listening to the ocean splashing against the sides of the ship. There was nothing out there—just the vast emptiness, the great void, and enormous openness. Now, Dolores and I both go to a lake near by. There we just stand, and look out onto a peaceful, limpid scene. It is especially lovely early in the morning when a fog hangs over the lake. Perhaps each of us can find some nurturing place to go, just stand, and look. Becoming very relaxed, we can let go of obsessive thinking long enough for a purer perception—a knowing—to surface.

Creativity and Generativity

Mystical awareness may also occur during moments of profound creativity when the mind "disengages," and we see an inter-connectivity of things. This vision often happens when two or more fundamentals, like words and musical notes or shapes and colors, come together in a new and pleasing way. It is thus that Cyril Connolly (1903–1973) an English art critic, once said, *"The reward of art is not fame or success but intoxication."*

We all need activity in which we can lose ourselves. According to an article on "Boredom" in the December 2007 issue of *Scientific American Mind*, people who *do not* experience boredom are those who are able to throw themselves fully into some activity that is bigger than they are. Folks like Thomas Edison, Albert Einstein, and Madame Curie were never bored. According to an article by Kelley A. Robb in the *International Journal of the Psychology of Religions* (Vol. 13 # II, 2003), British psychoanalyst Marion Milner says that the same psychological processes are involved in both creative expression and mysticism. Creativity breaks down the barriers between self and other. In both mystical and creative states, one finds elements of joy, ecstasy, absorption, loss of self-consciousness, and loss of time. Milner says mysticism is one dimension of the creative process.

People often describe heightened sensitivity while dancing, playing a musical instrument, painting or writing. According to Zen, a walk through a rock garden or the act of chopping wood can be just as "enlightening" as what is experienced during "sitting" meditation. Sometimes when we are talking or writing, and it's flowing smoothly, we may feel as though we're not doing it. It is not necessary to think about what to say next. It's as though it is being given to us. Mysticism is quite natural. In fact, when we are not experiencing the mystical state, something has gone wrong: the ego has grabbed hold.

Contemplative Prayer

Prayer is the center of all religious traditions. Indeed, prayer is the center of religious life. Devout Muslims pray five times each day. Buddhists, Hindus, Christians, and Jews pray daily. Even atheists pray when they are in trouble. As the old saying goes, "There are no atheists in fox holes." There is also no one who has not experienced what seems to be failure at prayer. When that happens, we can't help but wonder, "Is God listening?"

Bargaining with God

The object of most prayer is to
wangle an advance on good intentions.
Robert Brault

Prayer does not seem to interest most folks too much unless a need arises; consequently, most prayer is asking for something. A lot of times, we get around to praying when we get to, "Oh please, God, don't let this happen." Or, "Please don't let this be true." Sometimes when the need arises, that may be the prayer we need to say. This is not, however, the mystic's prayer. When we are in need, we may try to persuade God to see things our way. We may promise that we'll be good, that we will be more loving—that we will do His will.

Two shipwrecked sailors were adrift on a raft for days. In desperation, one knelt down and began to pray. "Oh Lord, I haven't lived a good life. I've drunk too much. I've lied. I've cheated. I've gambled. I've caroused with women. I've done many bad things, but, Lord, if you'll save me, I promise—" "Don't say another word!" shouted his shipmate. "I think I just spotted a ship."

Dr. Jacob Bronowski notes in his book, *The Ascent of Man*, that success in science does not come until science asks the right question. The answer is always there. First it is necessary to ask the right question. God cannot answer prayer with an illusion, nor is it possible to receive that which would not be helpful to us. Much of what we call prayer is asking God to help us. Contemplative prayer, however, comes not from need—it arises from love.

Prayer and Positive Thinking

According to the laws of the world, we may pray for physical rewards and success, and we may receive what this world can give us. There are many examples of the use of *positive* thinking or *possibility* thinking or *prosperity* thinking to get what we want. There are many popular speakers who espouse this philosophy, and it is easy to see why some of them achieve worldly success. Much power is gained through training and exercising the mind. There are plenty of CDs designed to pump up the mind. But, which mind are we pumping up?

The question is, "Into whose hands do I place my mind?" You can run needles through your body and not hurt yourself. You can walk on hot coals without getting burned. It is possible to endure long periods without sleep. You can lose a lot of weight. You can make a lot of money and amass great wealth and power. *The Guinness Book of World Records* is filled with amazing examples of mind over matter. These events, however, reflect the *magical*, not the *miraculous*, use of the mind. Also, we may not receive what we *ask* for. Not all prayer is answered. God can, after all, give only "good" gifts to his children. We can pray to the ego and receive ego rewards. Yet, insofar as it is not consistent with the truth of what we are, we actually received nothing. In fact, we have backed a little further from the truth and a little deeper into illusion. The ego is very subtle. It may persuade us, for example, to go into debt to obtain some earthly reward. The idea may be appealing, but the debt must be paid and with interest.

It is easy to confuse form and content. What matters is where the heart is, not where the head is. How we stand, sit or kneel when we pray does not matter. Our words are, after all, but symbols of symbols. A grandfather passed his granddaughter's room one night and overheard her repeating the alphabet. He asked her, "What on earth are you up to?" She explained, "I'm saying my prayers, but I don't remember the words, so I'm just saying all the letters. I'll let God put it together for me." Quieting the mind and looking out the window watching birds at the bird-feeder or watching a water fountain or reverently humming a chant or a hymn is as much a prayer as any formal words. It's not the words we say; it's the prayer of the heart that matters.

In prayer it is better to have a heart
without words than words without heart.
John Bunyan

What we ask for is what we receive. What are we asking for and whom are we asking? Before we choose to do anything, it's best to ask if the choice is in accord with Spirit. If we feel no fear, it's the right answer and the right choice. One way to get the wrong answer is to make up our minds about how we want things to turn out and then ask. In this case, we have not really asked. If the mind is already made up, what good does it do to ask? What is the difference between the Voice for God and the voice for the ego? To find the answer, we can look at the results. If we do not like the results, one of three things has happened:

1. We've been asking the wrong question.
2. We've been asking the wrong teacher.
3. We've been asking the wrong teacher the wrong question.

Once we cancel our own terms, the right question and the right answer can appear.

Sometimes the answer to prayer is not
that it changes life, but it changes you.
James Dillet Freeman

James Dillet Freeman (1912 –2003, USA) was an American Indian poet and a minister of the Unity School of Christianity. He is sometimes referred to as the "poet laureate for the moon" because his poems were twice brought to the moon. His "Prayer for Protection" was taken aboard Apollo 11 in July 1969 by lunar module pilot Buzz Aldrin and a microfilm of Freeman's "I Am Thee" was left on the moon by James Irwin on Apollo 15.

Mysticism is about thinking along lines that lead to Heaven. Our task is to align our minds with the One Mind—to be able to think free of attachments, judgments, petty ego concerns, and projections. When the answer is right—we know. There is no question. We do not have to solve problems on our own. We can ask for help from the ego or from Spirit. Whichever one we choose will give us an answer. When the ego answers our prayers, we are left wanting. When God answers our prayers, we find peace.

Contemplative prayer is a state of communion and a direct awareness of God. Communion is the natural state of those who know the divine.

Contemplative prayer is non-rational meditation. In contemplative prayer, God is *felt* as a living presence, an awareness that occurs when we stop incessant thinking.

Contemplative prayer is prayer of the heart. Although it is not a place of words—words may work in their own small way. Chants and mantras are thus used in different spiritual traditions to "quiet" or "still" the mind with one thought, phrase or word that is repeated many times.

Contemplative prayer is an experience of God as the ground in which we are rooted. While words may be used to focus the mind, it becomes less and less a matter of saying anything and increasingly a matter of quietude. Advancing in prayer life is more about *listening* than talking.

Contemplative prayer is observing without judgment, interpretation or analysis. Contemplative prayer is acceptance and an ongoing process of communion, a movement toward the divine, a deepening of spiritual life, and a freeing of ourselves from the fetters of the world.

Contemplative prayer is something we do all the time, something which becomes us.

I have lived to thank God that
all my prayers have not been answered.

Jean Ingelow (1820–1897, England),
poet, novelist, and friend of Alfred Lord Tennyson

Contemplative Prayer is an experience of God at the center of our being. Communion comes simply by letting God be God. Prayer is not supplicating or entreating. It's not magic or wishful thinking. It's not wanting in times of scarcity and lack, nor telling God what we need.

Contemplative Prayer is trusting. It is a way of living. It is something we do every minute of every day.

Contemplative prayer is the opening of the mind, the heart, and the whole being to God. At the core of contemplative prayer, there is silence. Contemplative prayer is spoken silently, deeply within, where there is an opening of the heart and a simple receptivity.

Prayer is a way offered by the Holy Spirit to reach
God. It is not merely a question or an entreaty.
It cannot succeed until you realize
that it asks for nothing.

A Course in Miracles

When we pray to God we must
be seeking nothing—nothing.

Saint Francis of Assisi

St. Francis of Assisi (1182–1226, Italy) is the founder of the Franciscan Order and the most popular of the Catholic mystics. His picture has been painted more than any other saint. It is said that Francis was so kind to animals that wild rabbits ran to him for protection. A famous story tells how he preached to birds, telling them to be thankful to God; he once removed a thorn from a wolf's paw. The movie made about his life is *Brother Sun, Sister Moon.*

The first course I took in the ministry as a pre-ministerial student in 1961 was Beginning Preaching. Jesus, however, never taught his disciples to preach—only to pray. When it came to preaching, he told them to open their mouths and follow inner guidance. When the disciples asked Jesus to teach them to pray, he said: "When you pray, pray thus. Our Father which art in Heaven, Hallowed by thy name, Thy Kingdom come, Thy will be done." There is no greater prayer than *Thy will be done.*

Prayer is
An offering
A letting go
A stepping aside
A giving up of ourselves
A means of communication
A time of listening and loving
A time of remembering.

Mysticism and Work

Contemplation implies nonattachment,
which does not preclude activity.
Dr. David Hawkins

Erik Erickson (1902–1994, Germany) was a Jewish German. His developmental psychology describes eight stages that we all go through in the process of maturation. Six of Erikson's eight stages occur in the formative years from infancy through young adulthood. The eighth stage, which Erickson calls the mature years, applies specifically to older people. The seventh stage, from young adulthood to the mature years is the longest stage and constitutes most of our working years. During this stage, says Erickson, we need to be "generative." We need to work, to produce, to create, to be responsible, constructive, contributing participants in this world. If we cannot be generative, the result is often frustration and despair.

Wealth and Happiness

According to a 2004 analysis of more than 150 studies on the topic of wealth and happiness, Sharon Begley of *The Wall Street Journal*, writes that researchers found income is an accurate predictor of well-being when it raises a person from, say, being homeless and unemployed to being financially secure. With increasing wealth, however, extra money doesn't buy extra happiness. Indeed, wealth is more a curse than a blessing if it keeps a person from working. People who inherit a great deal of money are often unhappy, the exception being those who have found some way to be creative and philanthropic. The happiest people on earth are those who experience depth in relationships, enjoy their work, and see life as meaningful.

The Alchemy of Work

Get happiness out of your work or you may never
know what happiness is.
Elbert Hubbard

Osho said that given sufficient practice, the meditative state can be achieved and maintained while performing everyday tasks. We can learn to strengthen meditation and carry it through the day. There is then an undercurrent of awareness in everything we do. Something peaceful underneath is continuously flowing.

With what can we compare the Kingdom of God?
Or, what parable shall we use for it?
It is like a grain of mustard seed, which when sown upon the ground, is the smallest of all the seeds on earth, yet when it is sown it grows up and becomes the greatest of the shrubs, and puts forth large branches, so that the birds of the air can make nests in its shade.

He told them another parable,

The Kingdom of Heaven is like leaven, which a woman took and hid in three measures of meal, till it was all leavened.
All this Jesus said to them in parables; indeed he said nothing to them without a parable. This was to fulfill what was spoken of the prophets: I will open my mouth in parables; I will utter what has been hidden since the foundation of the world.
Matthew 13: 31–35

The parables of the mustard seed, the leaven, and the seed that turns into wheat (and at the *right time* is ready for harvest) describe the process by which we may become aware of the Kingdom of Heaven within. Each suggests a subtle way in which the Kingdom is manifest. There is something deep inside that produces transformation. How, the gardener does not know, but it works. The inner working produces transformation. Alchemy, a medieval forerunner of chemistry, concerned itself with transforming base substances into gold. The alchemist was after something golden, but gold was merely the outward symbol of a transformation that had to occur within the alchemist. Thus, one of the ancient alchemical texts proclaims:

To the Seeker:
Let him forbear who believes that Alchemy is
concerned solely with the mundane,
mineral and metallic nature of things.
Alchemy is but a symbol used to reveal by analogy
the process of achieving "Spiritual Realization"
in a word that a man is at once the prime matter
and author of The Work.
Claude d Ygin

Work speaks to us in quiet ways. Work is a blessing and never a curse when we use it to help us in our transformations.

Every one has been made for some work, and the
desire for that work has been put in his heart.
Rumi

Hindu philosophy emphasizes karma yoga—the way of work. Mystics enjoy work. They love doing whatever they do. As we become involved in our work, we develop "mastery." As we develop mastery, we find ourselves being transported, promoted, advanced, or "fired out of" our work, into a yet deeper dimension of work. The radio announcers praise Fridays and bemoan Mondays because the "nine to five" can be burdensome and grievous. It's not that way, however, for the mystic.

There are two ways to wash dishes:
The first is to wash dishes in order to have clean dishes; the second is to wash dishes in order to wash dishes.

Thich Nhat Hanh

During the war in Vietnam, **Thich Nhat Hanh** (1926 – Present, Vietnam, France) worked for reconciliation between North and South Vietnam. His lifelong peace efforts moved Martin Luther King, Jr., to nominate him for the Nobel Peace Prize in 1967. He coined the term "Engaged Buddhism." He lives in exile in France, where he teaches, writes, gardens, and works to help refugees worldwide.

Work as Devotion

Karma Yoga, the way of work (and Bhakti Yoga, the way of love), calls upon us to work with devotion through the selfless service we render to others—our children, communities, and the world as a whole. When we work with dedication, whether peeling potatoes, sweeping the floor or cleaning up another's mess, it is not a chore. It is an act of love. Selfless service promotes awareness, and devotion develops wisdom, patience, and forbearance.

Work is rewarding when we are *engrossed, immersed,* or *wrapped up* in it. Then, we feel neither anxiety nor despair, only the perfection of doing what we are doing. Devotion is a way of being with oneself and God; therefore, any work done with devotion can lead to awakening—and be fulfilling. Throughout his entire life, Jesus understood clearly there was a specific work that was his life's purpose, and he was about doing it. At the age of twelve, he said to his mother and father, "Don't you understand I have to be about my father's business?" Regardless of the form of work, there is really only one work, and that is our Father's business. Several of Jesus' parables are about good and faithful stewards taking care of the master's work.

Mysticism, the Crafts and the Arts and The Knowledge of Hands

The "answer" is found with the hands, the head, and the heart. At the end of the movie *The Return of the Jedi*, in the final and most crucial moments, our hero Luke must trust "the force." (Remember the lines: "Use the Force. Let go, Luke. Let go, Luke. Trust Me, Luke.") Moving deeply into work, we can set aside the ego. Musicians do not think about where their fingers go. Their hands automatically make the decision. If they start thinking about which finger goes where and get anxious about how well they are doing, they might strike the wrong key or hit the wrong note and create discord.

When the Church descended into the Dark Ages (sometimes called a thousand years without a bath), the Crusades, and the Inquisition, mystical studies were forced underground and were conducted secretively with artists and craftsmen. During this time, the various trades or guilds were also being established. The Freemasons are one example of the outgrowth of a deep esoteric inner working that was neither happening nor allowed within the church. The word *Masons*, now used to describe an esoteric fraternity, comes from the word *mason* meaning "one who works with bricks and mortar." Carl Jung and Winston Churchill both laid bricks to invigorate themselves. The Medieval Mystics felt that work done with the hands provided knowledge unavailable to the leisured class.

During the time when an excessively corrupt and authoritative Church was unable to offer spiritual solace, people were finding comfort and mystical insight through the practice of their crafts and trades: blacksmithing, silver-smithing, carpentry, masonry, pottery, farming, architecture, printing, medicine, leather working, music, and more. Work is something that people do with their hands, heads, and hearts. Now, in the twenty-first century, hands touch computer keys and numbers on cell phones. Fewer and fewer people dig, drill, carve, chisel, mold, assemble, forge, cut, weave, sculpt, sew, paint or saw. The most respectable of ancient occupations were those in which people learned to do *fine* things with their hands. In art, music, and the trades, people were thus making mystical inroads without the aid of the Church.

The work is with you and in you in such a way that once you find it in yourself, where it always is, you have it always, wherever you may be, on land or sea.

Hermes Trismegistus,
The legendary founder of alchemy

The symbol for alchemy is the athanor, the furnace of the alchemists. A furnace is where things are transformed. The athanor of the body is the stomach, the place where digestion occurs. Mysticism in the alchemical sense involves turning things over, buffing, burnishing, rubbing, polishing, perfecting, improving, changing, and developing up to the point of ripeness and then harvest—the book is written, the house built, the concert performed, the painting completed, the Self realized.

Fire-tending is the most ancient alchemical stimulant. Human consciousness developed around campfires. Staring into a fire for hours on end leads to meditation. Imagine sitting looking at the eyes of your brother looking back through the flicker of the flames. For hundreds of thousands of years, fire was TV before there was TV. The earliest mystics were potters, smiths, cooks, and bakers. Pottery, glassblowing, working with bronze, and sword-making involve innumerable stages working with fire, leading to the final "perfected" product.

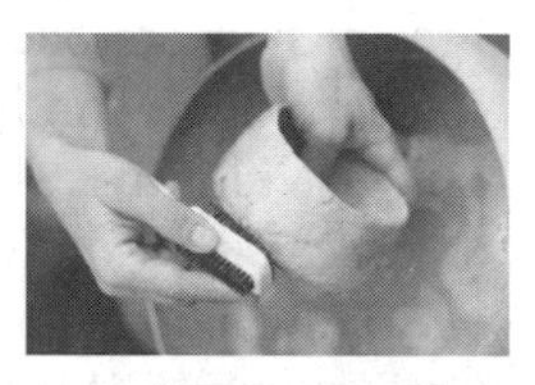

The oldest form of alchemy is fire-tending, the next is pottery. You take a very basic substance (the earth itself) and transform it into a useful vessel. First you take clay from the earth and throw the clay onto the center of a wheel. You add some water, and then you spin, center, shape, and form it. You mold it till you have something—perhaps a pot. Then you glaze and fire it under great heat till you have a useable container. The most common elements found at ancient sites are pottery shards.

Composting is alchemy.

Without a rose we cannot have garbage.
Without garbage we cannot have a rose.

Tich Nhat Hahn

Through the process of rot, or decay and putrefaction, material things are recycled, or turned into, brown gold—a primary ingredient in fertilizing soil.

Gardening is alchemy.

Planting seeds is mystical: you place little "gems" into the soil, water them, and then watch as they come forth from the dark earth, turning into fruit and flowers in the light of the sun. It takes sensitivity to the seasons and weather to know what plants need and when they need it.

Cooking is alchemy.

You take raw food matter, combine it with other foods. Then mix, beat, heat, and cool it until you have turned it into something that tastes good and nourishes the body. A woman once told me she had a mystical experience while washing macaroni.

Writing is alchemy.

Kierkegaard took his journal writing seriously. Once he wrote that his journal was his *"most trusted confidant."* When writing, you take an idea, jot it down, work it over, add to it, and work it over again. Then set it aside. Go away. Come back and approach the work with a fresh perspective. You edit: cut out the chaff, leave the gold, feed it with new ideas, sift through, synthesize—feed again, sift through again—until it's finally done.

Journaling or keeping a spiritual diary deepens the writer. I highly recommend such writing. Write questions to Jesus, for example. Or write to a teacher you admire, and see if he or she answers you. Writing is my practice. I write religiously, like some people practice the piano. I like to write early in the morning before the phone begins to ring, when my mind is fresh and uncluttered.

Ram Dass was once telling a group of people about one of his experiences with psychedelics. An older woman in the front row kept nodding her head as though she understood what he was describing. After the talk, he told her he was surprised that she seemed to understand what he was saying, and she said, "Yes, I crochet." Gandhi's alchemy was spinning. Your alchemy may be music; or you might knit, quilt, sail, sculpt or work with wood. There's a time when the wood speaks to the carpenter, the garden converses with the gardener, and the piano plays with the pianist. Such inner work is an ongoing process, rather than simply repetitive. It involves the discovery and unfolding of an insight that is progressively wonderful and fulfilling.

If you commit to it,
writing can take you as deep as Zen.

Dainin Katagiri
in Natalie Goldberg's *Long Quiet Highway*

Dainin Katagiri (1928–1990, Japan) In 1963 Dainin came to the United States, and in 1972, he became the first abbot of the Minnesota Zen Meditation Center in Minneapolis. Katagiri authored *Returning to Silence*, emphasizing the need to return to our original, enlightened state of being. A second book, *You Have to Say Something*, focused on how to bring Zen into daily life.

The choice of how to make one's living is crucial,
for the work we do makes us what we become;
The blacksmith pounds the anvil—but the anvil also
pounds the blacksmith. The clam shell turns golden in
the brown depths of the ocean, and in a more subtle
way is one's mind colored by the course of one's life.
When a man chooses his labor,
he chooses his future self.

Henry David Thoreau

When we love what we do, hear the call of destiny in it, understand God's plan, and throw ourselves into it, we discover even greater depths of creativity and expanding returns. While insight may be gained instantaneously in a lightning flash, for the vast majority who trek through this world of illusion, mystical maturing takes time. It's the "cooking," the gestation, the seed growing secretly, that brings character.

There are many ways of serving God. One way is not holier than another, but the way we approach it is holy—or not. As Swami Ramdas said, "Whatever act you do is worship when it is done with the thought of God." Whatever we are doing, cleaning house or writing a book, we do in service. We do it with devotion.

Swami Ramdas (1884–1963, India) was a philosopher and guru. His message is one of Universal Love. He lived on charity but never accepted money. His practice was to view the world as forms of Ram (God)—and thus to see everything that might befall him as the will of God. He knew and worked for a time with Ramana Maharshi.

Whence comes it then, that we have so many complaints, each saying that his occupation is a hindrance to him? Whence comes this inward reproof and sense of guilt which torments and disquiets you? Dear children, know that it is not your work which gives you this disquiet. No, it is your want of order in fulfilling your work. If you performed your work in the right method, with the whole aim to God and not to yourselves nor your own gain or pleasure, but only God's glory, in your work, it would be impossible that it should grieve your conscience.

Johannes Tauler

God must become an activity in our consciousness.

Joel Goldsmith

Joel Goldsmith (1892–1964, USA) was a teacher of "practical" mysticism, which he called *The Infinite Way*. He studied Christian Science, prayer and meditation. "Well being," he said, "is the result of attaining oneness with God." There is a transcendental awareness available to us here and now, which comes from "dying daily" of the old self and a rebirth of the new self, the son of God. He explored the ideas of God as Love, as Law, and as Oneness. He traveled throughout the world as a non-denominational teacher, helping others look inside themselves and thus find *The Mystic Way*.

Commitment

Buddhism emphasizes right livelihood. Right livelihood involves the integration of survival with doing what we are supposed to be doing. Right livelihood involves commitment to something we are happy doing for a lifetime. How long a project takes doesn't matter. Aging works in our favor for right livelihood. The more we do our chosen work, the better we get at what we do, the more we develop character and creativity. I watched a documentary on people in their nineties who were healthy and active and seemed destined to live past 100. All of them were working!

Work brings its own relief.
He who is most idle has the most grief.

Anonymous

You've seen bumper stickers that say, "I'd rather be flying" or "dancing" or "sailing," and so forth. What we *should be* doing is what we would *rather be* doing. People get paid for flying. The task is to focus on what calls the soul. As Joseph Campbell said, "Follow your bliss." When we integrate who we are with what we do and what we do with who we are, we cannot be other than happy. To the ego, work is a curse. To the mystic, work is nothing less than the happy means of returning Home. Work is central to who we *already* are. Work is grease on the hinge that opens the door to Heaven. Any work can be creative. The more creative it is, the more we enjoy it. The more we enjoy our work, the more we feel we are doing what we are supposed to.

When our avocation is our vocation,
we are always on vacation.

Contemporary mystic Barbara Marx Hubbard describes what she calls "vocational arousal" as your own deep genius turning on. It is your unique life-purpose activating you. Work to be *who you are*. Don't worry about money.

Work to become, not to acquire.

Elbert Hubbard

What work I have done
I have done because it has been play.
If it had been work I shouldn't have done it

Mark Twain

Forest Dwelling and Saging with Aging

A fellow in his mid-sixties came to one of my classes. He was retired, and he said he had decided to spend the rest of his life figuring out the meaning of life. He was, he said, going to spend the remainder of his life working on himself. He said he was an active reader and thus frequent visitor to Barnes and Noble. Also, he was actively meditating and studying his dreams. I thought that was great.

For everything there is a season. Hinduism divides life into three stages: in the first, you study; in the second, you become a householder; and in the third, you go become a forest-dweller. According to the Hindu texts, when you see your hair turning grey, it is time to take your wife or husband by the hand and head for the forest, where you live modestly and have time to think.

Life Mastery

Transformation comes through the mind, the heart, and the hands. If we learn how to read music but never play music, we will not *master* music; we will not be "skilled." Mastery is not about competition or the ability to do something better than anyone else. It is about refinement and polish. Mastery enables the creation of beauty, free of any mistakes. Mastery for the mystic is simply continual work and refinement of the soul until he or she obtains God.

The secret of joy in work is
contained in one word—excellence.
To know how to do something well is to enjoy it.
Pearl S. Buck

Only one who devotes himself to a cause with his
whole strength and soul can be a true master.
For this reason mastery demands all of a person.
Albert Einstein

Work is the grand cure of all the maladies and
miseries that ever beset mankind.
Thomas Carlyle

Section III — Six Great Illusions

What is Metaphysics?

Metaphysics as derived from **Aristotle** (384-322 B.C.E., Greece) is concerned with explaining the nature of the world. It is the study of "reality" or "being." Metaphysics asks: What is real? Is any "thing" real? What is man's place in the universe? Is my subjective experience real? Can anything be known purely objectively? Does the world exist outside the mind? What is the nature of the events which occur in our lives? Are these events meaningful or is it all happenstance?

Ontology, the central branch of metaphysics, investigates what categories of things are in the world and what relations these things have to one another. The metaphysician thus tries to *understand how* we *understand.*

"Metaphysics" also means that which is beyond physics. ***Meta*** means after, beyond, or transcending, such as meta-morphosis, as in the change of a caterpillar into a butterfly. The butterfly comes after or goes beyond the caterpillar. Physics examines the physical world. Metaphysics comes after physics and examines the relationship between mind and matter. An in-depth study of physics often leads to metaphysics and an in-depth study of metaphysics can lead us to mysticism and thus to God—as it did for Einstein.

Metaphysicians seek to understand what is happening on a higher level, a deeper level or a spiritual level: the mind and heart level—beyond the sound and sight of ear and eye.

To awaken to the truth of who we "already are," we remove (let go of) the blocks to the awareness of love's presence. Our hero or heroine (you—me) has fallen into a dream from which we can awaken. There are seven major blocks on the path to awakening. 1.) The World. 2.) Time. 3.) The Body. 4.) The Ego. 5.) Death. 6.) The Belief in Duality.

Chapter 7

Mysticism and the World

The world is a maladaptive solution
to a non-existent problem.
Dr. Kenneth Wapnick

The Dreaming of the World

The ego is based on the belief that we live in a material world, inside bodies, and subject to the passage of time. According to St. Augustine, only eternity is real. Everything else is fleeting. That which was not created by God does not exist. Evil, being ego-based, is not created by God—neither is it eternal. We have split minds. While part of our attention is given to God, a greater part is given to the self. This self, which we call "the ego," is a dream. It has no more eternity in it than last night's dream.

St. Augustine (354–430, North Africa), Bishop of Hippo in North Africa, tried to combine Greek Philosophy and Judeo-Christian Theology. He emphasized the soul's search for God and the illumination of the mind. His book *Confessions* written in 400 is the first "introspective" autobiography. (One of the next best is *The Story of My Misfortune* by Peter Abelard, 1079–1142, France) Augustine takes Christianity to an "intellectual" stage. God is a paradox, the container and the contained. He greatly influences most of the Christian mystics.

The perceived world is part of our attempt to maintain ego identification. Jesus in the Gospels says, "What does it benefit a man to gain the whole world and lose his own soul?" (Luke 9:25) We cannot lose our soul. We can, however, lose our awareness of it. After a lifetime of trying to possess the world, tyrants must come with sadness to the realization that there is no world to possess, and their dreams of dominance are a fleeting fantasy.

Sir Thomas Browne (1605–1682, England) said that the world is a vague picture of the real world. His major work *Religio Medici* (Religion of a Physician) was placed on the list of forbidden books by the Vatican. He influences Samuel Taylor Coleridge, Theosophist Madame Blavatasky, and Scottish Psychologist R.D. Laing.

The world one sees does not even exist.
Ramana Maharshi

What does it mean there is no world? The world seems so tangible. First of all, the world we see is *our interpretation*. There is no world because *we're always making up the world.* The world we make up as part of our fantasy is a dream—sometimes a nightmare, sometimes very ordinary. We may dream a happy dream—still, we are dreaming. Still, a happy dream beats a nightmare any day.

All "things" and all sentiments are interpretations
only, and interpretations cannot be real in any sense.
Wei Wu Wei

According to Wei Wu Wei, perceiving is itself pure, in other words, impersonal and real. The interpretation that follows introduces subject and object with a resulting concept that is unreal. The result is that we have an oneiric, or dreamlike, interpretation of what we call reality. The Australian Aborigines, perhaps the materially poorest people on earth—and the only group of people on earth who have no suicides in their culture—have always thought of this world as a dream. Similarly, the native tribes in Venezuela also speak of "waking" life as a dream.

Domestication

The dreaming of the world includes all of society's rules, morals, customs, beliefs, values, religions, myths, philosophies, psychological problems, and more. Our families, social institutions, and the omnipresent media constantly create and describe "society's dream." To some extent, we all are at the mercy of the culture into which we are born. We are domesticated; we have become addicted to dreaming, much the same way a dog is domesticated through a system of rewards and punishment.

Popular opinion is the greatest lie in the world.
Thomas Carlyle

Thomas Carlyle (1795–1881, Scotland) was an author, and historian. His parents wanted him to become a preacher. While a student at the University of Edinburgh, however, he lost his Christian faith, yet he remained deeply religious. This loss of faith along with his religious temperament made his work appealing during a time of social upheaval.

Another Scotsman, **R. D. Laing** (1927–1989), a psychiatrist who worked extensively with psychosis, felt that much of what we call insanity is the result of being unable to adjust to an insane world. People are put in difficult situations, where they are unable to conform to the conflicting and often contradictory expectations from parents, society, the church, and more. Unable to cope, some people just *check out*, leading to distress for everyone else concerned. According to Laing, society is crazy and some people have a hard time adjusting to the insane habituated patterns of the world.

There were few institutions that either Gurdjieff or Osho respected. Neither cared much for politics or self-righteous social trends. They both felt that dogmatic religions were outside the realm of the "real." The real world according to Gurdjieff was a place where cosmic laws held dominion. The world of social and political trends is contaminated by the laws of the ego. In this world, the law is "an eye for an eye and a tooth for a tooth." Man is caught, said Gurdjieff, in a world that is asleep, a world prone to psychotic and mindless fits of rage called "war."

In the first chapter of his book, *The Four Agreements*, Don Miguel Ruiz talks about "Domestication." According to Ruiz, all of what we hear and see is a dream. Dreaming is the main function of the mind, and we are constantly dreaming. What Ruiz calls dreaming, Eckhart Tolle calls "compulsive thinking." We might also call it "unconscious thinking." Society is "the dreaming of the planet"—a collection of billions of small dreams carried out in a wide variety of cultures.

Don Miguel Ruiz (1952 – Present, Mexico) was born into a family of healers. His mother was a *curandera* (healer) and his grandfather a *nagual* (shaman). He attended medical school and become a surgeon. A near-death experience changed his life.

In solitude we have our dreams to ourselves,
and in company we agree to dream in concert.
Dr. Samuel Johnson, in *The Idler*

Our world is "word" built. We use language to understand what is going on in ourselves and the world around us. Michael Talbot in *Mysticism and the New Physics* says, "Reality is a semantic creation largely constructed by cultural beliefs. What we believe to be true becomes true. What we call reality is learned."

Man has always sacrificed truth
to his vanity, comfort and advantage.
He lives not by truth but by make-believe.
W. Somerset Maugham

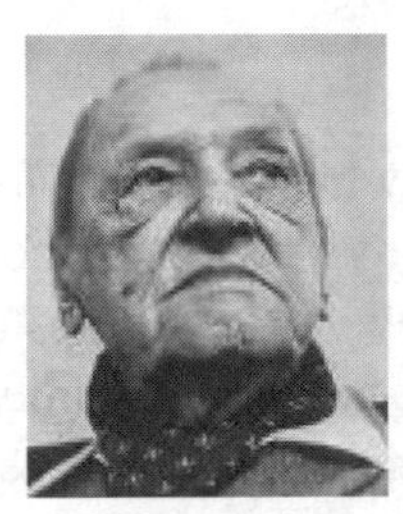

William Somerset Maugham (1874–1965, England) was one of the most popular authors of the early twentieth century and the best paid author of the 1930s. In his last major novel, *The Razor's Edge* (1944), the main character is a disillusioned veteran of World War I who abandons his wealthy friends, lover, and lifestyle to go to India seeking enlightenment. The story's themes of Eastern mysticism and war-weariness struck a chord with readers just as World War II was coming to an end.

If a woman walks bare-breasted down almost any street in the United States, she can be arrested for "indecent exposure." In certain South Pacific and African cultures, however, women walk around bare-breasted, and no one even notices because it's not regarded as unusual. In many Islamic cultures, a woman must have not only her breasts covered but also her ankles, hands, face—everything. Each of our social codes is based on diverse interpretations of reality. Which is right and which is wrong? None of them are right. None of them are wrong. They are just different interpretations. Yet, we kill each other over such interpretations of reality.

The individual has always had to struggle
to keep from being overwhelmed by the tribe.
If you try it, you will be lonely often, and sometimes
frightened. But no price is too high to pay for the
privilege of owning yourself.
Frederick Nietzsche

Someone once sent me the following email:

I Was Drugged

I had a drug problem when I was young.

I was drug to church on Sundays.

I was drug to church for weddings and funerals.

I was drug to family reunions.

I was drug to the bus stop to go to school.

I was drug by my ears when I was disrespectful.

I was drug to the woodshed and whipped when I disobeyed my parents.

Those **"drugs"** are still in my veins; and they affect my behavior in everything I do, say, and think.

The person passing around this email thought it was good having been "drugged" because now he knew what to do and was not on "drugs."

Every child is born a mystic, then we draw him
toward the school and the education and the serpent.
The serpent is the civilization,
the culture, the conditioning.
Osho

From infancy upward, we are told what the world is. This teaching is incessant until we perceive the prescribed world. After a while, we no longer have to be domesticated. We want to please others, and we act appropriately. Domestication is so strong that we even punish ourselves if we "get out of line."

The terror of society, which is the basis of morals,
the terror of God, which is the secret of religion
—these are the two things that govern us.
Oscar Wilde

Oscar Wilde (1854–1900, Ireland) was one of the most successful playwrights of late Victorian London. A novelist, poet, and author of short stories, he was well known for his pointed wit and his outlandish lifestyle.

Conform to the proper description of the world, make appropriate interpretations, and we are rewarded with money and prestige, fame and fortune, degrees and titles. The reality of day-to-day life consists of an endless flow of interpretations we share with the world. These shared interpretations are rarely questioned.

The mystic has the most disturbing awareness that
something is not quite right. The social order,
with its world of thought, sentiments, speech and
religion and its entire cultural network, determines
our thoughts and actions to such an extent that it is
hard to see or accept any alternative.
Bruno Borchert
Carmelite Priest and Mystical Researcher

Worlds Within Worlds

We can speak of different worlds, the worlds of the Babylonians, the Spanish conquistadors, Napoleonic France, or Nazi Germany—as though they represent certain states of mind or attitudes that existed once upon a time but exist no more. Looking at a wall full of magazines at a Barnes and Noble bookstore, I noticed that we have *Gun World*, *Motor Home World*, *Antique World*, *Fishing World*, *Wrestling World*, and *Craft World*, to name a few. You can choose whatever "world" you want to make a part of your own. Pick a world. Castaneda says to his teacher Don Juan, "Are you trying to show me the real world?" Don Juan said, "No, I'm not trying to show you the real world; I'm trying to show you that the world you see is just a view—it's just an attitude." One evening, I asked my then teenage daughter, Sarah, what she was watching on TV. She said it was a show called *The Real World*. "And what," I said, "what is '*The Real World*'?" She replied, "It's about teenagers who get drunk and have sex," So, now I know!

Man should be freed and not glued to the world.
We should be free of the constraints of time,
and from rushing after whatever diverts us.
Thomas Müntzer

Thomas Müntzer (1488–1525, Germany), an early reformer, thought that Luther had not gone far enough with the Reformation. Scripture alone was insufficient. We also need inner guidance. He taught the "living word of God" (continued revelation and prophecy). He led a group of peasants (The Peasants War) against spiritual oppression. Defeated, tortured, and beheaded, his head and body were placed on stakes as a warning to those who would defy the authority of the Catholic Church. Müntzer's thought is seen again in American Transcendentalism and what became known as New Thought.

If a man's choices depend on his passions,
or on propaganda, or on current conventions,
they are not free choices.
It is not the exercise of choice
that makes man free, but the determination
to choose the Truth.
St. Sharbel

Saint Sharbel (1828-1898, Lebanon) was a Maronite Catholic monk and priest. He lived as a hermit and his reputation for godliness compelled people to seek him out for a blessing. He followed strict fasting and was devoted to the Blessed Sacrament. After his death, people reportedly saw lights over his grave which is now a site for pilgrims.

We live in the *In-formation Age*—an age coming into form. As we have more and more information, we also have more reinforcement about what constitutes the nature of reality. At the same time, the more we discover in cosmology, the more we realize we don't know very much.

In the twenty-first century, electronic screens on the walls in our homes tell us what to believe about the world. Television teaches us what is valuable and real and which people are beautiful. It tells us what is most appealing to the eye: what's elegant, splendid, and sublime. It also shows us what's offensive, repugnant, and repulsive. We learn what's hip, cool, or hot and what's not. Daytime television is dominated by soap operas. Michael Lebowitz of Columbia University designed a computer program to write soap operas. All you have to do is to put in a few basic elements like hatred, revenge, lying, and cheating. Only one rule prevails: *nobody gets to be happy!* Characters in soap operas often have the best of what this world has to offer: the finest homes, cars, furs, and jewels. Yet every character is isolated, broken, deprived, sorrowful—suffering from spiritual malnutrition. If we watch a soap opera for one minute, we see that the characters are true to the "program"; each one is manipulating, lying to, and cheating on the other. Everyone is out for him or herself; no one is genuinely altruistic. We create our own soap operas and live them "out loud" with our families, neighbors, and co-workers. This is the way the ego works.

Some folks are "news addicts." They want to know what's going on. To know what is really going on, take a break from television, the internet, and newspapers. Jesus in the gospels suggests we go into the closet and shut the door. (I know one woman mystic who actually does this.) Sit down, shut-up, and wait! After a while, we have some idea about what is really going on. When Jesus says the "Kingdom of Heaven" is inside, he doesn't mean it's in our bodies. It's in the mind, which has always been connected to God. We can't see beyond this world until we stop making it up.

If you try to be a prophet and encourage people to see things differently, you may very likely get into trouble with the establishment. Mystics are often the agents of change by inspiring those who bring change. The Protestant Reformation was prefaced by the death of tens of thousands of mystics who in the name of truth gave up their bodies in the "bonfires" of the church.

The number of mystics beatified or canonized is much fewer than those burned at the stake.

Bruno Borchert

Why Don't Cocker Spaniels Have Tails?

As a part of our dreaming of the world, we sometimes do things and then forget why we started doing them. I once had a cocker spaniel named "Joyful" who inspired me to try raising cocker spaniel puppies. At the time I owned a mini estate in Katonah, New York, with a spacious dog run, perfect for puppies. So I had my "Joyful" dog bred.

When the puppies were born, they all came out with tails, even though their mother and father had no tails. I didn't have the heart to cut off their tails. I envisioned the little pups yelping their heads off if I tried that, and I couldn't inflict pain on something I loved. I couldn't have a veterinarian do it either. Consequently, my cocker spaniels grew up with tails. When they were about three months old and it was time to earn me some money, I found I could not sell my cocker spaniel pups. As the breeder explained to me, "They have no value—they have tails." The best I could do was to give them away.

I did some research to find out why it is necessary to cut off the tails of cocker spaniel puppies. About 200 years ago, most of the world was rural, and cocker spaniels were being raised in muddy barnyards both in America and Europe. Mud from the barnyard, cockleburs from the field, even their own dung—everything got hung up in their long hairy tails. The farmers, not wishing to have a ball of mud dragged into the house behind their dogs, started chopping off the tails of puppies to prevent this problem. Two centuries later, most cocker spaniels were living in apartments and suburban homes and never got close to muddy barnyards or cockleburs. The dreaming of the world is often driven by old ideas that no longer make sense.

Why are men circumcised?

I once asked the above question in a lecture, and some woman said, "Because they drag it in the mud." On another occasion, a woman said, "because, if you don't, they don't have any value. The best you can do is to try to give them away." And on a third occasion, yet another woman said, "Because women are always looking for twenty percent off."

People will sometimes say men are circumcised for hygienic reasons. If that's true, it's an argument similar to cutting off the tails of cocker spaniel puppies. There may have been some value in this practice several hundred years ago, when men did not shower every day. Now that we live in an age where most men shower every day, this argument is not valid. According to an article in *Men's Health* magazine, there are good reasons not to circumcise men. For one thing, circumcision reduces sensitivity during intercourse, as there are glands in the foreskin that promote lubrication.

Eighty per cent of all adult American males are circumcised. This operation is often done without any "serious" consultation with parents. Male baby boys are taken within hours of birth into a nursery. They are then strapped down with Velcro strips, and a portion of the most sensitive part of the human male anatomy is then cut off. Baby boys scream "their heads off" during this whole procedure—and women wonder why men are crazy. Men experience a major assault on the body within hours of birth. Here is the world's "proof" of the "fact" that we are bodies, egos, and victims.

Several years ago, after services one Sunday (when I was working as Minister of Interfaith Fellowship in New York City), a woman came up to me and asked if I would please pray for her little baby boy who was going into the hospital to have an operation. "My goodness," I said, "What's wrong?" "Well," she said, "You know the circumcision? They slipped and messed it up. We have to have reconstructive surgery done." "Why," I asked, "did you have him circumcised?" She said, "Well, my husband said, 'What happens when he is eleven years old, changing clothes in a gym someplace, and the other boys notice that he looks different? Let's fix it so he will not look different'." That was it! That was the reason. It was not a religious or hygienic reason. It was being done for the sake of conformity.

Fashion is a good example of another shared illusion. Who decides what color will be "in" each fall? One day at a men's store, I asked for a velour shirt because they are comfortable and great to sleep in when they get old. I was told that I could not buy a velour shirt because they were no longer in fashion. "Come back in a couple of years," the clerk said. "Maybe they will be back in fashion."

If men can run the world,
why can't they stop wearing neckties?
How intelligent is it to start the day
by tying a noose around your neck?

Linda Ellerbee in
The Seattle Post-Intelligencer

A minister witnesses a lot of foolishness around weddings and funerals. Some weddings, for example, are so *perfect* almost no one has a good time. Concerning funerals, I once went to a funeral home to perform a service and arriving ahead of the family, I had to sit in the waiting room. A copy of *Sunnyside* (a magazine produced for funeral directors) was lying on the coffee table face-down with a full-page ad on the back from a company that makes vaults to encase caskets. There was a picture of the leaded vault on the ground beside an open grave. Under the picture was the caption. "After 40 years the family is still happy." (About what—that the corpse did not decay as fast as it would have without the leaded vault?)

Saying that there is no world does not mean we are to deny the "seeming reality" of the world. To say there is no world does not mean that we can do whatever we want without *consequence*. While in Rome, we must do what the Romans do—pay our taxes and observe the speed limit, among many other things. It is very helpful, however, to see that the world as we have constructed it is simply a "construct."

To say there is no world doesn't mean we should not be appreciative of beautiful mountains, rivers, and forests or of flowers, animals, and good food. The mystic is a great "lover" of whatever presents itself: nature, music or another soul. We are not to "hate" the world. To hate the world is to make the world real in a negative way. Our task is to change our vision so that we regard all illusions with love and compassion, or what the Buddhists call "loving kindness."

In my 1976 experience, I got to see that there is no world. As I described it in *Missouri Mystic*:

> *Time started to collapse in a series of violent jerks. My life, my past, all was dying, turning to dust, disappearing. For a moment I remembered my father, my life on the farm, and that oh-so-ordinary reality which seemed like a space of bliss. I felt the most incredible sense of connection with the earth and that man. I then experienced what might be called the severing of the genetic-ego. The earth and every aspect of it flashed before me, was burned into a tiny crisp and disappeared in a jig-jagging line which now delineated a new universe. There was nothing left with which I could identify.*

There was nothing left with which I could identify as an ordinary ego, as a person who lived in a world filled with ego anxieties—regrets, nostalgia, and remorse or thoughts of sin, guilt, and fear.

But healing is the gift of those who are prepared to
learn there is no world, and can accept the lesson
now. Some see it suddenly on point of death, and rise
to teach it. Others find it in experience that is not of
this world, which shows them that the world does not
exist because what they behold must be the truth,
and yet it clearly contradicts the world.

A Course in Miracles

Mystical awareness is so incredible that this world fades away in the experience. In my 1976 experience,

I saw a jig-jagging line that delineated a new universe. The world disappeared, and there appeared in its place a multidimensional, multicolored grid that is impossible to describe in words because it involved another dimension. How do you describe another dimension? How would you explain to someone who had never smelled anything what a fragrance is? I'm not the only one to have described this grid. The ancient Hawaiians thought they were one with a divine source, which they called *Ke Akua*, and that everything was connected together. The Navaho also say there is a matrix of energy that connects all of us. The Navaho call it a web; the Tibetans call it a net. Modern cosmologists and astrophysicists call it the quantum hologram. Coincidently, we now refer to our ability to be interconnected by way of the computer as the *web* and the *net*. In my experience the grid was more "real" than this world. It exists in a place I've been to before. I was returning to reality, not losing reality. [For more information on the Hawaiian understanding of the grid, see Laurie Grant's website at www.archhealing.com].

The World is Temporal; Heaven is Eternal

Does your childhood seem like a dream, something that happened once upon a time in a distant land? If you have lived long enough to go through major moves and transitions, doesn't it seem that you've lived other lives that you now remember in a dreamlike way? In the morning, we usually forget our nighttime dreams, even those that were vivid and seemingly real. We forget dreams because they were only dreams. The day and the moment we are living through right now will soon be a memory, very much like a dream, and as time goes by we will forget more and more of what seems real in the moment.

This so-called "real world" is a place of separation, sadness, sin, sickness, and suffering. It is a realm of illusion, where the ego and the body are made real. In God's creation there is no suffering, pain, loss, separation or death because God's creation is love itself, an eternal, changeless reality that is sometimes called Heaven. Nothing in this world is eternal. In the world of form, illusions hold sway and Heaven seems like a fantasy. To the mystic, it's the other way around. Heaven is reality, and this world is a dream. To be free of the world and our attraction to it, we must forgive the world for all the things *we think* it has done to us. Paradoxically, as we forgive the world, we are freed from the world.

God did not kick Adam and Eve out of Heaven. We saw ourselves as separated bodies and egos, and we went off to try to make it on our own. In that sense, we are all prodigal sons and daughters. We have all split ourselves off from our Source. At any instant, our Source is ready to provide us with guidance that will help us return home to the eternal reality of love. It does not matter what we did or think we have done. What matters is our willingness to return home.

It is hard to understand what 'The Kingdom of Heaven is within you' really means.
The word 'within' is unnecessary.
The Kingdom of Heaven is you.
A Course in Miracles

The body is temporal and will die. The Kingdom of Heaven is eternally alive. We don't see Heaven because we are looking for the inside on the outside. We've got it flipped around the other way.

If I find in myself a desire which no experience in this world can satisfy, the most probable explanation is that I was made for another world.
C.S. Lewis

C.S. Lewis (1898–1963, Ireland) was an author and scholar residing in England. Influenced by the work of William Blake, he is known for his work on Christian apologetics, and fiction, especially the children's series entitled *The Chronicles of Narnia*.

We are made for another world because we are "of" another world. Heaven is not something we have to hope for or work to earn. It is not something that is going to happen *someday*. For the mystic, Heaven is "now" because there is no other time. A soap opera is not real; it is a melodrama. When we are living in a soap opera, we know it; we can feel something "artificial," something is not quite right. Hell is the experience of being caught in circumstances from which it seems there is no escape. When we come to recognize, as the mystic does, that Heaven is inside, we can see craziness around us and not go crazy; we can see hatred and not hate; we can see misery and not be miserable. Unaware of Heaven within, it is easy to go crazy, get angry, or sink into misery. To come to Heaven is to come to ourselves.

That there is no world, is corroborated on a deeper level of understanding by the modern insights of subatomic physics. The photons that comprise light have been observed to consist of waves or particles, but not both a wave and a particle at the same time. The observer's intent determines which one is seen (wave or particle), which is another way of saying that the observer's perception literally creates reality. With this understanding from sub-atomic physics comes the further realization that every "thing" we see in the world is a projection from our minds.

Max Planck (1858-1947, Germany), the "father of quantum physics," was one of the most important physicists of the late nineteenth and early twentieth centuries. When he received his Nobel Prize for Physics in 1918, he said, **"There is no material world as we know it.** All that we perceive to be matter is held together by a force, and this force is intelligence. As a man who has devoted my entire life to studying the substance of which the world is made, I can firmly state that mind is the matrix of all matter."

Modern Cosmology

There is something holding the visible universe together, and it's not just gravity. Gravity works within our own and other planetary and galactic systems, but it is not a sufficient force to explain why the Universe is not literally flying apart. *Something* is keeping everything together. The physical universe, what we call "atoms," makes up 4 percent of the universe. Another 23 percent is made up of *dark matter*. Although dark matter is not observable, scientists know that galaxies, clusters of galaxies, and the universe as a whole contain far more matter than that which interacts with electromagnetic radiation and can therefore be detected.

The remaining 73 percent of the universe is made up of what cosmologists call *dark energy*. No one is quite sure what dark energy is. There is, however, some force acting in opposition to gravity that holds everything together even though the Universe is expanding. Why don't we call this thing that has no form, has no dimension, and cannot be measured—Mind? We might also call it Love, for like Mind, Love has no form, no dimension, and it too cannot be measured. A mystic is someone who goes beyond physics and studies metaphysics. The question is, how do things work on the level of mind?

Nothing matters except insofar as we make something "matter" by bringing it into form physically or mentally. When distinctions created by imagination are taken to be real—especially the distinction between "subject" and "object," "I" and "other," "self" and "world," "we" and "they"—we lose sight of reality's wholeness and fall into an illusion of separation. Imagined separation is the cause of suffering.

The mystic strives for a higher vantage point, a realm wherein there is no separation and time stops. From this perspective, there is no judgment of the world, and there are no problems. We may continue to act in the world, but we need not "worry" about the world because we are driven by the instinct of spirit. The activity of spirit is eternal; the activity of the ego is limited and destined to end in time. If we find this world a confining place, we live in hell. When we are able to experience the unbounded vastness of spirit, we find Heaven. We can then "reflect" Heaven here in our daily, ordinary lives.

This world of time and space is often hellish. Pain, depression, and despair are hell. Hell is feeling alone, isolated, cut off, and separate. This illusory world is a place of duality where we witness and experience war, sickness, depression, poverty, and powerlessness. We can easily get caught in judgment and condemnation of this world; it is, however, much more fun to reflect Heaven here.

Heaven is not a place as we understand it. It is an awareness of oneness and the knowledge that there is nothing else. Nineteenth century clergy sometimes spoke of Heaven as a place where there were fine horses and carriages. I once heard a televangelist describe Heaven as a place of pearly gates and streets of gold. That was "his" Heaven—an idealized representation of this world. The world will not end in a bang or in a whimper. When its usefulness as a place of learning has passed, it will merely "seem to cease to be."

The world will end in joy,
because it is a place of sorrow.
The world will end in peace,
because it is a place of war.
The world will end in laughter,
because it is a place of tears.
A Course in Miracles

The mystic is one light with God and therefore there
is not in him either suffering or the passage of time,
but an unchanging eternity.
Meister Eckhart

Reading the World Right

It's important that we not blame our difficulties on the world. We need to remember that it is we who are *interpreting* the world. If we don't read the world wrong, it won't mislead us. It will just be what it is. Then we can be content in the world regardless of the misinformation it hands us.

Chapter 8

Mysticism and Time

Yogi Berra, the famous Yankee baseball catcher known for his tendency toward malapropism (The unintentionally humorous misuse of a word or phrase), once said, "I never said half the things I said." And "If the world were perfect, it wouldn't be." He was once asked the time by pitcher Tom Seaver, and he responded: "You mean now?"

His response is similar to the story of a priest who once said to the members of his flock, "All those who want to go to Heaven, stand up." Everyone stood up except one man who stubbornly kept his seat. The priest looked at him fiercely and said, "Don't you want to go to heaven?" "No," said the man. So the priest said, "Do you mean to tell me you don't want to go to Heaven when you die?" The man responded, "Of course, I want to go to Heaven when I die. I thought you meant now."

We might think of the "big bang" as the first projection. Before the "big bang," there was no time. Heaven is not in time. Heaven is eternal. By definition, there is no time in eternity. We always have been and always are in Heaven, unless we do not see it. When we are not conscious of Heaven, we say, "Thy Kingdom Come." One characteristic mentioned by all mystics is the timeless nature of the mystical experience. The experience seems to happen "outside of time," or time stops. Our human minds understand things when they happen sequentially, one after the other. We have past, present, and future "stories." Our lives are broken into years, seasons, and months; weeks, days, hours, minutes, and seconds.

According to **Moses Maimonides** (1135–1204, Spain, Egypt), a foremost mystic and intellectual figure of medieval Judaism, the idea of God creating the world at some point in time is a projection from our time-bound circumstances. God's being is not bound by time. Time conditions all space-bound experience.

Time and Relativity

Einstein said time is relative. It can speed up. It can slow down. What if it stopped? What if we could "freeze" everything for a moment? Would that not give us a new, higher perspective? Einstein's secretary once asked him to explain to her the theory of relativity, and he said, "Two hours with a beautiful woman seems like two minutes. Two minutes on a hot stove seems like two hours. That is relativity!"

Time in itself, absolutely, does not exist;
it is always relative to some observer or some object.

John Fowles (1926–2005) in *Aristos*
John Fowles was an English novelist,
philosopher and essayist.
His best known work is *The French Lieutenant's Woman*

If an astronaut were to leave earth, travel into deep space, and then return, his childhood friends would be old men and women while he himself would have aged very little. We accept this statement because the scientists tell us it is true, even though we may not understand why. There are several ways to state, and try to understand, this phenomenon. There is no time outside of time. Time is an illusion. Or, there is no time in Heaven. Or, Heaven is "now." There is no other time.

Time is the ego's way
of keeping everything from happening at once.

Time makes sense because we perceive events moving in a logical, linear sequence from the past, through the present, and into the future. Vision requires seeing in a non-linear way. In my 1976 experience, I could see-feel in 360 degrees. There was great *synchronicity* and *familiarity* about the experience. I felt like I was home, where I always have been—where we all always have been. Time continues as long as we need it. Eternity is a constant that always is. Eternity is permanent. Time is fleeting and momentary, or passing away. Eternity is endless, enduring, eternal—everlasting. The world and our bodies exist in time. The soul lives in eternity. For this reason, mystical awareness is sometimes seen as a "back flash," or a "flash back," of a memory of what already is.

Guilt and the Past

And Jesus said unto him, No man, having
put his hand to the plough, and looking back,
is fit for the Kingdom of God.

Luke 9:62

The ego lives in time: in a story or play, often a drama, sometimes a nightmare. We occasionally become preoccupied with thoughts of the past—of lost loves and unfulfilled ambitions—and with feelings of nostalgia, regret, and remorse. Because our minds are so preoccupied with thoughts of the past, we are unable to see anything as it is now.

Guilt is based on the past; otherwise, there can be no guilt. Remorse, penitence, and contrition are all experienced in relationship to the past. The older we get, the more past we have, the more we tend to live in the past. The younger we are, the more we tend to "project" the future. We have guilt in the past. We say, "If only, if only, if only. . . I had made a series of different choices in the past, I would have a different present." We did not, however, make different choices in the past, so our past has conditioned our "present."

Life is what happens
while we are making other plans.
John Lennon

John Lennon, (1940–1980, England), was an English songwriter, singer, musician, graphic artist, author, and peace activist who gained worldwide fame as one of the founders of The Beatles.

The best thing we can do with past memories is to let them remain where they belong, which is in the past. Through forgiveness, we undo the effects of the past (and remorse and guilt) in the present. Forgiving ourselves is acceptance of the fact that we could never have had a different past. The past is "not here now," and "now" is the only time there is.

Fear and the Future

What we tend to project into the future is fear-based. We have "if only" in the past, and "what if" in the future. "What if I get sick?" "What if I do not have enough money?" "What if there is nobody to take care of me?" Living in the past and projecting the future, we cannot be fully present. We cannot focus on what is "here now."

Again, the younger we are, the more we project the future. The older we are, the more we project (live in) the past. When we are middle aged, we are just as "neurotic" because we are living in the past and in the future. So we wind up feeling nowhere, experiencing a mid-life crisis. The mystic trusts in God and lets thoughts of the past and future go.

And He said to another, "Follow me."
But he said, "Lord, permit
me first to go and bury my father."
But He said to him, "Allow the dead to bury their
own dead; but as for you, go and
proclaim everywhere the kingdom of God."
Luke 9: 59–60

In the mystical experience, time stops—stands still. There is no past and no future because there is nothing (no ego) to have a past and a future. The mystical moment is incredible, effervescent, vivacious, vivid, and enthralling. There is then no "time" for time. The ego lives in time, rehearsing the past—*guilt*—and projecting the future—*fear*.

Judgment rests on the past. In fact, judgment is impossible without the past. The more we move into the moment, the more irrelevant time becomes. What happened in the past—whatever guilt or blame we place upon ourselves or others—is not in the moment. Fears of the future are meaningless in the moment. Nothing exists but this moment. In an emergency situation, there is only the moment. What is happening is precisely what is going on in the present moment and therefore requires our full attention.

Getting into Now

We don't want to experience Heaven now because we're afraid it would mean the loss of our individualities—our egos. Heaven is immediately available, but the ego wants to put God off until tomorrow. Time is a great illusion. It is either "something" in the past or "something" in the future.

There have been times for each of us when we have been so in the now moment that we forgot about time—it can happen for children when they are engrossed in play. As a child, I remember playing with colorful pebbles and becoming one with the pebbles, immersed in the moment of play. For a child, being in the moment is just fine.

Story Time

Stopping along a country road, a city slicker noticed a farmer lifting one of his pigs up to an apple tree and holding the pig there as it ate one apple after another. The farmer repeated this with a second and then a third pig. "Maybe I don't know what I'm talking about," said the city slicker, "but if you just shook the tree so the apples fell to the ground, wouldn't it save a lot of time?" "Time?" said the farmer, "What does time matter to a pig?"

When I come downstairs in our house in the morning, I often see our cat, Pockets, sitting by the door waiting to be let in. Sometimes, when I open the door, he just continues to sit there. Pockets has all the time in the world. Animals do not "spend time" in time as we do. Animals just are, and this is one of the reasons we love them so much. Animals do not have clocks. For animals, there are no such things as seconds, minutes, and hours. Animals are more present—much more "immediate." Their peaceful focus in the now is one reason we enjoy them so much. Were there no animals, the world would be crazier than it is.

I once asked a young man who I knew had had a number of mystical experiences how far he had gone (meaning progressed). He answered, *"Where?"* My question implied that there was a height to which he could ascend, or a depth or width of awareness that he might attain. These

are spatial and temporal limitations. Space and time are ego projections. The mystical state is timeless.

On this side of the bridge to timelessness you understand nothing. But as you step lightly across it, upheld by timelessness, you are directed straight to the Heart of God. At its center, and only there, you are safe forever, because you are complete forever.

A Course in Miracles

Eternity or Timelessness

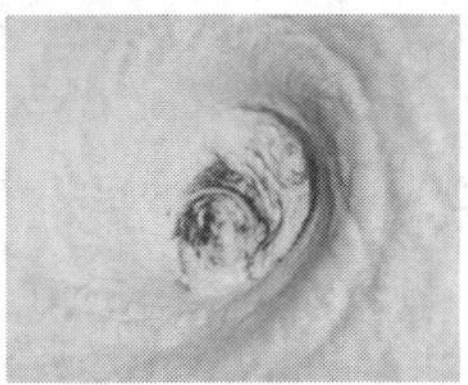

The center of a cyclone is a point of absolute stillness. Around the outside of the cyclone, there is an immense amount of chaos. In the center, everything stops, and there is complete silence. During ordinary, earthly life, it is possible to step into the center where chaos has stopped and only eternity remains. Everyone has had the experience of stepping away from time. It's just a matter of "remembering" it. You may see chaos, but you are not yourself part of it.

Eternity is "timelessness." God lives in timelessness. Love is "timeless." Christ is timeless. The Logos is timeless. We are timeless. Jesus stepped away from eternity and came into time, but he never forgot eternity. We step away from eternity, and we get caught in time. We get caught in histories; we get caught in dramas and lose sight of eternity.

Here is an anonymous description of a mystical experience from a 21 year old man:

I was lying in my bed; the lights were off, and out of what seemed like nowhere, a power entered me. From the crown of my head to the soles of my feet, in fact every fiber of my being resonated a vibration on an infinite scale. Into my mind came the pure understanding of the endlessness of all things, it was an infinite experience, my main thought at the time was WOW!!! Infinite possibilities!

Timelessness is reality. "God and the soul," says Meister Eckhart, "are not in space-time. They belong to the realms that are intrinsically or essentially real." "Time ends," he says, "where there is no before or after." ''We perceive," says Eckhart, "only a shadow of the real, living in a world created and sustained by our own cognition."

There is no time; it is one time.
There is no space; it is one space.

Edgar Cayce Reading

Only the ego lives in time. When we don't have to live in time, when we don't have to live up to an image or be caught up in our own personal dramas, we have an awareness of eternity. It is possible to be so in the moment that the past and future lose their significance. We can live so fully in the present that the past and future fail to imprison us. From this perspective, the past is not a place of guilt and the future is not a place of fear. Sin, guilt, and fear have nothing to do with Heaven. Sin, guilt, and fear lock us in time. There are no sin, guilt and fear in Heaven.

If you were to watch television ads from the 1950s, you might think people of that time were living with a strange interpretation of reality. Cigarette smoking, for example, was promoted on television as something you "should do" to relax. Likewise, people in the eighteenth century dressed in a way that we would think silly today. Wealthy men and women both wore fancy wigs and elaborate, ornamental blouses, pants, and shoes.

What if we could jump ahead to the year 3,000 and look back to now? From that perspective, would our present interpretation of reality not seem silly? At any moment, we can choose to see things as a mystic does. In any holy instant, we can transcend a limited view, let go of the soap operas, drop personal histories, and step out of time.

Take therefore no thought for the morrow:
for the morrow shall take thought for the things of itself.

Matthew 6:34

Happiness—Living in the Present—Focus

Do not dwell in the past; do not dream of the future, concentrate the mind on the present moment.

Buddha

Focus and Flow

A study done on "happy" people during the 1990s, showed that happy people live in the moment, and they have a great ability to focus on the task at hand. This heightened focus also enables them to get into a "flow" with their work, where they lose track of time.

Take up one idea.
Make that one idea your life—
think of it, dream of it, live on that idea.
Let the brain, muscles, nerves, every part of
your body, be full of that idea,
and just leave every other idea alone.
This is the way to success, that is the way
great spiritual giants are produced.

Swami Vivekananda

While we can imagine a future existence without the body, we cannot imagine any such existence without the mind. The mind is the determiner of everything. Heaven is here because there is no other place, and Heaven is now because there is no other time.

The Sufi is the son of time present.
Sufi Saying

Past and future veil God from our sight.
Burn up both of them with fire.
Rumi

Jalaluddi Rumi (1207–1273, Persia) is one of the greatest Muslim saints and mystics and is hailed by many as the greatest mystical poet of all time. Popularized versions of his poetry make him the best selling poet in twenty-first-century America.

Patience

Now you must learn that only infinite patience produces immediate effects. This is the way in which time is exchanged for eternity.
Infinite patience calls upon infinite love, and by producing results now it renders time unnecessary.
A Course in Miracles

Having made time, the ego becomes a slave to time. If there is no time, there is no reason to be in a hurry. The mystic is not in a hurry. The mystic has all the time in the world because she does not live in the world. The mystic is free and thus has infinite patience with her brothers, sisters, and herself. We thus say that someone who does not complain has the "patience of a saint." Mystics are patience. They can afford to be.

To be aware of Time is to be aware of the Universe, and to be aware of the Universeis to be aware of Time. To realize Timelessness is to attain nirvana.
Franklin Merrell-Wolff

Franklin Merrell-Wolf (1897–1985, USA)

"I am, Atman, identical with Nirvana."

Although a mystic does not have "a look," if there is anyone who looks like a mystic, it might be Franklin Merrell-Wolff (also his student Dr. John Lilly). Franklin graduated Phi Beta Kappa from Stanford and did graduate studies in philosophy at Harvard. His study of Kant convinced him that awareness transcends the intellect. He gave up a university career in 1929 to build a spiritual retreat in the Sierra Nevada Mountains. He considered Shankara to be his teacher. He believed we are to achieve a realization of Nothingness that is identical with our own Self. In the early 1970s, his student, Dr. John Lilly, persuaded me to read Merrell-Wolf's books *Pathways Through to Space* and *The Philosophy of Consciousness Without an Object*. They are not to be missed.

He who has no vision of eternity has no hold on time.
Thomas Carlyle

It is believed by most that time passes;
In actual fact, it stays where it is.
This idea of passing may be called time,
it is, however, an incorrect idea,
for since one sees it only as passing,
One cannot understand that it stays just where it is.
Zen Master Dogen Zenji

Dogen Zenji (1200 –1253, Japan) was a Zen Buddhist teacher and founder of the Soto school of Zen in Japan. He was a leading religious figure, as well as an important philosopher and teacher of zazen, or "nothing but precisely sitting", a kind of sitting meditation in which the meditator sits "in a state of brightly alert attention that is free of thoughts, directed to no object, and attached to no particular content."

Time does not move. It stands still.

For us believing physicists, the distinction between past, present and future is only a stubbornly persistent illusion.
Albert Einstein

The present is not a fleeting moment:
It is the only eternity.
In Time "lies" samsara
In the Present "lies" nirvana.
Wei Wu Wei

Note: *samsara* means "suffering or sorrow;" *nirvana* means "enlightenment." Awakened sages have a vertical rather than a horizontal relationship with the infinite.

It is at this moment that complete salvation is offered you, and it is at this moment that you can accept it.
Section 24 of "A Manual for Teachers" of
A Course in Miracles

Come out of the circle of time
And into the circle of love.
Rumi

If we can get the mind
to be still—we see.
We always have been.
We always will be.

Chapter 9

Mysticism and the Body

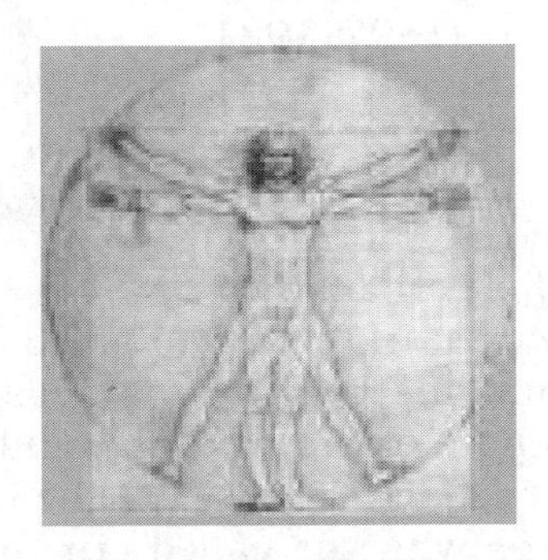

Mystics sometimes have a hard time knowing how to deal with the body. The appetites for food, pleasures of all sorts, and sex in particular, have always been confusing issues. Some of the early Christian mystics sought to punish the body through mortification of the flesh: by wearing hair shirts, sitting outdoors in inclement weather, flagellating themselves with whips, and fasting to the point of death. All these attempts to punish or escape the body, ironically, made the body seem more real. At the other extreme were the libertines who, while saying that the body was inconsequential, thought they could do anything they wanted and thus engaged in excesses of all sorts.

Heinrich Seuse (1295–1366, Germany) a famous Dominican mystic, is an example of a mystic with confusing issues regarding the body. He endured fasting, sleep deprivation, extreme cold, iron chains, self-flagellation, and a nail studded coat. He rubbed salt and vinegar into his wounds. Eventually he was healed of this obsession with suffering by a vision wherein he was told that God did not want him to hurt himself. Since he supported Meister Eckhart (who had been condemned by Pope John XXII), he was censured by his superiors and stripped of his teaching position. He suffered persecution by the Church until his death. Five hundred years later, he was made a saint.

Most of us have an ambivalent relationship with our bodies, sometimes loving them, sometimes hating them. Primitive man, looking at his face in a lake, must have wondered about this "thing" looking back at him. Plato called the body a "tomb." Seneca said it was an inn in which we stay only briefly; Palladas called it an affliction of the soul, a burden, a chain, and a tormenting punishment. Mohandas Gandhi called it a prison.

The body is a thing of shreds and patches,
borrowed unequally from good and
bad ancestors and a misfit from the start.
Ralph Waldo Emerson

The body is the ego's home. It is a school house, a place of learning and self-development. It is outside of us, but it seems to surrounds us. The body is "the central figure in the dreaming of the world." The Course says it is a "tiny fence" around a little part of a glorious and complete idea.

All whom Moses calls wise are sojourners.
Their souls are colonists leaving heaven for a new home. Their way is to visit earthly nature as men who travel abroad to see and learn.
So when they have stayed awhile in their bodies and beheld through them all that sense and mortality have to show, they may make their way back to the place from which they first set out.
To them the heavenly region where their citizenship lies is their native land; the earthly region in which they became sojourners is a foreign country.
Philo Judea

Philo Judea (30 B.C.– 45 A.D.) was an Alexandrian Jew who tried to combine the philosophies of Plato, Pythagoras, Stoicism, and Jewish mysticism. He wanted to show that the God of Abraham and Moses was the same as the Absolute (Logos) of the Greeks. He believed that the Unitive Reality experienced in the contemplative state is ever-one, unmoving, and unchanging. At the same time it is actively manifest in the world of form. There are limits to reason. Mysticism is more important than philosophical speculation. It was possible, he said, to actually "see" God.

Philo described the body as a tomb. From the mystic point of view, the body is a thought of separation projected by the mind into form. The ego-mind seeks affirmation of its separate reality through the physical body. The body places a limit on love. Also, our identifying with the physical body results in a split mind and thus bewilderment. While we intuit the illusory nature of the body, we nevertheless experience daily, overwhelming evidence that we *are* bodies.

The Ego's Use of the Body

The ego seeks salvation and gratification through the body. We are enamored with the body and its appearance. We live in an age of body painting, tattoos, facelifts, tummy tucks, and cryogenics. Vast sums of money are spent on cosmetics, clothes, and jewelry to adorn the body. The first thing each morning, we look in a mirror and think something like, "What can I do to fix this body up so it's presentable for other bodies to look at?"

If we are sick or overweight or believe we are ugly, we may hate the body and feel that it is not good enough to be our home. On the other extreme, we may be proud of our bodies and hope or pretend that they will last forever. We may project the desire for eternity into the body and external objects. We raise children, write books, paint pictures, and build institutions that we hope will continue a remembrance of us after we are gone. We have buildings and streets named after us, and we build mausoleums for our bodies, all in the "grave" hope of some earthly immortality.

Appetites are "getting" mechanisms. The ego seeks to satisfy itself through the body. We are easily addicted, and in trying to enjoy the body, we run the risk of addiction and over-satiation.

No one is free who is a slave to the body.
Seneca

We confirm bodily life daily by eating, drinking, making love, and sleeping. Almost all of our so called "thrills" are associated with our bodies. Some folks actively seek adrenaline rushes with skiing, roller coaster rides, bungee jumping, surfing, sky diving, and more. Now, in the twenty-first century, we are finding more refined ways of "pushing the envelope"—helicopter skiing from the tops of mountains, parachuting from tall buildings and the highest of cliffs, and racing cars and power boats. Bodily "stimulation" is often the name of the game.

A helpful technique when an appetite arises is simply to wait, rather than going for something to eat, for example. Merely wait. Appetites diminish when they are not fed. When we feed an appetite, it asks for more and can become insatiable—leading to addiction. It is possible to crave even so called good food, so when we choose our addictions, we should choose them well.

Westerners deal with their bodies by filling them with caffeine, alcohol, bad food, and anxiety, all of which keep them from seeing.
Carlos Castaneda *Journey to Ixtlan*

According to **Maharaja Nisargadatta** (1897–1981, India), our true nature is perpetually free, peaceful awareness. This awareness is the source of, but different from, the personal, individual awareness related to the body. While the mind and memory are associated with a body, awareness exists prior to mind, memory, and body. The idea that we are the body keeps us from living what he called our "original essence."

The Body is Neither Good Nor Bad

The notions of "good" and "bad" appear as the mind judges the functions of the body. The body can be a helpful tool for communication and learning. As the central figure in the ego's dream of the world, however, the body can separate us from others and thus from wholeness. To see ourselves as bodies only is depressing. When we refer to *our* bodies, we imply bodies are something we possess and are not synonymous with us. For the mystic, the Spirit, not the body, is reality. All matter, including the body, is a part of the world, and thus, of illusion.

In the 1980s during a PBS series on "The Power of Myth," Bill Moyers asked the then 80-year-old Dr. Joseph Campbell, "What is it like being an octogenarian?" He said it was like driving an old car. His body did not start as well in the mornings as it used to. It "chugged" when going up hill. It was covered with wrinkles, and the tail pipe was starting to drag. Joseph Campbell said he thought he was about ready to turn it in for a new model—six months later he was out of here. Likewise, mystics experience themselves as the awareness that animates or "runs" the body, but not as the body itself.

Thomas Jefferson and John Adams died the same day, July 4, 1826, exactly fifty years after the signing of the Declaration of Independence. They had been friends, but a rift developed between them. Then toward the end of their lives, they renewed their friendship. In the last letter Jefferson sent to John Adams, he inquired about his health.

John Adams wrote back saying that while he was fine, the house in which he lived had become quite dilapidated. The shingles had almost all fallen off (his hair was almost all gone). The windows were all fogged over (he could no longer see very well). He was fine, but his body was like a decrepit old house—just about to tumble over.

Who is Pulling the Strings?

If we watch a puppet moving around on a stage, it appears as though the puppet has life, yet we know there is no life in the puppet. The "activating agent" pulling the puppet's strings generates the appearance of life. It's easy to get caught up in the life of the body and the ego as though that life were somehow "reality." Yet, *Spirit*, by definition, is life, and *mind* is the "activating agent" of Spirit.

Transcendent Uses of the Body: Dancing, Singing, and Sexuality

The body is a harp for the soul.

Kahlil Gibran

Story Time

The famous violinist Ignacy Jan Paderewski once appeared on stage to play a violin. He told the audience that it was the most expensive violin in the world. He then proceeded to play a stunning number. At its conclusion, the audience stood with uproarious applause. After the applause had died down, Paderewski took the violin and smashed it over his knee. As everyone gasped, he said, "I was only kidding; it was a cheap imitation." Then he said, "I will now play on a violin that really is the most expensive in the world." After he played a number just as magnificent as the first, only a few said they could hear the difference.

Our souls make the music of our lives. The body is a communication medium that receives and sends messages. In the hands of the ego, it communicates pain, fear, separation, despair, and anger. From the mystic's point of view, the body communicates healing, love, unity, and joy. Beyond the appearance of the body—past the mascara, face lifts, wigs, porcelain teeth, and elevator shoes—is something that radiates us, thinks us, and feels us. That something is the Spirit that moves us all, and the body can be used in ways that makes the action of the Spirit more obvious.

Dancing and singing are at the heart of almost all religious traditions and are often associated with transcendence. Perhaps the best known "spiritual dancers" are the whirling dervishes of the Sufi order. Also, the Pentecostal church today (along with many of the evangelicals) encourages singing and dancing, swaying and chanting as an inducement to altered states.

The great spiritual philosophies of the East developed effective forms of prayer, meditation, movement meditation, and breathing exercises with profound spiritual components.

Stanislav Grof

Stanislav Grof, M.D. Ph.D. (1931 – Present, Czechoslovak, USA). I sponsored workshops with Dr. Stanislav Grof during the later 1970s, in New York City at Wainwright House in Rye, New York, and my own home High Rock Spring in Katonah, New York. He is one of the founders of transpersonal psychology and a researcher into the use of altered states of consciousness. He is especially known for his early studies of LSD. Following the legal suppression of LSD in the late 1960s, Grof discovered that altered states of mind could be explored without drugs by using breathing techniques which he calls "Holotropic Breath work."

The chanting of mantras can help us move into meditation. Mantras also can induce a semi-hypnotic altered state. While certainly enjoyable and even intoxicating, beating drums, chanting, and dancing are all transitory. When they stop the trance also stops, and we still need to do the work that brings us home to God.

There I leap into love,
From love into understanding,
From understanding into enjoyment
And from enjoyment beyond all the human senses.
There I shall remain and yet circle still higher.

Mechthild of Magdeburg

Mechthild of Magdeburg (1210– 1282, Germany) was born into a noble family. At age twelve she experienced a "disrobing" of the ego and longed for a life free of marriage, wanting only to spend her time in contemplation of God. She recorded her visions and religious teaching in her book, the *Flowing Light of the Godhead.*

Mysticism and Sexuality

Of the 21 categories leading to a mystical experience, the last one in Sir Alister Hardy's list is sexuality. While sexuality may well introduce us to the mystical, human sexuality is, we all know, an issue surrounded by much misuse, misunderstanding, division, and confusion. The story of Adam and Eve (basic to Judaism, Christianity, and Islam) associates sexuality with shame and guilt and the need to hide. Sexuality in the Eastern religious traditions is seen as natural and therefore neither shameful nor sinful.

When a man is intimate with his wife,
they are wafted by their desire to the eternal hills.
The Zohar (Judaism)

In Judaism, to abuse sexuality is to abuse what is holy. Hindu, Tantra, and Chinese Taoism advise us not to reject the body and its desires. Rather, through discipline, we should learn to embrace them in an "enlightened" way. Because sexuality leads to the most intimate of adult relationships, it brings up issues of possession and jealousy. Sexuality has proven a difficult challenge for all organized religions. Christianity has a complicated history of opinions regarding and reacting to sexuality. For this reason, Mary the mother of Jesus is seen as a virgin; early Christians could not accept the idea that she could have been "soiled" by sex. St. Paul saw marriage as an inferior state because of sex. He even went so far as to say, "I wish that all could be as I am"—namely celibate.

The early Christian Church advocated a strict sexual abstinence, and there remains to this day within the church a mistrust of sexual impulses. Both Christianity and Islam have resorted to judgmental renunciation and the overt, often forced, suppression of sexuality. Not surprisingly, the more any desire is repressed, the more it seeks expression in sometimes socially inappropriate ways. The deliberate choice to be celibate in order to focus one's attention beyond the physical and thus attain a more mystical awareness is most likely to succeed when the choice is *freely* made.

Those who enter the gates of heaven
are not beings who have no passion or who
have curbed the passions, but those who have
cultivated an understanding of them.
William Blake

The heart longs for union, and there is within each of us a great urge to be connected. We long to "fall in love." Lovers often feel they have found another world in which the traditional ways of seeing and living have been dissolved. Some mystics use sexual imagery to describe their experiences of union with God, as in "The Song of Songs" from the Bible. St. Bernard of Clairvaux and St. Teresa of Avila speak of being united with Christ in a holy "embrace."

When the beloved Soul shall have been perfected,
the Bridegroom will make with her a spiritual
marriage and they shall be two,
not in one flesh, but in one spirit.
Bernard of Clairvaux

Mystics speak of a union (*unio*) and communion (*communio*) of absorption, and of being completely taken by the experience. Osho says of sex, "Even though it lasts only a moment that moment is eternity. Everything stops. You forget all the worries, all the tensions."

According to Tantra, an Asian practice that seeks to channel Divine energy, sexual intercourse is a sacrament and a means of spiritual transformation. It is possible to experience moments in love making when boundaries dissolve, and there is a blissful merging, blending, and becoming one with the beloved and even more—union with the all of existence. There is ecstasy and self-forgetting in the sexual experience of being overwhelmed. Since sexual ecstasy is often short lived, Tantra aims to heighten and prolong the connection between a couple lost in the lover's embrace.

According to Tantra, if a couple intentionally holds off their orgasms, rather than rushing to a climax, the experience is taken to a higher and more intensely satisfying level. Tantra seeks to teach how to fuse opposites, how to transcend the apparent duality of the sensual world. According to the mystic, at the very depth of our souls, there is only God. Osho says, "For Tantra everything is holy."

There is an old joke that asks, "What does an atheist cry out at the time of orgasm? Why do we say, "Oh God!" when things are going very right or very wrong? Maybe such experiences are taking us back to the beginning of our being, back to oneness, back to the infinite, back to the void.

A sexual orgasm gives a glimpse into the infinite. For a few moments there is no time and no mind. Eternity is there and everything stops; for a moment there is silence and bliss. At other times, if we are not fully present in the sexual experience, we may feel alienated, separated, and alone. So much depends upon the conditions of the heart and mind. A mystic is not needy, and in desirelessness there is freedom. The task of the mystic is to be truly loving—giving without making demands. Obviously, the more we give in love, the more love we experience coming back our way.

The best way to deal with the body is to keep it healthy, active and functioning in the world so we do not become obsessed and possessed with its possible problems.

Chapter 10

Mysticism and the Self

I'm Nobody, Who Are You?

Behave as though the self does not exist.
Buddha

A senior minister walks into the chapel of his church, kneels down before the altar, and says,

"Oh God, I am nobody, I am so nobody."

The associate pastor walks by and, seeing the senior minister, goes into the chapel, kneels beside him, and he too says,

"Oh Lord, I am nobody, I am so nobody!"

The custodian is passing by and, seeing the two ministers on their knees, goes in and also kneels. He too says,

"Oh Lord, I too am nobody, I am so nobody!" Seeing the custodian next to him, the associate minister pokes the senior minister in the side and whispers into his ear, *"Look who thinks he's nobody!"*

I'm nobody! Who are you?
Are you nobody, too?
Then there's a pair of us, don't tell.
They'd banish us, you know.
How dreary to be somebody!
How public, like a frog.
To tell your name the livelong day
To an admiring bog!
Emily Dickinson

Emily Dickinson (1830–1886, USA) was a mystic, inspired poet, and a very private person who devoted herself to writing. Only ten of her nearly 1,800 poems were published during her lifetime. She was deeply tinged by the mysticism of William Blake and her contemporary, Ralph Waldo Emerson. According to philosopher Norman D. Livergood, she was "a mystic of the first order in the tradition of Rumi." Her world was the world of imagination. Along with Whitman, she is one of the leading mystical poets of the nineteenth century.

Specialness—Superiority and Inferiority

Someone once said, "I've had about as much of myself as I can take." At times, each of us has probably felt as though we've had as much of ourselves as we can take. This ego thing is so distracting. Wouldn't it be nice to be free of it? The truth is, the self we create is not who we are. According to *A Course in Miracles*, no one is special. *"You are not special. If you think you are, and would defend your specialness against the truth of what you really are, how can you know the truth?"* Specialness, our stories and dramas, can keep us from awakening by perpetuating *"the dreaming of the world."*

There are two extreme ways of being special. Some people have "big" egos. They are special because they have important jobs, make lots of money, are handsome and youthful, and so forth. There is nothing wrong with any of these things, but they do not make us special.

He who is in the habit of looking down upon others
has not got rid of the erroneous idea of a self.
Huineng

Huineng (638–713) was a Chinese Chan master who taught immediate, "sudden" enlightenment.

As we develop spiritually, we have to watch for specialness. We may think "I meditate. I'm better than people who don't mediate." Or, "I eat a clean diet. I'm better than people who eat junk food." Or, most insidious, "I'm non-judgmental so I'm better than people who are judgmental."

On the other extreme, we may see ourselves as special because of a sorrowful "victim" condition. "Woe is me. Look at what has happened to me." Mystics are *totally* and *absolutely* responsible for *everything* that comes their way. If we accept full responsibility, we cannot project; we cannot blame someone else or our circumstances. Blaming brings guilt and separation. We are each at our own unique level of development. No one here is special, different or better than anyone else. In this sense, the more nothing we are, the more freedom we have.

Right-Mindedness and Wrong-Mindedness

God whose love is everywhere
can't come to visit unless you aren't
there.
Angelus Silesius

Angelus Silesius (1624–1677, Germany) was raised as a Lutheran and educated as a scientist and physician. Influenced by Jacob Boehm, he enjoyed the paradoxes of mysticism. He converted to Catholicism, becoming a priest and bishop. He wrote hundreds of hymns. Many of them were adopted by the German Protestants.

The above quote from Angelus Silesius should be on the walls in our churches. God's voice speaks to every one of us every moment of every day. It's not that God is not there; when we are full of ourselves, however, we cannot be aware of the presence of God.

See yourself as nothing. Only one who is nothing can contain the fullness of the Presence.
Menahem Nahum

Menahem Nahum (1730–1797, Ukraine) was part of the Hasidic movement started by the Ba'al Shem Tov (1698–1760) that originated at a time when many European Jews felt that Jewish life had become too "academic" and that it no longer emphasized spirituality or joy.

When his friend Harrison Blake asked Henry David Thoreau if his adventure by Walden Pond had left him feeling a longing for society, Thoreau answered, *"No, I am nothing."* Thoreau had gone on retreat to Walden Pond to find himself—that is, to find God within. Thoreau could not identify with all the incessant business going on in Concord, as he wrote in 1845. How much busier and "seemingly" important is today's world? (*Letters to a Spiritual Seeker*, by Henry David Thoreau)

For the mystic, there is no making-up of the world; there is simply immediacy in all its pristine purity. The mystic perceives what is happening in the "now" without needing to change the moment. The mystic is not a projector, and doesn't want to be. As Aldous Huxley expressed it, our task is not to be thinking. Our task is to be "thought."

Mystic **Anandamayi Ma** (1896–1981, Bangladesh) said that she was completely empty with no sense of "I am." She was, she said, "nobody." She often objectified her body by describing her actions in phrases like "this body did this" or "this body went there." She once said, *"So long as the sense of 'me' and 'mine' remains, there is bound to be sorrow and want in the life of the individual."*

Anandamayi described four stages in her spiritual evolution:

1. The mind was "dried" of desire and passion so it could catch the fire of spiritual knowledge. As we get older, we may naturally find "things" attracting us less. The body is less preoccupied and obsessed with sex, food and drink, and the need for status loses it appeal.
2. The body became still and the mind drawn inward.
3. Her personal identity was then absorbed, she said, by an individual deity (God). As some distinction between form and formlessness still remained, however, she was able to function in the world.
4. Finally, there was a melting away of all duality, and the mind was free from the movement of thought with consistent, full consciousness, even in dreams.

When **Paramahansa Yogananda** (1893–1952, India), founder of the Self-Realization Fellowship and himself a mystic, met Anandamayi Ma and asked her about her life, she answered: "Father, there is little to tell...My consciousness has never associated itself with this body. Before I came on this earth, Father, 'I was the same.' As a little girl, 'I was the same.' I grew into womanhood; I was still 'the same.' When the family in which I had been born made arrangements to have this body married, 'I was the same.' And, Father, in front of you now, 'I am the same.' Ever afterward, though the dance of creation changes around me in the hall of eternity, 'I shall be the same'." Anandamayi describes a great void and a deep peaceful emptiness. We might think of the void as a farewell to all that is human. It is the cessation of the ego self—a total absence of self.

Why are you unhappy? Because 99.9 per cent of everything you think, and of everything you do, is for yourself—and there isn't one.
Wei Wu Wei

When I quote that line at various lectures, it often gets a nervous laugh—because we know that it is true.

Once at a public dialogue, a man said to the mystic **Jean Klein** (1916–1998, Austria), "Every time I come to hear you, I notice that you seem so clear and relaxed. You radiate peaceful, loving warmth. You seem happy. Yet, I am always discontent, often stressed out. There are times when I feel quite miserable. What is the difference between us?" Jean replied:

"You think that you are somebody
and I know that I'm not."

Jean, a medical doctor, said that one day his individual identity simply disappeared and was replaced by an all-pervading light, which he recognized as "the one reality." Dr. Klein defines life as awareness without fixation on one's identity.

Dropping Personal History

We gain the moment of great awareness "in the now" by dropping personal history. *"If we could erase personal history,"* says Don Juan of the Carlos Castaneda books, *"we would be free from the encumbering thoughts of others."* Don Juan points out to Castaneda that he, Carlos, has to renew his personal history daily by telling his family and friends everything he does. If we have no personal histories, no explanations are needed. When people know our personal histories, know exactly who we are, what we believe, and what we stand for, they have control over us. To express it simply, if you don't have a story, you don't have to fit it. *"One day,"* says Don Juan, *"I discovered I didn't need a personal history, so, like drinking, I dropped it."*

Don Juan says he knows all kinds of things because:

1. He doesn't have a personal history.
2. He doesn't feel more important than anything else.
3. His death is sitting right there beside him.

Only someone with an excessive sense of self-importance could think that his or her problems are more important than those of other people. When we lose the sense of self-importance, we realize that everyone has the same problems. In describing his mystical experiences, A.H. Almaas says, *"I learn a great deal of what I truly am when I am not trapped in the particulars of personal life and history. I am then the unchanging background witnessing."* Or, as Gangaji says it, *"I am not bound by the story of me."*

Rare Spontaneous Awakenings

Sudden mystical awakenings are rare but possible. One such description comes from **Susan Segal** (1945–1997, USA), author of *Collision With the Infinite*. At the time, she was a 27-year-old pregnant American woman married to a French doctor. She was about to board a bus in Paris when...

"I lifted my right foot to step into the bus and collided head-on with an invisible force that entered my awareness like a silently exploding stick of dynamite, blowing the door of my usual consciousness open and off its hinges. What I had previously called 'me' was forcefully pushed out of its usual location inside me into a new location that was approximately a foot behind and to the left of my head. 'I' was now behind my body looking out at the world without using the body's eyes."

A seasoned meditator, Susan could not figure out what had happened. She no longer had any wants or needs, cravings or desires. She found herself being an *observer* rather than a *projector*. She continued to live a normal life but everything had changed. She started going to psychologists to find out what had happened, but no one could figure it out. She was eventually diagnosed with a "dissociative personality disorder." Not having "wants" or "needs" meant she no longer had a personality. Finally, one of her therapists decided that she had experienced the disintegration of the ego, which some might equate with insanity. To mystics, however, such an egoless state means that one has gained sanity rather than lost it.

In my 1976 experience, I disappeared. This world, all of it, also disappeared. I no longer existed as a separate individual in the universe. Not only was the body gone, so was the personality. And yet something was seeing; otherwise, I could not now talk about the experience. I was given the opportunity to take a brief look at this personality and then let the story go. I really had no choice. It was frightening, but only for a moment. Once you jump into eternity, you float. You do not disappear.

O let me not exist! For Non-Existence proclaims in
organ tones, to Him we shall return.
Rumi

What was it then that was having this experience? There was still awareness. In fact there was more awareness than ever—much more. Sometimes when people describe near-death experiences, they talk about meeting their deceased loved ones or talking to people on the "other side." Love is attracted to Love. But there were no "bodies" as we think of bodies. There were no "individuals" to talk to, and yet there was tremendous awareness. The awareness was inside, outside, and all around. I was it. It was "what I was." There was no separation, no me and other. Inside and outside were the same. Nothing was lost; there was simply great depth of awareness. "Who" or what was having this experience? There was merely experiencing.

So long as the sense of "me" and "mine" remains,
there is bound to be sorrow
and want in the life of the individual.
Anandamayi Ma

We rely on our belief systems and "stories" for our identities. Being caught in stories or dramas is to be in conflict with or divided from other human beings whose identities are based on a set of beliefs different from our own.

Self-inquiry leads to
the realization that:
(Here is another secret!)
There is no inquirer
and nothing to attain.

Story Time

Four Catholic ladies are having tea together. One of them takes a sip of tea and says, "My son is a priest, and whenever he walks into the room, all the ladies say, 'Good evening, Father'."

The second lady takes a sip of tea and says, "My son is a bishop, and when he walks into the room, all the ladies say, 'Good evening, Your Grace'." Wow!

The third lady takes a sip of tea and says, "My son is a cardinal. When he walks into the room, all the ladies say, 'Good evening, Your Eminence'."

The fourth lady takes a sip of tea and says, "My son is a six-foot-two, hard-bodied male stripper. When he walks into the room, all the ladies say, 'Oh, my God!' "

His Holiness, the Very Right Reverend

Once you label me, you negate me.
Soren Kierkegaard

Thoreau says we should watch out for any profession which requires that we wear special clothes. When I was a young minister in the1960s, I wore a clerical collar. The Catholic folks in Brooklyn, near my home, practically tripped over themselves when they saw me coming, and everyone stared at my neck. I even had an Irish Catholic policeman apologize once for stopping me when he saw the collar. I had made a right turn on red where there was a sign saying "No right on red." And the Irish policeman said, "I know you didn't see that sign, Father." The clerical collar literally felt like a noose around my neck, and I stopped wearing it. Titles can be divisive; they are forms of separation that take us away from, rather than closer to, each other and thus the truth.

The dreaming of the world takes many forms,
because the body seeks in many ways
to prove it is autonomous and real.
It puts things on itself that it has bought
with little metal discs or paper strips
the world proclaims as valuable and real.
It works to get them, doing senseless things,
and tosses them away for senseless things
it does not need and does not even want.
A Course in Miracles

The more well-defined our position, the harder it is to be free. It is helpful not to identify with positions concerning worldly events, religion or anything else with which the world may call upon us to identify. It is best not to be a Democrat or a Republican, Liberal or Conservative, Catholic or Protestant. Titles are divisive. They separate us from one another. All man-made labels take us away from truth, rather than closer to it.

The more defined the position, the harder it is to be free. Be glad not to be famous. Famous people (like Marilyn Monroe, Elvis Presley, Freddie Prince, Princess Diana, and Anna Nicole Smith) have (or had) a very difficult time living in this world, which becomes for them increasingly artificial.

Routinely, people discover that the life
of a celebrity is onerous and burdensome
once the novelty has worn off.
Dr. David Hawkins

David R. Hawkins, M.D., Ph.D., is a psychiatrist, researcher, teacher, and speaker on the subject of advanced spiritual states, and the Realization of the Presence of God as Self. He is the author of the best-selling trilogy: *Power vs. Force*, *The Eye of the I*, and *I: Reality and Subjectivity*.

It is said of Marilyn Monroe that she reached "mythic" status. Myth means "not real." One month before she died, Marilyn Monroe did a recording for *Life* magazine called "Marilyn on Marilyn." She talked quite frankly about her feelings concerning herself and the image that had been made of her by Hollywood. She saw this image as a cardboard, cartoon character.

Being famous didn't seem quite real to me. I felt as
though it was happening to someone right next to me.
I always felt as though I was somebody else.
Being a sex symbol means being a "thing"
and I didn't want to be a "thing."
From *Coffee with Marilyn*
by Yona Zeldis McDonough

Marilyn was clear that it was all an empty fantasy. Hollywood had created an image of a sex goddess, and it wasn't her. Then she said in the most poignant way, "And, I let them do it." It was not, however, who she was. She was just Norma Jean.

It stirs up envy, fame does.
People feel fame gives them some kind of
privilege to walk up to you and say anything
to you and it won't hurt your feelings
like it's happening to your clothing.
Marilyn Monroe

Everything we perceive as the outside world is a part of ego identification. Dropping personal history gives us a taste of eternity, freedom, and happiness. Sri Ramana Maharshi says, *"The gross body which is composed of the seven humors, I am not; the five sense organs which apprehend their respective objects, I am not; even the mind which thinks, I am not."* It is easier to speak of what we are not than what we are. We are not our bodies, our occupations, our church, our city, state or nation. We are not our race, our clan or our families. We are not even our thoughts or that which thinks them, our feelings or that which feels them because thoughts and feelings which come from the ego are not true. Our real thoughts are the thoughts we think with God.

So Who or What Are We?

Ramesh Belsekar says, *"What is absent in enlightenment is duality, 'me' as a separate entity and 'you' as another separate entity. Consciousness is all there is."*

You live in illusion and the appearance of things.
There is a reality, but you do not know this.
When you understand this, you will see
that you are nothing. And being nothing,
you are everything. That is all.

Kalu Rinpoche

Kalu Rinpoche (1905–1989, Tibet), is a Buddhist meditation master, scholar, and one of the first Tibetan masters to teach in the United States. He pursued the life of a solitary living in the woods. The term *Rinpoche* is an honorific meaning "precious one."

Matter Doesn't Matter

When I lost awareness of my body in 1976 and again in 2007, I was surprised to see (as is anyone who dies) that awareness continues without an object. Is the mind a "thing?" Is "love" a thing? The brain is a computer, but who runs the computer? Everyone attests to the reality of love, yet love is beyond definition and description—even poetry doesn't do it justice. Poetry is still talking "about" love.

Neither do "things" exist. Things are meaningful only as we are attracted to or attached to them. Aldous Huxley, standing watching his house burn down in the Bellaire fires of 1961, said it was a marvelous *clean* feeling. Thinking there is something to "acquire" can get us into trouble. Remember our most basic question: "What is the wanting creature?" "What is it that 'needs' anything?"

If you are distressed by anything external,
the pain is not due to the thing itself.
It is due to your own estimation of it; and this you
have the power to change at any moment.

Marcus Aurelius

Marcus Aurelius (121–180, Roman emperor) was the last of the "Five Good Roman Emperors" and himself a stoic philosopher and mystic. His book *Meditations* is a literary work of art. It contains kindness unexpected from a Roman Emperor. Unlike previous emperors who got caught up in the world, Aurelius saw the folly of it all.

He is not accompanied by thingness,
nor do we ascribe it to Him.
The negation of thingness from Him
is one of His essential attributes.

Ibn Arabi

Ibn Arabi (1165–1240, Damascus) is known as "great master." He is an important spiritual teacher in Sufism. He emphasized the possibility of the human being to reach perfection. An inexhaustible writer and creative thinker, he was a proponent of the Unity of Being. He wrote over 300 works, including his magnum opus, the 37-volume *Meccan Illuminations*.

Through Love, I have reached a place where no trace
of Love remains, where "I" and "we" and the
painting of existence have all been forgotten
and left behind. As long as you are "you,"
you will be miserable and impoverished.

Javad Nurbakhsh

Dr. Javad Nurbakhsh (? – Present, Sufi Muslim, Iran) retired as the Head of the Department of Psychiatry at the Tehran University in 1977. He is master of the Nimatullahi Sufi Order.

To truly 'know' is to 'be,' at which point
one does not know; instead one 'is.'

Dr. David Hawkins

No one is special, different or better than anyone else. Our bodies have come through different terrains of biology, time, geography, and social circumstances. From the mystic's point of view, the more "nothing" we are the better for sanity. Gaining sanity, we find that what happens to our personal self, our hopes and dreams, our hurts and pains, is not a matter of life and death seriousness. We discover a Self beyond such selfishness, a place which is formless, spaceless, timeless, infinite, and empty.

The Soul is tied to no individual, no culture,
no tradition, but rises fresh in every person,

beyond every person, and grounds itself
in a truth and glory that bows to nothing
in the world of time and place and history.
We all must be, and can only be,
"a light unto ourselves."
Ralph Waldo Emerson

Meister Eckhart used words like *desert* and *barren* to describe his experience of illumination. St. Teresa of Avila speaks of the *still wilderness* or the *lonely desert* of the Deity. Yet this is the true country of the soul, a space free from desiring, where the ego does not reign. While Ultimate Reality constitutes the true nature of everything, in itself it is nothing.

You can call it the void. It wasn't just a void.
It was this pure awareness I always talk about.
I was aware that I AM THAT I AM.
I was aware of the whole universe.
Robert Adams

Robert Adams (1928–1997, USA) author of *The Silence of the Heart*, said he was enlightened at the age of fourteen while concentrating in preparation for a math exam. He studied with Yogananda and Ramana Maharshi in India and was a Jnana Yogi (knower of truth). He emphasized the transcendence of the individual "I" through the process of self-inquiry, realizing the one Self in all. He did not want his picture taken.

Emptiness is the ultimate nature
of everything that exists.
Lama Yeshe (1935–1984, Tibet)

There are neither good nor bad qualities in the Self.
The Self is free from all qualities.
Qualities pertain to the mind only.
It is beyond qualities.
If there is unity, there will also be duality.
The numeral one gives rise to other numbers.
The truth is neither one nor two. It is as it is.
Ramana Maharshi

To be nothing is to discover peace, expansion, and freedom from boundaries. You are nothing, and nothing is full, whole, infinite. It is everything, and it is everywhere. Being nobody is wonderfully refreshing. It takes all worry away.

The self you made is not the Son of God.
Therefore, this self does not exist at all.
And anything it seems to do and think means nothing.
It is neither bad nor good.
It is unreal, and nothing more than that.
A Course in Miracles

Who are we beneath, below or prior to this pseudo-self? If we succeed in finding release from the prison of individuality, what then? There follows in time another second and yet another second and what do we find in that second? We find Supreme Identity with the All, with Universal Spirit. What we find is the Soul, the Self, Spirit, unhampered by the ego. We are eternity. We are love. We are all the wonderful things we can name and more. This Self is pure witness. It exists prior to time—prior to the big bang. It is not born. It does not die.

I have a friend who takes part in a spiritual practice where people work in dyads, or pairs of twos. Each participant sits facing a partner, and the partners take turns asking each other, "Tell me who you are?" People respond by identifying themselves with their names and their occupations. They may talk about their families and where they live. After they stop talking or start another turn, the partner asks again, "Tell me who you are?" Other material may appear. "I'm so and so's wife or husband," etc. Eventually, the participants realize that none of the definitions will do. Who they are in truth then must be something that transcends all of these limiting definitions.

When the mirror of my mind became clear
I saw that God is not other than me, and this
non-dual knowledge completely destroyed all thought
of "you" and "I." I came to know that this entire
world is not different from God.
Lalleshwari

Lalleshwari (1320–1392, India) also known as *Lalla*, was a Hindu poet. Her verses are the earliest compositions in the Kashmiri language.

Although the self that we created is not who we are, beyond, above, and outside all the illusions of the world there is a Self that we are in truth. This Self is a holy child made in God's image, not our own. It is this Self, not the little self created by our egos, that holds the key to happiness and leads us once again Home. Our greatest happiness comes from knowing we are God's child and doing His will.

I ask you only to stop imagining that you were born,
have parents, are a body, will die and so on. Just try,
make a beginning—it is not as hard as you think.
Nisargadatta Maharaja

Chapter II

Mysticism, Madness, Illness, and Death

Illness as a Prelude to the Mystical

The sixth stimulant to a mystical experience, according to Sir Alistair Hardy's research, is illness. Several well known mystics had visions during the time they were ill and or dying. Suffering from a severe illness and thinking she was about to die, Julian of Norwich (1342–1413, England) had a series of visions that were the source of her major work *Sixteen Revelations of the Divine*. Likewise, Blasé Pascal was often sickly; after a near death experience, he had an intense mystical vision. From then on, he was subject to states of rapture.

While it would be wonderful to just "know" the truth, to just "see" the truth and "be" the truth, and although that's possible, most often we "learn" the truth through experience. We may wonder, why is someone born blind? Why does one body seem to have some form of imperfection while another seems nearly perfect? Sometimes, even when we exercise, eat right, and lead a healthy lifestyle, our health can change suddenly. It can come from the outside, as in an accident, for example. My plans for July and August of 2007 were to vacation with family, visit extended family and friends, and give several lectures and workshops. Instead, I spent three weeks in the hospital and the following five weeks recuperating at home.

I've had five NDE's (Near Death Experiences). A friend once joked that perhaps I had nine lives. Each of these experiences brought me back to the present, back to the moment, back to now. NDE's stop, at least temporarily, the dreaming of the world. Each of these experiences also included a *revelation* or *vision* and *hallucinations* that have little to do with revelation. Still each "vision" has introduced me to a different dimension of mysticism. The first experience was at the age of nine, when I had my tonsils removed. It was not too profound. I simply found myself being "hurled" though space. Comets and stars whirled past me as I jetted by them, or so it seemed.

The second experience in 1976 was clearly the most profound. I deliberately stepped into this experience, not knowing it would be as profound as it was. I literally did not think I could come back to ordinary, earthbound perception and was very surprised when I did. During this experience, it became clear to me that there is no time; we are not bodies; there is no world; life does not begin at birth or end at death. I clearly saw that there is no duality. There are no opposites—only one—that the script is written and Love or God or Life or Eternity are all synonyms and the only Reality.

Twenty-two years later, in 1998, there was a third experience when I had a quadruple by-pass at Columbian Presbyterian in New York City, where Helen Schucman received much of *A Course in Miracles*. The surgeon was Dr. Memet Oz, the now famous Dr. Oz often seen on Oprah. I wasn't afraid during this experience and did not think I would die. It was next to the least profound of my NDEs and yet an important event. The majority of people who come out of bypass surgery report similar experiences namely, a deeper appreciation for life.

When we finally know we are dying,
and all other sentient beings are dying with us,
we start to have a burning, almost heartbreaking
sense of the fragility and preciousness of each
moment and each being, and from this can grow
a deep, clear, limitless compassion for all beings.
Sogyal Rinpoche (1950 – Present)
Tibetan Buddhist Teacher living in the USA

After this experience came the wonder of looking at life and the joy of talking with Dolores and taking walks in August where I could spend some time each day immersed in observing the white lady's mantles, black-eyed Susan's, and blue bachelor buttons with bees buzzing, busily moving about amidst the presence of small, white butterflies. Even though our bodies are temporary, being fully alive in the moment of Now is a magnificent experience.

In 2001, there was a fourth NDE in connection with cancer. This time I had to take a good look at physical death. Before the ultimate state of existence can be experienced, there must not be a "me" needing something to happen. By *letting go*—or not "needing" to exist—it is possible to be more aware of the whole of existence.

Then six years later, in 2007, there was a fifth experience. One day, I discovered mosquito bites all over my arms. The next day I felt like I was coming down with the flu, finding it more and more difficult to concentrate on my work. I don't remember any of the next few days. This is what I am told. I was standing in my office when my assistant Fran asked what I was doing. I told her I was sleeping. She responded, "Standing up?" Fran called Dolores, and she asked me some more questions to which my responses were nonsensical. An ambulance was called, and we were off to the hospital. I was admitted to the hospital hallucinating with a temperature of 106! 106 can "fry" the brain. Fortunately, mine just got scrambled.

I went into a coma, was put on life-support, and stayed there for several days. A coma does not mean total blackness. The body may have shut down, but the mind may be very awake and "seeing." The world we *normally* see is not available in a coma, so it's like living in a dream world. The main thing to remember when in a coma is that you are dreaming—that it is a dream—and not think that what you are now seeing is "reality." If you see that you are dreaming, you can have some control in the dream. You do not have to give in to fear, and if you relax, you can have a good time observing the universe up close. What universe? Any universe. The universe right in front of you. It is your creation, so pick one. It's your choice.

I had contracted Viral Lacrosse Encephalitis, which causes swelling of the brain. My trip back to what we call reality was slow and gentle and took several weeks. Fortunately, there were some very nice nurses and doctors. Dolores was there a lot, and Fran took care of the office. I did not eat solid food for several days and lost my appetite, along with 37 pounds in about 37 days. It was a good two months before I regained my energy. Now food is once again delicious and distracting. After I came out of the experience, my neurologist, cardiologist, and internist each said they had not expected me to live. As my cardiologist stated, "You do not know how sick you were. You are a miracle."

Hallucination and Visions: Psychosis or Gnosis?

Mysticism and psychosis are examples of naturally available, altered states of consciousness. In his article "Mysticism and Schizophrenia," Kenneth Wapnick discusses the similarities and differences between the mystical and the schizophrenic experiences. Both schizophrenics and mystics follow similar paths of development. However, the mystics tend to follow a structured, controlled, meditative process, while the schizophrenic is "...over-whelmed, with no means of dealing with his experience and no conviction that he will survive it." (Kenneth Wapnick, "Mysticism and Schizophrenia," *Understanding Mysticism*).

During my coma, I kept leaving planet earth and then coming back—leaving and coming back again. What was most fascinating was the rawness, the closeness and intimacy of everything. I also saw that I bring judgment into everything. At one point in the night, I awoke, held up my right hand and looked at it with amazement, thinking: "This is a hand! What an incredible thing a hand is." I wondered how I knew the name of this "thing."

Dolores came to visit me and I kept asking her to marry me. Of course, we're already married. Two nurses came in the room to take blood and insert IVs. I was convinced that this was happening outdoors in the center of the little town of Washingtonville, near where we live. The nurses were indeed there, but we were not outside.

At one point, I was so far gone that I wanted to die, except it was unpleasant to think of what this would mean for Dolores and Sarah, my sister Ann and my other family members. I continued to think that I had unfinished work to do. I then saw something I saw before in 1976—it was a web, a net, a gigantic multicolored grid with zigzagging lines throughout the whole universe. It was a hologram in which everything was connected through dots where the various points in the grid connected. These points were stars. What we don't normally see is the lines connecting the dots, forming a gigantic DNA-type molecule grid.

For more than two weeks, I briefly came into this world, left, and returned again. I saw again as I had in 1976 that what we call reality is not reality. Our time in this world is spent in an oneiric, or "dream-like" world. This was, I knew, a world of my own making. Fortunately, I knew I was making it up despite its *seeming* reality. Neither the world of our dreams nor what we think of as the ordinary world is real. I also had moments of "vision" and the experience of "perfect" love, often when other people were presents—nurses, doctors, family members, and friends. I felt the deepest love for them. They were loving to me and trying to help me; how could I do anything except love them?

Death

From the standpoint of the ego, death is witness to the reality of the body. If the body dies, it must have lived. This means that its creator, the ego, must be real. There is only Life. God is Life. God is Love. These sentences are tautologies. They can be read from the left or the right, and they still make sense. A little logic also tells us that if God is Life and God is Love, then Love is Life and Life is Love. So the more in Love we are, the more we know of Life, the more we know of Love—the more we know of God.

People living deeply have no fear of death.
Anaïs Nin, *Diary*, 1967

There are many states of being that are not physical. Love that is real does not have a form. Eternity does not have a form. God does not have a form. Truth does not have a form. All there is, is Life. Life is not dependent on form. The body is ephemeral. To say that life is eternal does not mean that we go from one body to another, that would be a continuation of dreaming. Who wants to go from story to story, from soap opera to soap opera?

Those Who Die Before They Die
Don't Die When They Die.

The dissolution of the body is simply the quiet laying down of the body and the transformation from a dream, or an awakening, into life. When the body disappears all there is, is life. Whatever is all encompassing has no opposite. God is all encompassing. There is no opposite of God.

When your body and your ego and your dreams are gone, you will know that you will last forever.

Perhaps you think this is accomplished through death, but nothing is accomplished through death, because death is nothing. Everything is accomplished through life, and life is of the mind and in the mind. The body neither lives nor dies, because it cannot contain you who are life.

A Course in Miracles

Anything that rusts or rots or decays, or is turning from one form back into another, is not permanent and therefore, not eternal. Only the mind, only spirit, is eternal. Jesus did not believe in death. He did not resist the crucifixion because it meant nothing. He willingly went to the cross to show us that although his body could be killed, he could not be killed. As a line in Martin Luther's hymn "A Mighty Fortress" says: *"The Body They May Kill, God's Truth Abideth Still. His Kingdom is Forever."*

The ancient Greeks had a saying—*"soma sema"—"the body is a tomb."* The body is the ego's chosen home. It is also its prison. According to the mystics we have nothing to lose, not even our bodies. To lose a body is just to lose a body. Death of the body is not the end. It's not the beginning. Death is no big deal. It is birth into this world we should be concerned about. Spirit cannot be limited to a specific experience in space and time.

If the story of the wandering Jew be true, indeed if there was a man who could not die, would he not be the unhappiest of men?

Soren Kierkegaard

Who wants to live forever in the body? Woody Allen jokingly said, "I do not want to gain immortality through my work. I want to gain immortality by living forever." Woody Allen is immortal and will live forever, not in his body, not in his works and not as Woody Allen. None of these things are eternal. Nothing physical is immortal.

Death is no more than a turning of us over from time to eternity.

William Penn

William Penn (1644–1718, England, USA) is best known as the founder of Pennsylvania. He was a close friend of George Fox, the founder of the Quakers, and traveled with him in Europe and England. The Quakers obey their inner light, a presence of God within each person. They also believe that God speaks to everyone. In order to hear His voice, one must learn to be still and listen.

Who wants to be here in the realm of duality, of time and space, forever? Why not escape, why not know truth and freedom? I'm not suggesting that we do away with our bodies. The body is a tool, and we've been given this tool in order to learn a lesson. It is best we learn the lesson before we move on. Still, there is no eternity in the body—the form of "the thing" is never "the thing."

Death may be the greatest of all human blessings.

Socrates

Story Time

A five year old girl who was returning home from her grandmother's funeral in a car with her other grandmother asked, "Where did grandma go?" "We believe she went to be with God," the other grandmother replied. "How old was she?" "She was eighty years old." "How old are you?" "I'm eighty-three." The little girl then said, *"I hope God hasn't forgotten you!"*

To die is to awaken. It is a coming back to life, not a loss of life. It is a rising of consciousness, not a loss of consciousness. It is an awakening from a death. In *Conversations with God*, Neal Donald Walsh writes:

Death is not an end, but a beginning, not a horror, but a joy. It is not a closing down, but an opening up. The happiest moment of your life will be the moment it ends. That's because it doesn't end but only goes on in ways so magnificent, so full of peace and wisdom and joy, as to make it difficult to describe and impossible for you to comprehend.

Only the dream disappears—only the ego and its attachments, hates and prejudices—only those things die that have no reality. Yet the truth is that they don't die. They simply disappear into the nothingness from which they came—just like a dream. Illusions cannot be part of eternity. Illusions do not exist. Prejudices, fears, and hatreds are part of an illusion that will disappear because it has no truth in it—no eternity—no reality.

Nothing real can be threatened. Nothing unreal exists, herein lies the peace of God

A Course in Miracles

As we awaken, we see a happy dream in which the body, the ego, and the illusory world, are not there—because they literally are not there! The illusory world is nothing in light of the reality of God. To be truly awake is to be free of dreaming. To share in the vision of Christ is to see Christ in everyone. We love all people by letting them be who they are. Getting on with fulfilling our destiny, we help others fulfill theirs. The body has no eternity. The body is only form. You are not form. There is nothing to be afraid of, and there is no one we need attack. We only have to speak truth to gain entry into Heaven. The truth is simple and can be spoken easily. At the gate, when asked your identity, say simply you are a Child of God.

For what is it to die, but to stand
in the sun and melt into the wind?
Kahlil Gibran, from *The Prophet*

Khalil Gibran (1883–1931, Lebanon, USA) was a poet, artist, and mystical writer. Born in Lebanon, he spent much of his life in the United States. Gibran's best-known book, *The Prophet*, is composed of 26 poetic essays. During the 1960s, *The Prophet* became especially popular with the American counterculture and the New Thought and New Age movement.

If you are mindful of death, it will not come as a
surprise—you will not be anxious.
You will feel that death is merely like changing
clothes. Consequently, at that point you will be able
to maintain your calmness of mind.
Dalai Lama

Live as if you were to die tomorrow.
Learn as if you were to live forever.
Mahatma Gandhi

Chapter 12

Mysticism, Moninsm—Heaven and Hell

Words create distinctions and hence duality. Mysticism is monistic. There is one God, a singular experience of Love beyond all names, words, and religions. *Love*, *God*, and *Heaven* are synonyms. According to Fichte, "Being is absolutely singular, not manifold; there are not several Beings, but one Being only." For Edgar Cayce, the essence of mysticism was a belief in the underlying unity of all things that otherwise appear to be distinct. To Cayce, mysticism meant going beyond differentiations, or distinguishing between inner and outer, dark and light, good and bad. As Cayce said, "Only in Christ Consciousness do the extremes meet."

Edgar Cayce (1877–1945, USA) channeled answers to questions on theology, physical and psychological health, the past and the future. The Association for Research and Enlightenment in Virginia Beach continues his work to this day. (See *The Essential Edgar Cayce* by Mark Thurston).

Though it is impossible to be separated from God, the ego tries to create a world devoid of God—a world in which God is a fantasy. From the viewpoint of the ego, Heaven seems like a fantasy, and this world looks like reality. The most common experience for the mystic is unity and connectedness—the sense that everything is whole and complete.

Mind, which is without beginning, is unborn and indestructible. It transcends all limits, measures, traces and comparisons.
Huang Po, 9th Century Zen master

If we are in unity with Spirit, we are in unity with each other, and so we are all one.
Plotinus

There is but one wisdom, to understand how all things are steered through the All.
Heraclites

In essence, things are not two but one. All duality is falsely imagined.
Lankavatara Sutra (Buddhist)

If we will see things truly, we are strangers to that which creates distinction.
Meister Eckhart

Our consciousness is shared, one with all humanity.
Krishnamurti

The overall number of minds is one.
Edwin Schrödinger, quantum physicist

According to the Heisenberg Principle, it is impossible for the perceiver not to affect the object perceived. Thus the mind determines the reality of everything. We are constantly superimposing our interpretations on everything, but believing that we see things as they really are.

We delight in one knowable thing,
which comprehends all that is knowable;
in one apprehensible, which draws together
all that can be apprehended; in a single being.
Giordano Bruno

Giordano Bruno (1548–1600, Italy) was one of the most interesting and important mystical philosophers of the Renaissance. He advocated nature mysticism with a scientific slant. He said that the universe was infinite, that it contained an infinite number of worlds inhabited by intelligent beings. The Catholic Church had him burned at the stake. Bags of gun powder were hung around his neck, and he was gagged so that onlookers would not be seduced by his heretical lies.

The following is a description of oneness from the files of the Religious Experience Research Center established by Sir Alister Hardy:

"In 1956 at the age of 23 my husband and I were walking the cliff path from St. Ives in Cornwall to Zennor. It was a bright sunny day in September, bright but not a garish mid-summer sun. My husband was walking his usual forty yards ahead and disappeared over the prow of an incline, so to all intents and purposes I was entirely alone. Although there was no mist the light seemed suddenly white and diffused and I experienced the most incredible sense of oneness and at the same time 'I knew what it was all about' it being existence. It struck me that the oneness was in part explained by the sensation that the air and space and light was somehow tangible, one could almost grasp it, so that there was not a space which stopped because my human form was there but that my form was merely a continuity of the apparently solid space. The experience was unbelievably beautiful, and I will never forget the quality of that bright white light. It was awesome."

Who Is the Devil?

Traditional Christianity is dualistic. It teaches that there is a Heaven, but also a hell (a place of eternal punishment for sinners) and a devil. Both are quite real in traditional Christianity. According to monism, only Heaven exists. Hell is a bad dream that can happen only in time, not in eternity.

Evil, and evil spirits, devils and devil possession, are the outgrowth of man's inadequate consciousness of God. We must avoid thinking of evil as a thing in itself—a force that works against man or against God.
Eric Butterworth.

Eric Butterworth (1916–2003, Canada, USA) was the senior minister of The Unity Center of New York City from 1961 to 2003. The church I served in New York City (Interfaith Fellowship 1989–2002) was only a few blocks from Eric's church, and he was thus something of a wonderful rival. A number of our members also went to see Eric. He was an expert on Emerson and Thoreau and a highly respected innovator of New Thought. He was the author of 16 best-selling books on mysticism and metaphysical spirituality.

In the world of Christian fiction, the hottest novels today are those of Frank Peretti, a Pentecostal author who writes spiritual thrillers dramatizing a supernatural warfare between angels and demons in small American towns. Catholics update their pledge once a year to "renounce Satan," while ritually renewing their vows at Mass. Sixty percent of "born again" believers report that they have been tempted by the devil. According to Rev. Jerry Falwell, Satan is "the enemy of family and of children—the force behind drugs and a program straight from hell."

If men were born free, they would,
so long as they remained free,
form no conception of good and evil.
Benedicts de Spinoza

Benedicts de Spinoza (1632–1677, Holland) along with Rene Descartes and Gottfried Leibniz, Spinoza is one of the outstanding "rationalists" of the seventeenth century. He was familiar with writings of the mystics Moses of Cordova and Moses Maimonides, philosophers with ideas similar to Gurdjieff. According to Spinoza, all reality consists of one substance: God, or Nature. The intellectual love of God frees us from desire and brings immortality. His emphasis on *freedom of thought* paved the way for the Enlightenment and got him excommunicated from his synagogue. The romantic thinkers Lessing and Goethe and the English poets Coleridge and Shelley embraced his philosophy because it had nothing to do with religious dogma. His *magnum opus* is the *Ethics*.

The word for devil in the Greek of the New Testament is *diabolos*, which means "slanderer." Paul and the earlier gospel writers call the devil *Satan*, meaning "the adversary, accuser or separator." From the mystic's point of view, the devil is a projection of the ego in an attempt to displace guilt or responsibility onto an external agent. If evil is "out there," we can justify attacking it. Once we have duality, we have good and bad, and the world is seen as a battleground between these energies or forces. War is the ultimate result of believing that we are separated from God, or a single unifying reality. War subtracts; peace brings abundance. In the hell of war, everybody loses.

The devil is a belief, and we can be free of the devil by seeing it for what it is: a projection of the ego. When we make illusions real, we give them power over us. During the 1970s, the Iranians painted President Jimmy Carter as the devil, while Americans painted the Ayatollah Khomeini as a devil, each pointing the finger at the other. Such cross-demonizations obviously continue today between Christians, Jews, and Muslims, feeding the ceaseless religious conflicts of the Middle East.

The devil exists only insofar as the ego exists, and the ego no more exists than does the devil. The devil is a shadow, a bad dream perhaps (but not a physical being), and the bad dream is not eternal. As angels are symbolic extensions of the thoughts of God, the devil is a symbolic extension of the thoughts of the ego. Angels are symbols of the light and protection of God that always surrounds us; the devil is a symbol of separation, fear, anger, and aggression.

Man has created the devil; he has created him in his own image and likeness.
Fyodor M. Dostoyevsky

The belief in a supernatural source of evil
is not necessary; men alone
are quite capable of every wickedness.
Joseph Conrad

The Temptation Story

The temptation story from the Bible is not recorded in *Mark*, the oldest of the gospels. Matthew and Luke, however, view the event as an essential element in the story of Jesus. The temptation story occurs after the baptism of Jesus and just before he begins his ministry. Not until after the wilderness journey does Jesus offer his first sermon. After his baptism Jesus goes off alone, apparently to think through his mission. According to the Bible, he is led by the Holy Spirit into the desert for this time of testing.

The word *temptation* comes from the Latin *tenatio* and means "trial," or "test." Bishop Atterbury, banished from England as a Jacobite in 1723, says, "A temptation is only another word for an experiment, or trial." We experience temptations each day through our inclinations to listen to the ego, rather than the voice for God. With each temptation comes the opportunity to choose once again. There is always a peaceful choice and a choice that will lead us into greater separation and guilt. Every second, we get to choose again until we choose wisely.

The three temptations put before Jesus are descriptive of Abraham Maslow's hierarchy of needs: 1) the need to satisfy the body, 2) the need to show off, and 3) the thirst for power. Whenever we are afraid, the ego encourages our fears and tells us to choose in favor of security, status, and possession.

A major contribution to contemporary mysticism was made by **Dr. Abraham Maslow** (1908–1970, USA), one of the founders of humanistic psychology. In *Religions: Values and Peak Experiences*, he defined a mystical or peak experience, as one of those times when the entire pretense of the personality and all fear drop away, and we seem to be in touch with the whole universe.

The temptation to immediate need. The first temptation experienced by Jesus in the wilderness is to satisfy immediate needs. It occurs when he is hungry from his long fast. We are easily distracted by the murmurs, rumbles, and cravings of the stomach. Don Juan says, "A mystic should always be a little hungry." It is better to control the appetites than to have them control us.

The temptation to show off. Jesus knew he was called. He had a mission to fulfill, but how was he to do it? How would he get people's attention? He could do something really spectacular and give a convincing sign of his power and authority. If he threw himself off the temple and was not hurt, people would worship him. The temptation was to listen to the ego, instead of God. And Jesus said, "You shall not tempt the Lord your God." The imperfect cannot affect the perfect.

The temptation to power. An incredible destiny awaits Jesus; he will be a king, but what kind of king? The third temptation is to create his own world over which he would exercise temporal power. It is a typical ego temptation. Jesus could have controlled, molded, and manipulated, but these were all earthly demands. His kingdom was not of this world. There was another higher possibility, namely to follow the will of God and find entrance into the Kingdom of God.

The object of temptation is to induce us to substitute something else for God. To obscure God.

R.H. Stewart

Division (the work of Satan) has no place in God's kingdom. Temptation has only the power we give it; otherwise, the power isn't there. Letting go of an addiction, we see that whatever we were addicted to, we did not need.

What do you lose when you lose an illusion?

If the man we know as Jesus had given in to any of the temptations, there would be no "Jesus story." Jesus never gave in to the seductions of the ego and maintained an awareness of His true identity. Unlike the "Jesus story," in most hero stories the hero gets seduced by the ego. Inevitably then, there is a need to overcome failure, come to the Self again, and find the way out of darkness.

Jesus went into the desert to encounter the devil. St. Anthony, Buddha, and Saint Teresa of Avila, were similarly assailed. We all go through trials and tribulations, caught up in our complexes, compulsions, and battles for status and control. We often give in and listen not to the voice of Holy Spirit, but to a voice that calls upon us to show off, forget about God, and build our own world wherein we judge, condemn, and exert our power. The temptation to engage in separation keeps us in a hell made with our own hands. Fortunately, this state is not eternal and therefore not real.

Our Enemy: Ourselves

Man's chief enemy is his own unruly nature and the dark forces pent up within him.

Ernest Jones (1879–1958, England), psychiatrist, friend, and biographer of Sigmund Freud

We can look at the selfish, separating ego-self and then look beyond it. By not ignoring the dark side, we take away its power. A mystic looks at the ego not to affirm its reality but to see beyond illusion. We cannot let go of the ego until we see its illusory quality. If we try to kill or attack the ego, it grows stronger. But there is nothing to fear. We are in truth *one Self united with our Creator*, and that means we have no enemies, not even within ourselves.

Although in truth there are no enemies, during the daily course of our lives, it is possible to run into occasional resistance and hostility. One of the most important lessons we can learn is how to disagree with someone without attacking. Those we may perceive as our enemies can help us discover our own deeper truth.

Our enemies are those who strengthen
our nerves and sharpen our skill.

Edmund Burke

Jesus' truth was frightening to the Pharisees, who saw him as a threat to their power. What he said was true, and it frightened them. Martin Luther did not want to leave the Church; he was excommunicated and thus had no choice but to go on his own. In remaining true to himself in the face of powerful opposition, Luther helped birth the Protestant Reformation. Jesus, Gandhi, and Martin Luther King, Jr., changed the world by peacefully facing their opponents.

The Oceanic Quality

Freud coined the term *oceanic* to describe the falling away of the borders of consciousness and the pleasurable experience of oneness. Melting into oneness and unity is not an altered state. It is just seeing without contamination. There is no block to awareness. There is just awareness.

When it's cold, water freezes into ice; when it's warm,
ice melts into water. Similarly, when you are
confused, essence freezes into mind; when you are
enlightened, mind melts into essence.

Muso Kokushi

Muso Kokushi (1275–1351, Japan) was one of the most influential early garden designers in Japan

The soul which is reduced to the Nothing, ought to dwell therein; without wishing, since she is now but dust, to issue from this state, nor, as before, desiring to live again. She must remain as something which no longer exists in order that the Torrent may drown itself and lose itself in the Sea, never to find itself in its selfhood again; that it may become one and the same thing with the Sea.

Madame Guyon

Madame Guyon (1648–1717, France) was an advocate of quietism, a doctrine considered heretical by the Catholic Church. Deeply attracted to mysticism, she devoted her life to the quest and was known for her imposing appearance and the eloquence with which she explained mysticism. In 1688, she was arrested as a heretic but released with the help of friends. She was arrested again and placed in the Bastille from 1695 to 1703. She had a tremendous influence on the philosopher Schopenhauer.

This is the way mystic Robert Adams describes an oceanic experience:

I was the center and also the circumference, expanded throughout the universe, and I was able to feel the planets, the stars, the galaxies, as myself. And this light shone so bright. It was beautiful, it was bliss, and it was ineffable, indescribable. I was able to feel, and understand, that all of the planets, the galaxies, the people, the trees, the flowers on this earth, everything were myriads of energy, and I was in everything. I was the flower. I was the sky. I was the people. Then I was everything. Everything was the I. The word "I" encompassed the whole universe.

The mystic is absorbed by such a boundless ocean, a great sense of connectedness with the whole. According to Sufism, if the whole is likened to the ocean and the part to a drop, then when the drop becomes one with the ocean, it sees with the eye of the ocean. The mystic loses the sense of personal self, like a drop of water disappearing into the ocean.

But I'll tell you what hermits realize.
If you go into a far, far forest and get very quiet,
you'll come to understand that
you're connected with everything.

Alan Watts

...I felt that I was vast, limitless in size.
A feeling of all pervasiveness swept over me.
I was everyone, and everyone was me.
There was one continuous principle pervading everything. Everything was one.
I felt love pouring out of me. Compassion streamed forth from me. No one was baser or inferior to me.
There was no sin, no badness,
no punishable instinct...

Deepa Kodikal

Deepa Kodikal (1941 – Present, India) is a scientist, painter, and musician. She disovered as a child that she could direct her dreams and achieve a samadhi-like state of absorption. The description of her mystical experiences (galaxies within galaxies) provides a picture of an infinite colossal tapestry in motion, different dimensions of time in different spatial dimesions and yet other dimensions not available in ordinary awareness. It is the most "cosmological" description I've ever read and one of the closest to my own experience.

When you fall in love, you become identified with the beloved. You want to become one with her, and then with the world. My wife Dolores and I often think the same thought at the same time and say that thought out loud. In those moments, we are literally of one mind. Jesus meant it when he said, "I and the Father are one."

The fundamental dysfunction of our minds takes
the form of a separation between me and other.
We falsely grasp at an "I" on which attachment
grafts itself at the same time as we conceive of an
"other" that is the basis of vision.
Bokar Rinpoche

God is one's very own Self, the breath of one's breath,
the life of one's life, the Atman.
Anandamayi Ma

The Mystical Surrender

The mystic is not in charge of the mystical experience. When you are experiencing the mystical, something happens to and through you. You are not the author, which accounts in part for its overwhelming beauty. Teresa of Avila insisted that the special quality of the mystical state is that although you can prepare for it, you cannot attain it by your own efforts. It comes at last by grace. If the ego tries to control, manipulate or label the experience, the experience fades. If you are experiencing *déjà vu*, for example, and you say to someone, "I'm having a *déjà vu* experience," you lose the experience. The best way to sustain mystical awareness is to surrender and just "hang out" with it, without analyzing or interpreting what is occurring. To surrender is similar to being carried as a child is carried. Can you remember as a child falling asleep in the back of the car at night and having your parents carry you to bed? Remember the gentle feeling of trusting your body to the arms of your mother or father. Surrender is like that, a willingness to go with the flow—a willingness to be carried.

Chapter 13

Mysticism, Accidents, Coincidence and Synchronicity

"God! How could you do this to me?"

The only survivor of a shipwreck washed up on a small, uninhabited island. He prayed feverishly for God to rescue him. For days he scanned the horizon but he saw nothing. Exhausted, he was finally able to start a fire and he eventually managed to build a little hut to protect himself from the elements, and to store a few possessions. One day, after scavenging for food, he arrived home to find his little hut in flames, with smoke rolling up to the sky. The worst possible thing had happened. Everything was lost. He was stunned with disbelief, grief, and anger. He cried out, "God! How could you do this to me?" The next day, he was awakened by the sound of a boat approaching the island! "How did you know I was here?" asked the weary man. *"We saw your smoke signal."*

Remember our earlier discussion of falling asleep in the back of the car, and having your parents carry you to bed? Remember the gentle feeling of trusting your body to the arms of your parent? Surrendering to God's Will is like this—it is, as I said, a willingness to be carried. One advantage of getting older is that the longer we live, the more we may understand why life went the way it did. According to an article in *Scientific American Mind* in 2007, as we get older, one of two things happens. Either we get grumpier, more mean spirited, and projective; or we become more open minded, laid back, loving, and receptive. Which way do you want to go? Fortunately, most folks choose the more loving response.

Time is a trick, a sleight of hand, a vast illusion
in which figures come and go as if by magic.
A Course in Miracles

In everything, even things which do not make sense or seem significant, there is a plan. The script is written. Our passage through time and space is not without design. When we come to revelation, we come at last to the knowledge of "What already is!"

Consciousness of Coincidence

The Celestine Prophecy, by James Redfield, popular during the early 1990s, lists nine insights. The first insight is becoming more conscious of *coincidences*. Coincidence is an unplanned alignment of events; things happening in a way that seems planned, even though it is an accident. We wonder how life is going to work out, and then we go someplace or meet someone or read something that is just what we needed. Mystical awakening means becoming progressively aware of coincidence, and experiencing coincidence makes life more exciting.

Jung, Synchonicity, and Serendipity

Carl Jung was fascinated with the concept of synchronicity—a coincidence in time of two or more seemingly unrelated events having the same meaning. We experience synchronicity when we meet a friend in an unexpected place. Joe Campbell loved to play with paradox. He once said, "Unless you allow for serendipity, you will never find your way." Serendipity occurs when we find valuable or agreeable something we weren't looking for or expecting to find, but it is exactly the right thing. Sometimes, to find ourselves we have to get lost. We go on a detour and there discover what we need. Sometimes, at the precise moment you think things cannot or will not change, everything changes.

There is a French proverb which says that *we often meet our destiny on the road we took to avoid it.* From 1982–1990, I taught college classes in philosophy inside Sing-Sing Prison. It was a privilege to have had such a captivated audience. (Sorry about the pun.) I wanted to work in prison and teaching philosophy and religion was ideal. I've had prisoners tell me that they were glad they got caught. They couldn't keep running, hiding, and acting out forever. The only way out was getting arrested.

Chinese theories of medicine, philosophy, and architecture are based on a *science* of coincidence. Chinese texts do not ask what *causes* what, but what *likes to occur with* what. According to the Chinese, certain events "like" to cluster together. Everything makes sense at the level of archetypical configuration. There is a pattern to everything and everything flows naturally from one thing to another even if it does not look that way in the world of form.

Patterned events are more clearly seen during "crucial" phases in spiritual development. Dr. Carl Jung noticed prior to World War II that many of his patients were having horrific dreams of fire, war, destruction, and death—absolutely apocalyptic images. He was concerned that his patients were going mad. Later, he realized that their dreams portended the coming war. Once, Dr. Jung watched a beetle crawl up the curtain behind a patient, while the patient was describing a dream about an Egyptian beetle scarab. The movie *Crash* is a good example of how synchronistic events occur. People come "crashing" into each other but there are a host of decisions by each individual leading up to this moment and then another host of experiences that result from the crash, all of which actually leads to fulfillment of their destiny.

Responsibility: Facing Life Straight On

We've all had the experience of having something happen and then saying: "I would never have chosen this." When I lost a country inn I owned in 1989; left the Methodist ministry and lost nearly everything I had, financially speaking, I asked, "Why is this happening?" I later realized that it "had to happen." I had to go through this crash and burn and I had to step away from the institutional church to gain perspective. I had "chosen" this experience and it was necessary to go through this purification to experience life at a deeper level. In 2001, dealing with cancer and possible death enabled a letting go of planning. The only way ahead was to let go, accept the real possibility of physical death and live in the moment—doing so miraculously brought everything to life.

According to the Dalai Lama, when everything is falling apart something else is trying to be born. Accepting responsibility for what is happening helps us through loss. Life then takes an upward turn. We are not driven by external, purposeless events. Everything comes our way as part of our spiritual journey and no accidents are possible in God's Universe. As Einstein expressed it, "God does not play dice with the universe." Every accident is a lesson. We are constantly learning. The older we get, the more we learn about daily life and life beyond this life. There is no sickness, no physical loss, no financial difficulty, no interpersonal problem, and no death—no experience, however extraordinary or mundane—that does not come our way as it should.

The problems people bring me often find expression in terms like "Why is this happening?" as though some cosmic force was behind everything. Problems are doors that lead us home. Vaclav Havel (1936 – Present), the former President of Czechoslovakia says, "Hope is not the conviction that something will turn out well, but the certainty that things make sense, regardless of how it turns out."

With one exception, each of the Roman Emperors got involved in the ego's world. Mystic Emperor Marcus Arelius once said, "All things happen as they should." That is, after all, the way they happen. We are here, our best thinking got us here, and we have to be responsible for being here. Our journey through time and space is not by chance. We can't help but be in the right place at the right time.

In February 1997, Ram Dass, author of *Be Here Now!*, had a stroke that left him partially paralyzed, after which he wrote a new book called *Still Here*. Ram Dass looks at life before and after his stroke as two different incarnations. Since the stroke, he said, he has learned to play with this new incarnation. *"I was a golfer—a pretty good golfer and I was a cellist," in the first incarnation. "I had a sports car that had a shift that...oh, boy!" he continued, his face lighting up as he mimed slamming his car though the corner of a winding road, "Oh boy! Those three things!"*

When we hear of someone who has gone through some difficulty or has perhaps been born with a disability and has gone ahead to live to the fullest despite that difficulty, we cannot help but be impressed. One of the purest, clearest *seeing* of the mystics is Helen Keller (1880–1968, USA). Scarlet fever left her blind and deaf at 19 months of age. Despite severe disability, with the aid of her teacher, Anne Sullivan, Helen graduated from Radcliff and she wrote twelve books. The title of her autobiography, *Light in Darkness* says it all. Keller once said, *I thank God for my handicaps, for through them, I have found myself, my work, and my God.*

Accidents, Coincidence, and Destiny

No one comes to us by accident. No meeting of any two people is unplanned. It does not matter if the encounter lasts one second or a lifetime. Even in the simplest encounter as a smile, it is possible for two people to lose their sense of separation. As you walk around in a mall, look people in the eyes. See how many look back at you. Smile and see how many smile back your way. Giving a smile is just a little positive boost—a little love energy in the engine of God.

In *The Lazy Man's Guide to Enlightenment*, Thaddeus Golas says, "Enlightenment doesn't care how you get there." One of the characters in the movie, *Buckaroo Bonsai* says, "Wherever you go—there you are!" No matter where we are, no matter what is going on, we are responsible for being here—in this marvelous place—at this marvelous time!

I was once counseling someone who said her problems were because she lived in New York. Her problems, of course, had nothing to do with the "state" of the nation. They did, however, have something to do with the state of her mind. We can procrastinate and we can find innumerable excuses for not paying attention. Eventually, we have to face life straight on and deal with whatever stands in front of us. Eventually, all bills must be paid or forgiven.

I was listening to a 15-year-old girl describe a death experience and all she kept saying was, "It's all connected." Suzuki Roshi (1904–1971, Japan), the former head of the Zen Center, in San Francisco, says we cannot make a date with enlightenment. *Enlightenment is an accident and Spiritual practice makes us accident-prone.*

Choosing God is choosing our own greatest happiness. Choosing with the ego means despair. In this moment "right now," we either know the peace of God or we do not. The next moment is the same, as is the next. We have a choice as to how to view the moment. The power of decision is our *"last remaining freedom."* As we change our minds about the mind, we change the world. Letting destiny unfold in accordance with God's will is beautiful. Every one has a mission. Those who find a way to fulfill their destinies tell us time and again that they "knew" there was something they had to do. Destiny "had" to be fulfilled, and the best thing was to fulfill it.

Psychiatrist **Victor Frankl, M.D., Ph.D.**, (1905–1997, Austria) a neurologist and a Holocaust survivor and author of the bestselling, *Man's Search for Meaning*, said that the people who handled the trauma at Auschwitz best, were those who somehow knew that even in the horror of this situation there was some purpose. He found in Auschwitz two types of people. It did not matter what class or ethnic group they were from, there were still two types: *decent* and *non-decent, loving* or *not loving, trusting* or *fearful.*

Those who impeccably pursue their destinies are the happiest people, though they may choose to remain single, turn down wealth, or even be crucified. No step that anyone makes along the road is inadvertent. As a matter of fact, we've already walked this road, so it is a matter of remembering what we already know. We are already at home resting in the arms of God. The story has been played through. We have attained entrance to the Kingdom. We are already perfect and whole. We were just dreaming a "silly dream." In Maya's (illusions) house are many mansions. Heaven is reality, not a dream.

So how does this work with freewill?

Computers today are 1 billion times more powerful than they were 25 years ago and this growth is exponential. The more it grows, the faster it grows. Behind everything there is something analogous to the genetic code of the universe. There is a "reason" why each of us are going through life the way we are. It's amazing to think how much information can be put into a little MP3 player and it's getting ever smaller. Look at how much is contained in an iphone. Jesus tells us in the gospels that "Even the hairs on your head are numbered." And, "not even a sparrow falls to the earth without God's knowledge." Look at DNA and we see how miniscule everything can be. DNA is proof of the fact that in everything there is the whole.

Lesson 49 from *A Course in Miracles* says, "God's voice speaks to me all through the day." God's voice does speak to each of us every minute of every single day. WGOD is broadcasting a "program" we could follow if we want things to work out well. His plan is the best plan. We have freewill, the ego has its own plan and we are much more attentive to WEGO than we are to WGOD.

GPS—God's Plan for Salvation

A GPS system tells you where to go, "make a left," "make a right," mile by mile, sometimes even foot by foot. God has an amazing GPS system designed to direct us back home. Right now anyone on earth can pick up a cell phone and within seconds be talking with another person on the other side of the world with micro-waves sent through the air. God's got your number and guidance is being sent to each and every one of us every moment of every day. The Course tells us that for each of us the path is *highly individualized.* What I've got to go through to get back to God is different from the terrain you've got to travel.

What happens if we choose some diversion or some detour? You may think, "This guy is cute, I'll chase after him for awhile," or "I think I try materialism and see if I can make a lot of money." Or, perhaps "I'll get hooked on a drug." We have freewill and just like the prodigal sons and daughters that we are we can go off and try to do it our own way.

If we choose not to follow God's plan we will still get home. Taking detours, however, makes the trip longer and there are often rough places along the way, bumps in the road like divorces and bankruptcy. Rather than seeking the entrance to God's Kingdom, we can try building our own kingdoms. God's plan is all laid out and should we choose to follow it, we'll find that the path is fairly straight and smooth.

Enter in at the straight gate: for wide is the gate,
and broad is the way, that leads to destruction
and many there be which go there in.
Straight is the gate and narrow is the way,
which leads to life, and few there are that find it.
Matthew 7: 13-14

Few of us find the straight path and the narrow gate because we're busy stumbling down some diversion, some distraction, some habituated activity perhaps, or we're off trying to build our own world.

Recalculating

God's guidance system, remains operative at all times and it's persistent in its gentle guidance regardless of the detour we may have chosen. God's voice does speak to each and every one of us, every moment of every day. The question is: Are we paying attention to guidance?

If you're driving with a GPS system and you decide to turn off the prescribed route for lunch, perhaps, or for gas, the GPS system will start saying, "Recalculating—Recalculating." Every single moment of every single day each and every one of us are receiving direction from **G**od's **P**lan for **S**alvation. Should we chose to slip into denial, anger or projection, should we go off course, God's guidance system immediately recalculates the way back to the main road and thus home once again.

Hope is not the conviction that something will turn out well, but the certainty that something makes sense, regardless of how it turns out.

Vaclav Havel (1936 – Present), president of Czechoslovakia and opponent of communism.

Jesus was crucified, and it looks like a tragedy, yet there is a *purpose* in the event. So too, as we face our problems, we find the "purpose" for whatever we are experiencing, though we may not see it at the time. The more clearly we pursue the purpose we understand to be our unique function, the more our lives have meaning. Those who impeccably pursue their destinies are often the happiest people, though they may choose to remain single, turn down wealth or even be crucified.

Life is neither accidental nor arbitrary.
Don't push the river. Let destiny unfold.

Section IV — Being a Mystic

Chapter 14

Mysticism and the Senses

Rasa, Living Liquids, and Aesthetics

The branch of philosophy called *aesthetics* studies sensory values: judgments of sentiment and taste. It is the science of how things are known via the senses. Very early the Indian minds asked the question, what does a poem, drama, sculpture or painting address—man's intellect or his emotions? According to Indian aesthetics, a spectator witnesses a dramatic performance or work of art for the enjoyment of *rasa*. The word *rasa* is derived from the Sanskrit meaning "taste, essence, nectar of delight." Rasa is what occurs for us when we look at, or experience, art. While some mystics place emphasis on the intellect, or the mind, and some on the heart, others also emphasize the senses. This is true for example of Richard Rolle of Hampole.

Richard Rolle of Hampole (1300–1349, England) was a Bible translator, religious writer and hermit. He studied at Oxford and emphasized the physicality of religious experiences (feelings, colors, sounds, heat, etc.) Regarded as a saint after his death, he was never canonized.

What Does the Mystic See?

We often equate mysticism with seeing visions and hearing voices. The soul has many faculties. Hearing and seeing are primary. One may also, however, like Helen Keller, reach mystical vision (knowing) without seeing or hearing. There are no "unnatural" powers, and we each possess abilities of which we may be unaware. In the past 100 years, technology has opened us to an awareness of x-rays, gamma rays, infra-red rays, microwaves and more. No doubt greater vision welcomes us as we progress further into the twenty-first century.

Dr. John Lilly, author of *The Mind of the Dolphin*, spent much of his life studying interspecies communication, in particular the relationship between humans and dolphins. While the average human has a hearing range of .02 to 17 kHz, the range that dolphins hear best is 40 to 150 kHz, ten times that of the human ear. There is a whole world of sound we know nothing about because we have no way to hear it other than through sophisticated electronic technology. How much more exists that our sense cannot tell us about? The Course talks about Great Rays, which it describes as the extension of the light of God. These rays are of spirit and have nothing to do with the body; still they may be seen "without eyes."

In the holy instant, where the Great Rays replace the body in awareness, the recognition of relationships without limits is given you. But in order to see this, it is necessary to give up every use the ego has for the body, and to accept the fact that the ego has no purpose you would share with it.

A Course in Miracles

Communication is not limited to the small range of channels the world recognizes. God's voice is available to everyone, all the time. The question is, are you tuning in? There are senses beyond the five basic senses: the mystic's vision surpasses the body's eyes.

The fact that perception is involved at all in a vision removes the experience from the realm of true knowledge. True knowing extends into infinity. Visions, however holy, do not last. Perceptual images may also arise when we are appreciating nature, art or music and when we are meditating, quiet or just peaceful. The more we develop awareness, the more conscious we may also become of lights and auras, of intuitions and other forms of awareness that have nothing or little to do with the body's eyes. Archetypical images, as we sometimes encounter them in dreams, are among the first forms that appear out of Spirit. Indeed, visionary experiences often begin in dreams that become quite vivid. It's not unusual to have visionary encounters when the body is ill or very near death.

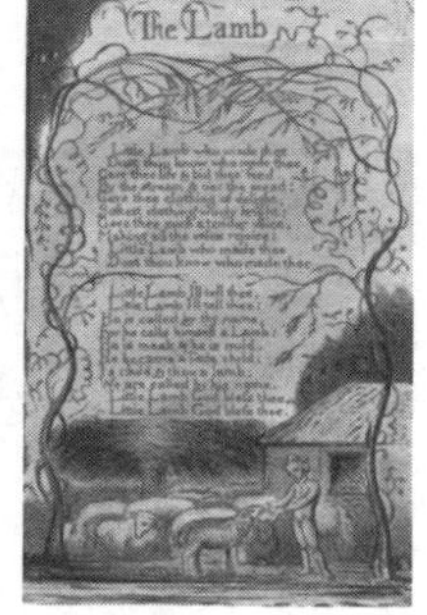

The Lamb
by William Blake

From a young age, William Blake claimed to see visions. At the age of nine he reported seeing a tree filled with angels "bespangling every bough like stars." On another occasion, as he watched haymakers at work, he thought he saw angelic figures walking among them. His wife Catherine recalled the time he saw God's head "put to the window." The vision, Catherine reminded her husband, "set you a screaming." Blake's visions were often associated with beautiful spiritual themes and imagery and therefore inspired him further with spiritual works and pursuits.

One of the best known visions that occurred with both seeing a light and hearing a voice, is found in the story of Saint Paul on the Road to Damascus. Paul, then Saul of Tarsus, was engaged in the persecution of Christians. No doubt his actions were weighing on him when he was blinded by a brilliant light and heard a voice saying, "Saul, Saul, why persecutest thou me?" Paul later regained his sight. Like many a convert, he then became a true believer in Christianity. His letters compose the major part of the New Testament.

When it comes to visions and voices, mysticism and madness occasionally mix. Hallucinations and distressful images sometimes come to people when they are ill, when they are fearful or after they have been fasting for a long time. St. Anthony was thus tempted by the devil in a vision. One of the qualities of a vision is that it seems quite real, even *more real* than what we might think of as *ordinary* reality. During her illness, Julian of Norwich saw the "horrible showing" of the devil, red with black freckles. It even clutched at her throat with its claws. St. Teresa said she likewise had visions of Satan, who left behind, she said, a smell of brimstone. Just as Dorothy got rid of the Wicked Witch of the West in *The Wizard of Oz*, St. Teresa got rid of Satan by dousing him with water. We see what we "can" see and what we've been trained to see.

Referring to such visions, or hallucinations, Evelyn Underhill says, "Visions can tend toward the psychopathic." They are also often incredibly cathartic. After an unpleasant vision, one feels better, as one does after throwing up. The ego itself is a hallucination which seems very real. The world too seems very real. Hallucination is not sanity. Sometimes hallucinations are fearful—more often, however, they are beautiful. The mystic's vision sees through the eyes of love. For this reason, the experience is one of blessedness and grace. Beautiful mystical visions bring calmness to those who have them. Such experiences have a life-enhancing quality.

On the whole, mysticism has nothing to do with visual sight or audible sound. Mostly it's a profound inner knowing and an awareness of the interconnectedness of all things—a sense that everything is perfect just the way it is. God, as a matter of fact, is in charge. Here is the description of a visionary experience by **Ramakrishna** (1836–1886, India):

The room with all its doors and windows, the temple and everything around me vanished from sight. I felt as if nothing existed, and in their stead I perceived a boundless ocean of intelligence. Whichever side I turned my eyes, I saw from all quarters huge waves of ocean rushing toward me, and in short falling upon me, engulfing me completely.

Thus getting suffocated under them, I lost my ordinary consciousness and fell down to the floor of the room, completely lost in the ecstasy of the vision. I was perfectly unconscious as to what had happened outside, and also how that day and the next had passed. The one thing which I was internally conscious of was my soul rolling in an ocean of ineffable joy, the like of which I had never experienced before. At the same time I was also conscious, to the inner core of my being, of the hallowed presence of the Divine Mother. (From Christopher Isherwood, *Ramakrishna and His Disciples*)

Voices

While visions may seem more dramatic than perceived sounds, mystical experiences are more frequently auditory, rather than visionary. Imagine that we are each two-way radios able to send and receive. Our tuners are set to WEGO, and WEGO is coming in loud and strong, although also a little statically, and not always with good news. It tells us of our guilt and reminds us of our fear. Busily listening to our own soap operas, we are not receptive to hearing. Our receivers are not tuned in to a "higher" frequency. The mystic is receptive, while the ego is projective. Which would we like to be? Which station do we want to hear? To hear the voice for God, we have to be quiet.

Each one of us is an outlet to God
and an inlet to God
Ernest Holmes

Ernest Holmes (1887–1960, USA) the founder of Religious Science, sometime called "Science of Mind," a part of the New Thought Movement is especially remembered for his book *The Science of Mind* and for *Science of Mind* magazine. He denied any "special revelation." He describes Science of Mind as "a" way, not "the" way. He was influenced by Emerson, Emma Curtis Hopkins, Phineas Quimby, and the texts of all the world's various religions.

Socrates (470–399 B.C., Greece) and his student Plato are thought of as the founders of Western philosophy. According to Socrates, the culmination of the philosophic path and the final vision of the form of the Good are arrived at from a mystical perspective. Socrates said he had a little spirit that whispered into his ear and told him what *not* to do. When he paid attention to this spirit, it always led him in the right direction.

Our task is to simply learn how to turn down the volume on WEGO so that WGOD can come through more clearly. It's not a matter of turning up the volume on WGOD. We don't know how to do that. What we can do is to turn down the volume on WEGO. The voice for God is *always* there, and it is *always* soothing, gentle, and compelling. Most of the time, listening to inner guidance does not involve anything as dramatic as hearing a voice that seems external to one's own being. The most common experiences of inner guidance are truly inner and intuitive. God's voice is always comforting and reassuring. The Holy Spirit is identified in the New Testament as the great Comforter, the Healer, the Teacher, and the Guide.

If we have ears to hear, God speaks to us in our own language, whatever that language is.
Mahatma Gandhi

Mahatma Gandhi (1869–1948, India) may be the best known of all mystics. Is there anyone who has not heard of the father of Indian spirituality and political leader in the Indian movement for independence, the pioneer of non-violent resistance? He was the inspiration for civil rights and freedom across the world. Spiritually, he led a life of simplicity, silence, chastity, and vegetarianism.

When we finally give up on the ego, it's not surprising that we can then hear the voice of God telling us something very simple, clear, and comforting. A man about to undergo an operation heard, "Fear not, I am always with you." A man who had just been fired and asked for help heard, "I just did help you." A woman whose husband was having a heart attack heard, "Patience, patience."

Sensory Deprivation is the primary form used by all of the world's various religious orders to enhance spiritual intuition and receptivity. Sensory deprivation involves closing the eyes and cutting off as much external stimulation as possible through erasing sound or learning not to be distracted by it. Dr. John Lilly invented the isolation tank—a lightless, soundproof tank in which subjects float in salty water at skin temperature. The idea is to remove as much external stimulation as possible in order to focus deeper within.

The wisdom of God is sought through stillness, prayer, contemplation, solitude, asceticism, and isolation. The experience of receiving inner guidance almost always comes when we are by ourselves. While a formal meditation practice is one of the best ways to access inner wisdom, there are also many informal opportunities we can access in the course of an ordinary day:

Messages Received

Martin Luther King, Jr., tells a story of once being terribly afraid. His life and those of his family had been threatened. One night when he could not sleep, he got up and sat at the kitchen table. He was considering calling off a civil rights march. In the middle of the night, in the darkness of his kitchen, he began to pray. He asked: *What am I supposed to do?* As with most prayers, he is asking a question, but he is also saying to God, "I want to see this situation the way You do." He then sat quietly in the dark, and there in the middle of the night, despite his terror, he heard a voice say, *"Do not to be afraid."* He got up from the table with a renewed sense of peace and went on with the march despite the threats that were converging upon him.

After I wrote an earlier book, *Listening to Your Inner Guide*, I led a number of workshops with the same title as the book. During the workshops, I asked people to tell me things they had heard, not just intuitively, but things they thought they had actually heard, as though they were hearing an external voice. It is not necessary to perceive the voice as being physically audible. Sometimes, however, we need to hear so badly, it seems that way.

When folks first begin to hear messages, they usually receive simple phrases and sentences that are very comforting. Often a voice speaks in the first person. Here are some examples of what various people told me they have heard.

- *I am the source.*
- *I am the antidote.*
- *I've been waiting for you.*
- *I will tell you when you are ready.*
- *I will always love you.*
- *I have always loved you.*

Sometimes people hear voices that give them specific information or inspiration, such as the following:

- *You are never alone.*
- *You can do it.*
- *You just need to be.*
- *You need do nothing.*
- *You are on the right track.*
- *You are my beloved daughter in whom I am well pleased.*
- *You never did anything wrong.*
- *You will never smoke again.*
- *You are not a bad person.*

- *You are strong*

Other messages include:

- *There is another way to look at this.*
- *This need not be. It doesn't matter.*
- *Trust me!*
- *It takes time to be healed.*
- *It's time for you to go.*
- *There will always be enough.*
- *Everything is going to be okay.*

Sometimes people hear very direct instructions:

- *Sit down and write.*
- *Divorce your mother.*
- *Look to the light. Teach only love.*
- *Turn on the computer—and it will come.*
- *Go for a walk.*
- *Don't hide. Don't panic.*

What is heard may have a psychic quality, forecasting how the hearer might be helpful to others in a way he or she could not know rationally. One woman heard, *"Step up to the window,"* where she saw someone in need. A nurse driving home heard, *"Get off here and go home the other way,"* where she passed an auto accident in which her friend was hurt.

Sometimes the Answer is "No"

A "no" answer to a prayer or request for guidance never comes with a negative intent. Remember also that you ask for this answer, else you would not have received it. "No" simply means—"Don't go this way. If you do, you are bound to delay your progress." "Do not attack someone." "Don't make a judgment here." "Don't spend the money." "Don't ask for a second helping." "Don't drink too much." "Don't talk too much." We have free will. We can act contrary to our inner guidance. We are always at choice. Which voice do we wish to hear—the voice for the ego or the voice for God? The answer is clear, and we know what it is.

Deeper guidance comes after these simple, initial declaratives. The voice sounds like your own—because it is your own. It is also the voice we share. Many mystics from St. Teresa of Avila to Emanuel Swedenborg, to Edgar Casey, to Helen Schucman received a direct form of ongoing inner communication. Such revelation usually begins in short sentences and aphorisms. My dear friend Dr. Robert Weltman hears a form of esoteric poetry.

In a Flash

Revelation sometimes comes all at once. Saint Teresa of Avila and Saint Hildegard of Bingen both received inspirations in a flash. Suddenly they knew all they needed to know. After that, it was just a matter of putting it down on paper. They didn't have to think about what to say. This information transcended their own knowledge and proved helpful to thousands, even millions, of others. Sometimes when I'm writing or talking, I won't be doing it with conscious forethought. The words come without thinking. These are the most wonderful moments; whenever I'm speaking thus I notice everyone is paying attention. Then true communication occurs.

Extroverted and Introverted Mysticism

Mystical researcher W.T. Stace says there are two kinds of mysticism: extroverted and introverted. The introverted experience is received by direct insight or inspiration without stimulation from the outside world. The path of meditation involves introverted experience. An extroverted experience is more sensory, intellectual, and emotional. It looks out from, or "feels through," the material world to a perception of spiritual reality behind the physical. Stace identifies an extroverted mystic as someone like Walt Whitman, who *deliberately* looks through the physical senses into the external world and finds the One there. Mystics perceive the same world of trees and hills and cities that anyone else does. Mystics, however, see things in such a way that their innate unity shines through. This unified vision often occurs in nature. It can happen, for example, when we look into the face of our beloved or an animal companion. It can happen all the time.

Walt Whitman (1819–1892, USA), was a transcendentalist, a contemporary of Mark Twain, and a friend of Ralph Waldo Emerson, Henry David Thoreau, and Richard Maurice Bucke. He was one of the most colorful and controversial characters of the nineteenth century. He wanted to live life fully—*out-loud*—to enjoy every moment of it. The world of his poetry is devoid of any religion as conventionally understood. Many people of his own day saw him as an affront to Victorian values. (See on DVD, *Beautiful Dreamer* the story of the relationship between Whitman and Richard Maurice Bucke.)

Mysticism, Nature and Sacred Places

The goal of life is to make your heartbeat
match the beat of the universe,
to match your nature with Nature.
Joseph Campbell

The third major stimulant for mystic awareness according to Sir Alister Hardy's study, is nature, and the tenth is sacred places. Our farm in Missouri during the 1940s and 1950s was for me a place of sanctuary and inspiration. There was one site on the back of our farm I called my "Heavenly Spot." I went there whenever I had a little free time—to think, to be quiet. I would take my horse Flicker bareback out to the field, have him stop, and then I'd lie backward over his broad hindquarters and look straight up into the blue sky—trying to see how far I could see. (Try lying down quietly on the flat earth in an open space and look straight up. You'll see what I mean.) Many years later, mother told me this spot was where she too went when she needed to be alone.

While *any place* can be inspirational, *no place* contains "magical" power. *Any place* might be a breathtaking space of inspiration, even our own bedrooms. Mountains, rivers, lakes, and streams; our homes, cemeteries, churches, monasteries, mosques, and temples have "meaning" in our minds. What we bring to the experience matters more than the place itself does. The farm I grew up on and the one room country schoolhouse I went to as a child are sacred to me, while to another they are just old buildings.

If we could see the miracle of a single flower
clearly, our whole life would change.
The Buddha

Even the most primitive of men, standing looking at a waterfall, a vast expanse of valleys or mountains or flowers in the spring must have felt some sense of connectedness, awe, and wonder at what he saw in front of him.

We have not the reverent feeling for the rainbow
that the savage has, because we know how it is made.
We have lost as much as we gained
by prying into that matter.
Mark Twain in *Tramp Abroad*

The mystic is an observer. Being receptive, mystics are sensitive to everything—another face, a flower, even a parking lot lined with trees.

The experience of being one with nature
in which everything hangs together
is the oldest form of mysticism.
Bruno Borchert

The introverted mystic is receptive. The extroverted mystic is participatory. Either way is fine. Although being participatory "seems" to have an added dimension to it, both ways of *looking* have their own depth. When it comes to being inspired by and appreciating nature, we might observe it as a sightseer. Or, we might participate in nature as does an outdoorsman, gardener or farmer.

The tree that moves some to tears of joy is in the eyes
of others a green thing which stands in the way.
William Blake

When it comes to the realm of the musical, we can either listen to or perform music. Music is a different experience for someone who reads music, plays the notes, and knows the various cords than it is for someone who *just* listens. Whether we participate passively through listening or actively through performing, music can lead to a sense of oneness and wonder.

I have no other masters
than the beeches and the oaks.
Bernard of Clairvaux

Bernard of Clairvaux (1090–1153, France) said that whatever he knew about divine things and Holy Scriptures he learned in woods and fields. For him, nature is the book written by God but not to be confused with God. It is not pantheism.

I, the fiery life of divine essence, am aflame beyond
the beauty of the meadows, I gleam in the waters,
and I burn in the sun, moon, and stars.
I awaken everything to life.
Hildegard of Bingen

Saint Hildegard of Bingen, (1098–1179, Germany) was born into a family of nobles who sent her as a tithe to the church. She was put in the care of Jutta, a Mother Superior. On the death of Jutta, Hildegard became the Mother Superior of the community. She was subject to receiving visions and felt commanded by God to *"Write what you see."* Her best known work is "Order of the Virtues," an oratory for male and female voices. She was canonized, not by the church but by the people who started calling her St. Hildegard. Her contemporary in Italy, St. Francis of Assisi, was also called saint by his own contemporaries.

Glance at the sun. See the moon and stars.
Gaze at the beauty of the green earth. Now Think!
Hildegard of Bingen

Nature mysticism is an expansion of awareness triggered by the natural world. In the changing of the seasons, the rise and fall of ocean waves, and the ceaseless changes of wind and weather, there is constant movement and beauty. Hindus celebrate Shiva, as the destroyer (enabling change), Vishnu, as the preserver (of life), and Brahma as the creator. The *Upanishads* contains our oldest account of nature mysticism, describing an innate order in all things including the innocence of sexuality. Taoism and Shinto are both nature based religions.

Lift up the stone and I am there.
Split wood and I am there.
The Gospel of St. Thomas

St. Francis of Assisi is known for his deep love of nature in its entirety. It is said that he even cherished the lice in his hair and clothes as "heavenly pearls." The following is from St. Francis of Assisi's *Song of the Sun*:

Glory to you, my Lord, for all your creatures. Especially our brother, the sun who is the day, and by whom you give us light: He is beautiful and radiant with great splendor and bears witness to you, most high One. Glory to you, my Lord, for sister moon and the stars You have made in heaven clear, precious, and beautiful and all the different weathers by which you sustain all creatures. Glory to you, my Lord, sister water who is very useful and humble and precious and pure. Glory to you, my Lord, for brother fire by whom you illumine night and he is beautiful and joyful and robust and full of power. Glory to you, my Lord for sister mother earth who sustains and governs us and produces different fruits and brightly colored flower and grass.

Nature mysticism brings with it a sense of the unity of all and a cosmological understanding of how things fits together—as seen in poetry by Rumi and Wallace Black Elk. Rumi captures the cosmological connection with the universe and all of life in the following poem:

I am the dust in the sun light; I am the ball of the sun. To the dust I say: Remain. And to the sun: Roll on. I am the mist of the morning. I am the breath of evening. I am the rustling of the grove, the singing of the sea. I am the mast, the rudder, the steersman and the ship. I am the coral reef on which it founders. I am the tree of life and the parrot in the branches. Silence, thought, tongue and voice; I am the breath of the flute, the spirit of man, I am the spark in the stone, the gleam of gold in the metal, the candle and the moth fluttering round it, the rose and the nightingale drunk with its fragrance. I am the chain of being, the circle of the spheres, the scale of creation, the rising and the fall. I am what is and is not. I am—O you who know, Jalaluddi, O say it! I am the soul in all!

Wallace Black Elk (1921–2004, USA) was a Lakota Elder and mystic whose visionary experiences were recounted in the book *Black Elk Speaks*. Raised on the Rosebud Reservation in South Dakota, he was one of the original spiritual advisors to the American Indian Movement. He was present at the occupation of Wounded Knee in 1973, was instrumental in the passage of the American Indian Religious Freedom Act in 1978, and served as the Native American Representative to the United Nations.

You are part of everything!
You are part of the fire, you are part of the water, you are part of the green, you are part of the stars, and you are related to everything.
You are related to the stones, to the trees, to the fish, to the creepy-crawlers, to the ones that fly, to the ones that walk on all fours, and to the ones that walk on two legs. Everything is sacred and, therefore, you are sacred too. That's what we mean when we say, Mitakuye oyasin.
Wallace Black Elk, Lakota Spiritual Elder

All blades of grass, wood and stone,
all things are One.
Meister Eckhart

In this light my spirit suddenly saw through all,
and in all by all, the creatures:
even in herbs and grass knew God.
Jakob Boehme

Mystics speak of the mysterious vitality of primeval forests, and the regular cycles of life. Take a walk through the ancient Sequoia tress and experience their silent enchantment. Tennyson's "flower in the crannied wall," Blake's "world in a grain of sand," and Vaughan's "Each bush and oak doeth know I AM" are each reports of mystical visions. In nature we can make contact with the "great Life of All" and through its rhythms sense the timeless truth of "all that is, and was, and evermore shall be."

Jacob Boehme

Jacob Boehme, (1575–1624, Germany) worked as a shoemaker. He experienced a religious epiphany in 1600 when a ray of sunlight reflecting in a pewter dish catapulted him into an ecstatic vision of God as penetrating all existence. His thought drew on the teachings of Paracelsus, the Kabbalah, and alchemy. His first work, *Aurora*, brought him a following. The Church tried to silence Boehme, but he continued writing in secrecy. He was then banished from his own house. His writings influenced Hegel, Schopenhauer, Nietzsche, Bergson, Heidegger, Paul Tillich, Martin Buber, and Carl Jung.

God had done me a singular favor in that in the winter, seeing a tree stripped of its leaves, and considering that within a little time the leaves would be renewed, and after that the flower and fruit appear,

I received a high view of the Providence
and Power of God which never left my soul.
Brother Lawrence

One of the finest descriptions of nature mysticism is that of the Cambridge Platonist John Smith (1618–1652, England).

God made the universe and all the creatures contained therein as so many glasses where in He might reflect His own glory. He copies Himself in the creation and in this world; we may read the lovely characters of the divinity: goodness, power, and wisdom. Divine wisdom and goodness shine out in different degrees upon several creatures, till they sweetly repose themselves in the bosom of the divine. True religion never finds itself outside of the sphere of the Divine.

For Immanuel Kant, two things fill the mind with ever-increasing awe: the starry heaven above and the moral order within. These combined provide a basis for the apprehension of the Divine. Likewise, Thoreau's *Walden* pulls at the heartstrings of every nature mystic: "I am a mystic, a transcendentalist and a natural philosopher to boot," wrote Thoreau. Thoreau withdrew from work, from incessant labor and the machine-like nature of the world. He went alone into the woods. There he could spend an entire morning sitting in his doorway just looking and *seeing*—finding himself and his spirit. He developed a nondominating, mystical relationship to the woods and animals, to light and water and air and ice. Sitting alone beside Walden Pond, he discovered in the calm, clear lake a depth he could not find in "polite" society.

I went to the woods because
I wished to live deliberately, to confront the
essential facts of life and see if I could learn
what it had to teach, and not, when I come to die,
discover that I have not lived.
Henry David Thoreau, *Walden*

Thoreau's cabin at Walden Pond

Gerard Manley Hopkins (1844–1889, England), a Victorian poet, Jesuit priest, and scholar, developed the idea of "inscape," or unique essence, of natural objects. Similar to the way we now talk about the "inner universe," each thing is unique and different from every other thing, yet a "force of being" holds things together. This truth is known by the mystic. Hopkins has written some of the greatest poems of both faith and doubt in the English language. Spirit is, he says, *"a falcon hovering in the wind, the harvest under the silk-sack clouds, the dare-gale skylark, the moonrise, the starlit night with its circle-citadels, the very air we breathe all speak of God."*

Some keep the Sabbath going to Church,
I keep it staying at Home—
With a bobolink for a Chorister,
And an Orchard, for a Dome.
Emily Dickinson

Richard Jeffries (1848–1887, England) was a farm boy and nature mystic. He was a contemporary of Walt Whitman and, like Whitman, was a journalist. Jeffries wrote a delightful little book titled *The Story of My Heart* published in 1883. The following is an excerpt:

There came to me a delicate, but at the same time a deep, strong and sensuous enjoyment of the beautiful green earth, the beautiful sky and sun; I felt them, they gave me inexpressible delight, as if they embraced and poured out their love upon me. It was I who loved them, for my heart was broader than the earth; it is broader now than even then, more thirsty and desirous. After the sensuous enjoyment always come the thought, the desire: that I might be like this; that I might have the inner meaning of the sun, the light, the earth, the trees and grass, translated into some growth of excellence in myself, both of the body and of mind; greater perfection of physique, greater perfection of mind and soul; that I might be higher in myself.

For esoteric philosopher **Rudolf Steiner** (1861–1925, Austria) nature was a "Mode of the Infinite." Steiner said that when it came to developing a love for the mystical, a person was especially fortunate to have grown up surrounded by nature. He describes his own childhood in Austria thusly:

The scenes amidst which I passed my childhood were marvelous. The bald rock face of the Schneeberg caught the sun's rays, which when they were projected on the little station on the fine summer days, were the first intimation of the dawn. The gray ridge of Wechsel's mountain made a somber contrast. The green prospects which welcomed the observer on every side made it seem as if the mountains were thrusting up-

wards of their own volition. The majestic peaks filled the distance, the charm of nature lay all round.

The following description of nature mysticism from **Forrest Reid** (1875–1948, England) contains a strong oceanic quality. He was a novelist, author of boy's books, literary critic, and translator.

It was as if I had never realized how lovely the world was. I lay down on my back in the warm, dry moss and listened to the skylark singing as it mounted up from the fields near the sea into the dark clear sky. No other music gave me the same pleasure as that passionate joyous singing. It was a leaping, exultant ecstasy, a bright, flame-like wound, rejoicing in itself. And then a curious experience befell me. It was as if everything that had seemed to be external and around me were suddenly within me. The whole world seemed to be within me. It was within me that the trees waved their green branches, it was within me that the skylark was singing, it was within me that the hot sun shone, and that the shade was cool. A cloud rose in the sky and passed in a light shower that pattered on the leaves, and I felt its freshness dropping into my soul, and I felt in all my being the delicious fragrance of the earth and the grass and the plants and the rich brown soil. I could have sobbed for joy.

The following is mystical researcher Rudolf Otto's description of nature mysticism:

The sense of being immersed in the oneness of nature, so that man feels all the individuality, all the peculiarity of natural things in himself. He dances with the motes of dust and radiates with the sun; he rises with the dawn; he surges with the wave.

Although J.G. Krishnamurti is not generally thought of as a nature mystic, there is a strong sense of earth-based mysticism in the following from his work *The Only Revolution.*

The sun wasn't up yet; you could see the morning star through the trees. There was a silence that was really extraordinary. Not the silence between two noises or between two notes, but the silence that has no reason whatsoever, the silence that must have been at the beginning of the world. It filled the whole valley and the hills. The two big owls, calling to each other, never disturbed that silence, and a distant dog barking at the late moon was part of this immensity. The dew was especially heavy, and as the sun came up over the hill it was sparkling with many colors and with the glow that comes with the sun's first rays.

Our ordinary human consciousness can at times be experienced as a kind of curse, a trap, a prison from which one can find no freedom, yet freedom is found paradoxically in our connections with each other and with nature.

A human being is a part of a whole, called by us
universe, a part limited in time and space.
He experiences himself, his thoughts and feelings as
something separated from the rest...
a kind of optical delusion of his consciousness.
This delusion is a kind of prison for us, restricting us
to our personal desires and to affection for a few
persons nearest to us. Our task must be to free
ourselves from this prison by widening our circle of
compassion to embrace all living creatures
and the whole of nature in its beauty.
Albert Einstein

What Makes a Place Sacred?

Sacred sites are the most loved and visited places on our planet. The oldest places draw the greatest attention. Since prehistoric times, spiritual folk have made pilgrimages to sites like Stonehenge in Britain and the pyramids in Egypt. Some places, Lourdes in France, for example, are believed to heal the body. They are places that stimulate enlightenment of the mind and awaken the soul. On January 27, 1799, when French soldiers under the dispatch of Napoleon came for the first time upon the great temple of Karnak in Egypt, without being given an order to do so, they stopped, formed rank and with the accompaniment of fife and drums, presented arms. What made them stop and offer their respect?

The mind is its own place,
and it can make
a hell out of heaven or
a heaven out of hell
John Milton in *Paradise Lost*

John Milton (1608–1674, England), one of the greatest poets of the English language, is best known for his epic poem *Paradise Lost.* His powerful prose and the eloquence of his poetry had an immense influence on eighteenth-century verse. He was a strong defender of freedom of thought and religious rights.

For Hindus, the ancient Ganges is a sacred river. It is the place where people come to die, to turn their lives back over to God. For the native people of Australia, Ayers rock, (Uluru to the Aborigines), the world's largest sandstone monolith, is a place of eternity. For Buddhists, the Bodhi tree in Bodhi Gaya, located in a temple complex, is said to be a descendant of the Bodhi (ficus religiosa) tree under which Buddha reached enlightenment. Why go off to look at the Grand Canyon, the Galapagos Islands, the Great Barrier Reef, the Harbor of Rio de Janerio, Mount

Everest, or Victoria Falls or any other of the majestic and moving sites to be found in this world? Dolores and I love to go out each fall to look at leaves turning color. It's one constant "Oh!" "Ah!" and "Look at that, Honey!"

The Center of the World

For the ancient Greeks, Delphi, the home of the ancient oracle, was sacred. Here the oracle sat on an elevated tripod chair above a fissure in the earth where, scientists now believe, ethylene gases escaped inducing a hypnotic-like trance. From this position above the fissure, the oracle answered questions. Delphi was revered throughout the Greek world as the site of the *omphalos* stone, (which looks like a gigantic phallus). This site was thought to be the center not only of the earth but the whole universe. In like manner, for the Incas, the city of Tiwanacu (constructed from 500-900 on the shore of Lake Titicaca in what is now Bolivia) is thought to be the birthplace of mankind. Similarly, according to the Shinto religion, Japan is the center of the world. Famous as a national symbol, Mount Fuji is perhaps one the most perfect volcano cones in existence and it is the highest peak in Japan.

The Pueblo and Hopi Indians of the Southwest U.S. have their *Kivas*, a round (or sometimes square) shaped underground room used for religious rituals. Here, the Indians re-enact the cycle of what Mircea Eliade called "the eternal return." The Kiva is entered from a hole in the ceiling; inside there is a fire pit and ventilation shaft. The kiva is a place were people return to their origins, pass on ancient knowledge, and perform rites of passage. In such places, people sing, dance, meditate, pray, and listen to the stories of their shamans and elders.

The Pilgrimage

For many folks, a pilgrimage to one of these holy spots is both an inner and outer spiritual journey. So it is for Muslims who at least once in their lives (if possible) must make the *hajji* (sacred pilgrimage) to the Kaaba and the holy black stone (an ancient meteorite) in Mecca. For many Christians, a pilgrimage is made to Jerusalem, the Vatican in Rome, or perhaps one of the great Cathedrals, like Notre Dame or Santiago de Compostela in Spain.

More than 500,000 people per year visit the temples of Angkor Wat, built between 800 and 1220. They are among humankind's most astonishing architectural achievements. Originally built in honor of Vishnu and then taken over by the Buddhists, it is now sacred to both faiths. Lhasa, the home of the Palace of the Dalai Lama, is a sacred place to Tibetan Buddhists. The palace is a magnificent 13-story, 1,000 room multiplex built in the seventeenth century on a structure dating back to the seventh century. While Lhasa is forever sacred to the Tibetans as the home of the Dalai Lama, it is safe to say that, if the Dalai Lama had not been driven out of his home, he would not have had the broad calming influence he has in this world today.

Perhaps sacred space to you is a more personal holy trek you make to the grave of your ancestors and other loved ones, or perhaps to the home in which you were born. I try to make a pilgrimage each year to the farm in Missouri, to my "Heavenly Spot" if possible, to the grave of my parents, grandparents, great-grandparents, and great-aunts and uncles. Their graves are out in the country on the open plain near a wonderful little one room country church.

Mysticism and Music

Music alone shares with
great mystical literature
the power of waking in
us a response to
the life-movement
of the universe.
Evelyn Underhill

Great music moves us because it is the wordless language of God, a message from the Beloved that awakens love within us. Music makes us dance, spurring an instinctive ritual that brings the body into a celebration of the divine. Music is a mystical form of breathing that reminds us of the original rhythm of creation itself.

There is geometry in the humming of the strings...
there is music in the harmony of the spheres.
Pythagoras

Pythagoras (569–475 B.C., Greece) was the first to realize that music is mathematical. He taught that the beating of the heart and the inhaling and exhaling of the breath are the basis of musical rhythm. There is, he said, a sound both without and within that is music.

People who excel in math often excel in music. Math can be written as music and music, as math. Because of the work of Pythagoras, we can talk about half, quarter or full notes. For the mystic, the true purpose of music is to inspire us to become musical in our thoughts, words, and deeds.

Beauty addresses itself chiefly to sight.
There is a beauty for the hearing too, as in certain
combination of words and in all kinds of music, for
melodies and cadences are beautiful and minds that
lift themselves above the realm of sense to a higher
order are aware of beauty in the conduct of life...
Plotinus

Music is the most sacred of the arts. Its multi-toned sacredness can be heard in the beautiful Kyoto music of Japan, the ringing of Tibetan bells, the Gregorian chant of Christian monks, the gospel music of rural America or the beating of a shaman's drum. St. John of the Cross, sensing the "unheard melodies" of the spheres, loved to spend time under the starry sky experiencing the "silent music, and the euphonic solitude."

Song is in a plenteous soul, the sweetness of eternal love and thought into song is turned, and the mind into full sweet sound is changed.

Richard Rolle

Music aids in the unfolding of the mystic's soul and the opening of intuitive faculties. I once surprised myself by bursting into tears while listening to Chopin's Polonaise. Music lovers can tell of many such experiences. Music charges us with enthusiasm and passion, inducing a form of rapture. The following is a description of such rapture in the classic *Samuel Pepys' Diary* from 1664:

The 27th.—Up and then with my wife and Deb to the king's house to see Virgin Martyr. That which did please me beyond everything in the whole world was the wind music when the angel comes down, which is so sweet that it ravished me and indeed in a word did wrap up my soul so that it did make me really sick just as I have formerly been when I fell in love with my wife. Neither then nor all the evening going home and at home was I able to think of anything remaining all night transported so that I could not believe that ever any music hath that real command over the soul of a man as this did upon me.

Mysticism in Groups

While mystical awareness almost always comes upon us when we are alone, mystical experience may also occur when we are with other people, as in church, for example. When this happens, however, it usually is not spoken of until after the experience has passed. *Participation in worship* is the 4th way of coming to a mystical experience, according to Sir Alister Hardy. The 5th way of arriving at a mystical awareness is from *an experience of literature, dramas or films*; the 7th way is from *listening to music*; the 10th way is from *visiting sacred places*, and the 11th way is from *viewing visual arts*. We may or may not be alone in any of these experiences.

A fellow once told me that he played in a symphony orchestra. Something wonderful happens, he said, when you are playing in an orchestra and all the musicians are in tune and on note. No one speaks. Everyone is literally in harmony, and everything is working perfectly. The audience knows it is perfect. The conductor knows it is perfect. The musicians know it is perfect. There can occur at that time an experience he described as electrifying and beyond ordinary human perception—a merging and coming together of awareness. Then, he said, you get wonderful, spontaneous standing ovations. This truly is an experience resulting from *the philharmonic* (the love of music).

A dance troupe leader told me of an experience that occurred when three musical elements were working together in perfect harmony: an orchestra, a chorus, and a dance troupe of which she was a part. The music was perfect, and the dancers were all "on point." When the performance ended, the dancers froze together for a moment looking away from the audience, and the leader of the troupe whispered so only the members of the dance troupe could hear her, "Did you feel that?"

To sing once is to pray twice.

St. Augustine

In a similar fashion, people sometimes have mystical experiences while singing together, perhaps in a choir or as a congregation in a church or while doing chanting in a very long kirtan (ecstatic devotional music of India). The singing of the sacred hymns set to music is one of the pillars of Hinduism and Sikhism. The Sikhs place tremendous value on this type of singing, and a Sikh is duty bound to listen and/or sing Guru-Kirtan as frequently as possible.

God respects me when I work;
but God loves me when I sing.

Rabindranath Tagore

Rabindranath Tagore (1861–1941, Bengal) a poet, philosopher, artist, and composer was Asia's first Nobel Laureate, winning the Prize in 1913. Humanity and the divine are, he said, engaged in a creative process—which is giving birth to goodness in the world. Goodness is possible only when humans work together *with* divinity.

Mysticism and Art

Painting as well as music and poetry exists and exults in immortal thoughts.

William Blake

The topic of art and mysticism is so expansive that I can neither do justice to it nor ignore it. Art is often connected to spiritual transformation. Great art and architecture have the power to transcend and transform the physical. Great art can grab our attention, make us stare, and sometimes even leave us awestruck. As music conveys the sound of the ineffable, art is a "language" that seeks to make visible what the mystic "sees." According to **Marsilio Ficino** (1433–1499, Italy), a famous alchemist mystic, art provokes the human soul's ascension to higher levels of beauty. Artistic creation plays a role in enlightenment for both the artist and the observer. During artistic creation, a dance takes place between creator, creation, and created. Then separation between the artist and the work of art falls away—the two are united as one—the actor becomes the character, the artist the art, and the seeker that which is found.

Art enables us to find ourselves
and lose ourselves at the same time.
Thomas Merton

For many artists, like many mystics, life is spent in isolation, devotion, and reflection. Some of the highest and most inspired mystical moments occur when we are absorbed in creation. Something seems to take over, and there is a forgetting of self and a merging with the object of creation. Many impressionists and abstract artists of the late nineteenth and early twentieth centuries were mystics—their work a bond between aesthetics and mysticism. Art gives us answers. From the perspective of "positive mysticism," nature is a mystery to be looked at and penetrated. The artist as mystic enters nature so that the inner structure of reality—its beauty—is revealed. Beauty is hiding in every form. We know it's in the snow flake (every one really is different). We know there is beauty too in micro-biology and the beating of the human heart. The artist and mystic simply draw it out.

Symbolic, surrealistic, and visionary artists often engage in a spiritual pursuit while also seeking though their art to transcend the world by opening themselves to a wider vision. Surrealism as an artistic movement began in the 1920s. In his *Surrealist Manifesto* of 1924, Andre Breton defined *surrealism* as "pure psychic automatism." Surrealistic art often features the qualities of amazement and revelation.

The French painter **Eugene Delecroix** (1798–1863, France) described contemplation as "a condition of indifference, liberty, and peace, an elevation above the world, a sense of beatitude where the subject ceases to perceive oneself in the multiplicity so that a deeper and purer soul substitutes itself for the normal self." In this state, consciousness of "I" and consciousness of the world of form disappear.

Claude Monet (1840–1926, France), the master of impressionism, was a true nature mystic. On his eightieth birthday when a photographer came to take his picture, Monet said, "Come back next spring and take a picture of my flowers in the garden. They look more like me than I do."

Vincent van Gogh's (1853–1890, the Netherlands) mysticism verged upon madness. In his younger years, van Gogh was a preacher like his father, Theodorus, and wanted to devote his life to the deepest truth. He did not, however, find it in church. Instead, he found God in trees, cornfields, and flowers. Many of his paintings are said to be sermons. When we look at one of Van Gogh's works, we are viewing the essence of Vincent, for there is a total union between art and artist. Van Gogh's madness increased his intensity, while his addiction to color made his paintings come vibrantly alive. You can feel the life force flowering in his work. He was a clear visionary.

Marc Chagall (1887–1985, Russia), like Blake, is inspired by love and the joy of life. He often used Biblical themes portrayed with curved, sinuous figures. Although his own life as a Russian-born Jew was difficult, his work with its highly vivid colors, nevertheless communicates happiness and optimism. Chagall once painted himself (together with his wife) as a mystic observing the world as if through a stained-glass window.

Fantastic Realism

Ernst Fuchs (1930 – Present, Austria), one of the best examples of Fantastic Realism in art, is also a visionary artist, architect, sculptor, poet, printmaker, and one of the founders of the Vienna School of Fantastic Realism. The paintings of the Fantastic Realism School often combined religious and esoteric symbolism. A student of the sermons of Meister Eckhart, he also studied the symbolism of the alchemists and read Jung's *Psychology of Alchemy.*

Psychedelic Art

Sometimes, as in the case of **Alex Grey** (1953 – Present, USA), inspiration is drawn from psychedelic experiences. *Psychedelic* means "mind manifesting." Grey is best known for his vivid paintings that "X-ray" multiple dimensions of reality, interweaving physical, psychic, and spiritual energies. He believes that mystically inspired art can arouse its viewers to transcend materialism and lead to an awareness of authentic spiritual reality. For Grey, artistic creation enables the transcending of the mind and opens viewers to a fuller expression of spirit. Alex and Allyson Grey are the co-founders of the Chapel of Sacred Mirrors, a not for profit institution supporting Visionary Culture in New York City. (Go to www.alexgrey.com.)

Whether through art, music, poetry or dance, mystics inevitably seek to express what they see and know. Thus it is that God is found in all the senses, in the intellect, in the heart, in love, in union—in every way known to man and many ways revealed only to the mystic, yet available for everyone who can open more fully to the divine.

Mysticism, the Mind, Paradox, and Poetry

Devise No Words—Ineffability

A lot can be said about what cannot be said.

What can't be said can't be said.
It can't be whistled either.
Ram Dass

Apophatic Mysticism

Apophatic mysticism comes from the Greek, *apophasis*, meaning negation. According to apophatic mysticism, it is easier to say what God is not, than, what God is. For example, God is not angry, jealous, hateful or hurtful. Similarly, almost nothing can be said of mystical experiences because they are absolutely indescribable, unutterable—or *ineffable*. Evelyn Underhill says ineffability is the foremost characteristic of mysticism, and all other researchers in this field mention ineffability. Perhaps the first thing we can say about mystical experiences is that nothing can be said—words are inadequate. Zen Buddhism speaks of the Satori experience as a *"wordless realization."* While such topics as God and the mystical experience cannot be captured by words, we have music, art, nature, emotions, physical sensations and intuition—all of which can provide intimations of God and the mystical. Words are, however, the primary tools we have to work with in this world, so we do the best job we can with what we have.

An example of apophatic mysticism is seen in the classical Tao text *Tao Te Ching*, which begins with the words, *"Even the finest teaching is not the Tao itself. Even the finest name is insufficient to define it. Without words, the Tao can be experienced, and without a name, it can be known."* Apophatic mysticism calls for an emptying out of our neurotic thinking in order to make room for the apprehension of God.

Words are a distraction
to enlightenment. Getting rid of
conceptual thinking means enlightenment.
Ramesh Balsekar

The word *mystic* is related to the word *mute*; both are derived from the Greek root *mustes*, meaning "close-mouthed." Thoughts and words automatically create distinctions and, thus, duality. The act of naming something creates duality as it distinguishes the thing named from other things. The deep dysfunction of our minds takes the form of a separation between "me" and others.

Nothing but duality enters speech's playing-field.
Rumi

Words and sentences are produced by the law of
causation and are mutually conditioning.
They cannot express highest Reality.
The Lankavatara Sutra (Buddhist)

That One which is beyond all thought is
inconceivable by all thought.
Dionysius the Areopagite (Christian)

Pseudo-Dionysius the Areopagite (anonymous theologian and philosopher, late 5th to early 6th century, Greece), also known as *pseudo-Denys*, is an anonymous mystic of the fifth century. His body of works shows strong Neo-platonic influence. He uses Plotinus' well known analogy of a sculptor cutting away that which does not enhance the desired image in order to get to the true identity buried beneath the surface.

He is the spirit of the cosmos, its hearing,
its sight, and its hand. Through Him the cosmos
hears, through Him it sees, through Him it speaks,
through Him it grasps, through Him it runs.
Ibn Arabi (Muslim)

Mind comes from this sublime and completely
unified source above; it is divided only as it enters
into the universe of distinctions.
Menahem Nahum (Jewish)

Define Love. Define God. You can't do it. You can try. You may write beautiful poetry, but that's not it. Socrates said that while he could not show us what the "good" is, he might be able to show us what "a child of the good" looks like; so we might then have some idea about what the parent—the thing itself—"looks like." Still, the picture is not the thing.

After my 1976 experience, I was completely dumbfounded. I could not talk because I realized that anything I said would be a "construct." It would be an attempt to try to put into words something that did not fit into words. I sat for two hours just looking at my right hand. I could hardly believe that I had reintegrated myself back into this old and familiar body. I had actually stopped talking to myself—all I could do was sit in awe and wonder. Even when I did start talking again, my words were such a poor attempt to describe what had happened.

The here-and-now mountain is a tiny piece of a
piece of straw blown off into emptiness.
These words I'm saying so much begin to lose
meaning: Existence, emptiness, mountain, straw:
Words and what they try to say swept out
the window down the slant of the roof.
Rumi

St. Thomas Aquinas (1225–1275, Italy) is a father of the Catholic Church and the greatest of the medieval scholastics. Six months before he died, he had a profound mystical vision—after which he said all of his writings were just so much "straw." The Catholic Church is built on this "straw." To express Aquinas' theology simply, "God is that He is." We say that God is, and then we stop talking. In the face of God, there is nothing we can say. Words are inadequate.

The beholding, whereby the soul can behold
no other thing, is so profound that it grieves me
that I can say nothing of it. It is not a thing which
can be touched or imagined for it is ineffable.
St. Angelo de Foligno

Myrtle Fillmore, (1845–1931, USA) became a convert to New Thought after she heard a presentation on Religious Science; she decided that by changing her mind she could cure herself of tuberculosis, which she did. She is the founder, along with her husband Charles Fillmore, of the Unity Church movement. In describing her own mysticism she writes:

I have come so close to breaking right through into the wonderful things of the kingdom; and at times I seem most bursting with beautiful, powerful realities that I would have humanity see and realize. But these great impressions and surges of power don't seem to put themselves into words and I can but radiate them.

A.H. Almaas says of his experience, "The more one perceives that it is indefinable, the more there is insight about it." Mysticism transcends human comprehension. Words are "physical" things. A written word is a physical thing. A spoken word is a physical thing; a sound vibration that strikes the ear is a physical thing.

I'm trying my best to speak intelligently and trying to
use words to explain what happened, but you can't.
Robert Adams

Mysticism and the Mind: The "Noetic" Quality, Revelation, Intuition, Illumination, and Intellectual Vision

Rationality can take you only so far.
Wei Wu Wei

You need not listen to me;
listen to the Logos within. When you do,
you will agree that all things are One.
Heraclites

Using the Mind to Go Beyond the Mind

Objective understanding, whether from perception or reasoning, is simply not enough, according to the mystics. It cannot get us all the way there unless we utilize Jnana Yoga, "the path of knowledge," to take us beyond the mind into the essence of being. Objective understanding of the world of form is inadequate. Objective understanding alone is a dead-end street. No matter how much we know, intellectual knowing (subject/object perception) alone is never enough. Such knowledge alone is dry and barren. According to many mystics, looking is judging and must therefore be abandoned.

According to the Sufis, there are three ways of knowing:

1. Intellectual knowledge (perception).
2. Spiritual knowledge (learning).
3. Knowledge of reality (vision).

There is a difference between perception and knowledge. The ego limits perception to our brothers and sisters' bodies and to the things of the world. When we first meet someone we have not seen for some time, we often ask them how they are and then give them our usually "positive" opinion of how we think they look. They then may in turn, critique us (our bodies). This is perception and judgment, not vision. *Vision* enables us to see God in everything. Our task is making this shift permanent.

Avicenna wrote mystical treatises that express the theme of the creature's love of the Creator. Once we are ready to know God, we can. God is ready now. If we are ready now, we are also there. Why wait for Heaven? There is nothing partial about knowledge. Knowledge is whole. It has no separate parts and no degrees. It just looks that way. You—I—we are not separate from God.

Wisdom and Knowing

The truth of our identity cannot be grasped by the reasoning mind alone. Intellectual knowledge is based on information, facts, and associations gathered from life. Wisdom is knowledge of reality as "simple" and all pervasive. It is the direct perception of essence. It is not emotional or purely intellectual. It is a permanent inner knowing, a form of "mystical illumination," a deep and profound insight into essence. The experience is not bodily or sensuous. It is inaudible to and unknowable by the intellect—yet it is known and known without doubt.

Plotinus speaks of "Another Intellect," different from that of reason and "rationality." It is not irrational; rather, it is "trans-rationality." Dionysius the Areopagite speaks of an "unknown knowing." For Shankara and Eckhart, the way of salvation is the way of knowledge or *revelation*. Revelation is an intensely personal experience. It is a direct contact with God that transcends time and abolishes fear. Inevitably, mystics say that they now know something that they did not know before. Although they may not be able to tell you what it is that they now know (because it is ineffable), they have received unquestionable insights and revelations beyond doubt.

Revelation is literally unspeakable because it is
an experience of unspeakable love.
A Course in Miracles

D.T. Suzuki (1870–1966, Japan), the man who brought Zen Buddhism to the West, taught university courses and wrote several books on Zen. Carl Jung and Thomas Merton both praised Suzuki for making clear the teachings of Buddhism. According to Suzuki, mystical awareness cannot be described, as such experience stands *above* or *outside* of the boxes of words and reason. Suzuki says, "When language is forced to be used for things of this world (the 'transcendental world'), it becomes warped and assumes all kinds of crookedness: oxymora, paradoxes, contradictions, absurdities, oddities, ambiguities, and irrationalities."

He says of "mystical intuition" that:

Sometimes it asserts, sometimes it negates and declares that A is not A and therefore it is A. This is the logic of mystical intuition.

Satori, the spiritual goal of Zen Buddhism, is individual enlightenment, or sudden awareness. Both a knowing and an intuitive awareness, Satori is a permanent and deep experience. The "feeling" is that of infinite space freed of concepts.

Mozart said he would receive an entire sonata in an instant. It was then just a matter of putting down what he heard (saw). There was no need to think it through. Divine revelation often comes that way. Revelation as a direct communion with God has nothing to do with words or time. It can happen in an instant. You now "know" something you did not know before.

Recollection

This act of perfect concentration,
the passionate focusing of the self upon one point,
when it is applied, "with a naked intent"
to real and transcendental things constitutes in the
language of mysticism the state of recollection.
Evelyn Underhill

In my 1976 experience, I was seeing what I had already seen. Yet, it was not in time. This sounds paradoxical, and it is. The experience suggested something Plato talked about 2,400 years ago in his discussion of *recollection*. Plato says our task in life is a matter of *remembering*, or *putting back together again* what the soul already knows. The *re-collection* is not of this world but our real home—a place free from the dreaming of the world.

A memory that is not alive to the present does not
"remember" the here and now, does not "remember"
its true identity, is not memory at all.
Thomas Merton

What Do the Mystics See?

- *Perhaps we have a clearer understanding of human nature and how the mind works and how we are to live in order to keep our minds in line with the One Mind.* We are not concerned about projecting onto others, knowing that "thoughts" affect everything.
- *Perhaps we have some insight into the human comedy.* Mystical insight often brings joy and laughter.
- *Perhaps we see something of the web of consciousness;* perhaps we see "the" inner connection of everything within the cosmology of the universe. It all fits together, and it goes on infinitely.
- *Perhaps we know that there is no such thing as death* and we understand that the body is ephemeral. True mystics do not fear death. Consciousness extends well beyond the limits of physical life. Indeed the body is a "limitation" on seeing.
- *Perhaps it is an experience of unspeakable love!*

Mysticism and Paradox

Take paradox from the thinker
and you have a professor.
Soren Kierkegaard

Paradox is a universal feature of mysticism. A paradox is that which is "contrary to expectation." Zen quotes are inherently paradoxical, as the goal of Zen cannot satisfactorily be described in words. Zen Masters seem to be talking in riddles as they try to point toward the Buddha nature. For example, Zen Buddhism speaks of obtaining a state of mind beyond both thought and "no-thought." In this sense, Zen Buddhism is pointing to a state in which there is no more striving, and the labeling of things has ceased. It is then a state of mind free of judgment.

Divine Folly

A man who has realized God shows certain characteristics. He becomes like a child or a madman, or an inert thing.
If you must be mad, why be mad for the things of this world?
If you must be mad, be mad for God.

Ramakrishna

Much madness is divinest Sense
To a discerning Eye—
Much Sense—the starkest Madness.

Emily Dickinson

One of the things I love about both Gurdjieff and Osho is their irreverence. At one moment, they each could be deeply reverent—in their appreciation for meditation and the experience of God, for example—and at the next moment completely irreverent—in their discussions of the ego, matters of the world, and the games of society. Gurdjieff and Osho both loved jokes. Osho said that his most important teachings were his jokes. Irony is basic to mysticism. We need to see the joke that is ourselves in the world of ego and form. Emptiness is the ultimate nature of everything that exists, yet emptiness, or no-thingness, is not a vacuum. It is glowing with awareness, consciousness, spirit—light. Speaking of mysticism, Arthur Koestler says:

The reflections I have put down so far were all still on the rational level...As we proceed to others in an inward direction, they will become more embarrassing and more difficult to put into words. They will also contradict each other for we are moving here through strata that are held together by the cement of contradiction.

Arthur Koestler (1905–1983, Hungary, UK) was a journalist, novelist, and social philosopher. He was the author of many books including *The Yogi and the Commissar.* His most famous work *Darkness at Noon* is a novel about the purges of the Soviet state during the Stalin area.

He who sees inaction in action and action in inaction, he is intelligent among men;
He is a man of established wisdom and a true performer of all actions.

Bhagavad-Gita IV.18

Paradox as a teaching device in mysticism helps us to stop thinking. It is also a way to transcend duality. This does not mean that mysticism is unreasonable, it just means, as Zorba the Greek says to his wealthy American companion while dancing on the beach in Crete, *"There is only one thing wrong with you boss! You need a little madness!"* We've got to step out of the usual egoistic way of thinking. We've got to step out of tradition and—dance. We've got to go beyond orthodoxy and solidified reasoning. A Shinto priest when asked about his theology told Bill Moyers, "I don't think we have a theology. We dance."

There was creation going on, and yet there was no creation. There was no creation taking place, and creation was taking place. Sounds like the thoughts of a mad man and it seemed normal. There is absolutely nothing strange about this at all, being nothing and everything at the same time.

Robert Adams

Ronald A. Knox (1888–1957, England), a theologian and mystery writer, identified seven paradoxes in mysticism:

1. The mystic has a sense of being carried away by a force stronger than self, yet merits the apprehension of God.
2. The apprehension of God in becoming more direct becomes less distinct.
3. In loving God, one makes less use of affection.
4. The will becomes more the center of our prayer, while its acts become less and less perceptible.
5. The more you pray, the less you ask for.
6. The more one enters into Self, the less self-consciousness there is.
7. The mystic is less, not more conscious of being virtuous.

The mystic who tries to speak logically and formally of unity consciousness is doomed to sound very paradoxical or contradictory.

Ken Wilbur

Mysticism is filled with paradox.

- You use the mind to go beyond the mind.
- A lot can be said about what cannot be said.
- God is darkness behind the light.
- God is not material—
  yet God is "visible" in all things.

- Mysticism is the doing of undoing, or the undoing of doing.
- You must close your eyes in order to see.
- Mysticism is non-nihilistic negativity or —All there is is God.
- We have knowledge without comprehending.
- Matter does not matter.
- Consciousness is something and nothing.
- Being is being without being.
- Mystics are loners—yet connected.
- To die is to awaken
- As we forgive the world our guilt— we are free of the world
- Pure consciousness is not a consciousness of anything.
- The static is the dynamic.
- The stillness is the dancing.
- There is silence at the center of the world of flux.
- The passivity at which the mystic aims is a state of intense activity.
- It is a "dazzling darkness."
- Pure unity exists without multiplicity.
- Mystics cease to be individuals, yet they retain individuality.
- To find yourself, you must lose yourself.
- The one who reaches nirvana neither exists nor does not exist.
- What do you lose when you lose an illusion?
- To say, "of myself I can do nothing" is to gain all power.
- What we thought we were seeking is seeking us.
- The best way to get somewhere is to let go of the need to be anywhere.
- The ancient Paradox of Poverty is that we only enjoy true liberty in respect to such things as we neither possess nor desire.

In the *Isa Upanishad* we read: *That One, though never stirring, is swifter than thought...Though standing still; it overtakes those who are running... It stirs and it stirs not. It is far, and likewise near. It is inside all this, and it is outside all this.*

The Tao Te Ching describes the Tao in this way:
When you look at it you cannot see it;
It is called formless.
When you listen to it you cannot hear it,
It is called soundless.
When you try to seize it, you cannot hold it;
It is called subtle....
It is up, but it is not brightened;
It is down, but it is not obscured.
It stretches endlessly, and no name is to be given....
It returns to nothingness.
You face it, but you cannot see its front.
You follow it, but you cannot see its back.

Consider the following by T. S. Eliot:
In order to arrive at what you do not know
You must go by a way which is the way of ignorance.
In order to arrive at what you are not
You must go through the way in which you are not.
And what you do not know
is the only thing you know.
And what you own is what you do not own.
And where you are is where you are not.

Thomas Stearns Eliot, (1888–1965, USA, UK) was a poet, dramatist, and literary critic. He received the Nobel Prize in Literature in 1948. Born in St. Louis, he moved to the United Kingdom in 1914 and became a British subject in 1927.

Mysticism and Poetry

Contemplation is the mystic's medium.
It is an extreme form of that withdrawal of attention from the external world and total dedication of the mind which also, in various degrees and ways conditions the creative activity of musicians, painters and poets.
Evelyn Underhill

Because the mystical is so hard to talk about, we might use imagery, poetry, song or dance. We might paint a picture or write a story. It says in the gospels that Jesus *always* spoke in parables because—"in seeing they do not see and in hearing they do not hear." Mystics are often poets. Sometimes, as with William Blake, Rabindranath Tagore, or Kahlil Gibran, poetry, art, and mysticism mingle together in one experience. Poetry is one of the most practical expressions of a mystic's experience. Though mysticism is ineffable, through poetry it is possible for the mystic poets to give a glimpse of what is seen: like a finger pointing to the moon, moving words offer a description of lofty experiences. Poetry combines imagery and feeling. It "proposes" something. The Vedas of Hinduism, our oldest spiritual literature, is poetry. The Bible is also filled with poetry: The Song of Solomon, Psalms, and Proverbs. Many of the medieval mystics were poets. Consider the following from St. Teresa of Avila:

God alone is enough.
Let nothing upset you,
let nothing startle you.
All things pass;
God does not change.
Patience wins all it seeks.
Whoever has God lacks nothing:
God alone is enough.

Sufi Poets

There are many Sufi poets, including Rumi, Hafiz, Kabir, Ibn Arabi, and Hazrat Inayat Khan. One of the most prominent of the Middle Eastern mystic poets, **Kabir** (1440–1518, India) preached an ideal of seeing all of humanity as one. He scorned religious affiliation and was viewed as a threat by both Muslim and Hindu. His ideas of loving devotion to God are expressed in metaphor and language from both the Hindu *Vedanta* and *Bhakti* streams and Muslim *Sufi* ideals. The following is from Kabir:

Are you looking for me?
I am in the next seat.
My shoulder is against yours.
You will not find me in the stupas,
not in Indian shrine rooms, nor in synagogues,
nor in cathedrals: not in masses, nor kirtans,
not in legs winding around your own neck
nor in eating nothing but vegetables.
When you really look for me, you will see me
instantly—you will find me in the tiniest house of time.
Kabir says, Student, tell me, what is God?
He is the breath inside the breath.

Hazrat Inayat Khan (1887–1927, India) was born into one of the most musical families in India. His grandfather was known as the 'Beethoven of India.' Hazrat became intensely absorbed in spirituality and adopted the Sufi path, eventually becoming head of the International Sufi movement. Here is one of his poems:

Thou art my salvation and freedom is mine,
I am not, I melt as a pearl in sweet wine!
My heart, soul, and self, yea, all these are thine;
O Lord I have no more to offer!
I drink of the nectar of truth the divine,
as Moses thy word, as Yusuf they shine
who walk in thy ways; and Christ is thy sign:
Thou raisest to life everlasting!
Thou art as Muhammad to them that repine,
My spirit is purged as the gold from a mine!
I only know that my heart beats with thine,
And joys in boundless freedom!

The English Metaphysical Poets

You are as prone to love, as the sun is to shine.
Thomas Traherne

William Blake (1757–1827, England) is one of our best examples of a poet/mystic. A visionary painter, and engraver, he spent most of his life in London. He was attracted to the writings of Emanuel Swedenborg, and from his early years, he experienced visions of angels. Like Traherne's, Blake's poetry shows childlike innocence and warmth. His poetry is filled with energy, combined with simplicity and clarity. He was opposed to slavery and sexual inequality. For Blake, *imagination*, the Divine in everyone, supersedes reason. While some desires cause suffering, the desire for familial love, sexuality, food, and shelter are from God. In 1790 Blake engraved *The Marriage of Heaven and Hell*, a book of paradoxical aphorisms. "If the doors of perception were cleansed everything would appear to man as it is, infinite." Thomas Merton did his master's thesis on William Blake. Perhaps the best remembered verse of Blake is:

To see a world in a grain of sand
And heaven in a wild flower
Hold infinity in the palm of your hand
And eternity in an hour.

Wordworth's verdict after Blake's death reflected the opinions of the time:

"There was no doubt that this poor man was mad, but there is something in the madness of this man which interests me more than the sanity of Lord Byron and Walter Scott. No one is a great poet, without being at the same time a profound philosopher. For poetry is the blossom and the fragrance of all human knowledge, human thoughts, human passions, emotions, language."

Samuel Taylor Coleridge (1772– 1834, England) was a poet, critic, and philosopher who, along with his friend William Wordsworth, is one of the founders of the Romantic Movement in England. He is best known for *The Rime of the Ancient Mariner* and *Kubla Khan*. He was interested in Kant's transcendental ideals.

Poets like Rumi and Kabir (also Whitman) are examples of the extroverted mystics and *Via Positiva*, a mysticism that embraces the world with love. Many of the other mystical poets include such more contemporary poets as Langston Hughes and Maya Angelou. The Romantic poets Coleridge, Byron, and Keats are renowned and respected for their ability to poetically convey the truth. Some other of the best known Western poet-mystics include William Wordsworth and Alfred Lord Tennyson from England and Emily Dickinson and Walt Whitman from the United States.

William Wordsworth (1770–1850, England) is accredited along with Samuel Taylor Coleridge with ushering in the English Romantic Movement. He is also a nature poet as in:

My heart leaps up
when I behold a rainbow in the sky:
So was it when my life began:
So is it now I am a man:
So be it when I shall grow old or let me die!

Notice Wordsworth's seeing, as in the following description from the morning of July 31, 1802, as he and his sister Dorothy were traveling in a horse drawn coach over Westminster Bridge in the city of London.

Earth has not anything to show more fair
Dull would he be of soul who could pass by
A sight so touching in its majesty
This City now doth like a garment wear
The beauty of the morning; silent bare
Ships, towers, domes, theatres and temples lie
Open unto the fields, and to the sky
All bright and glittering in the smokeless air.

Alfred Lord Tennyson (1809– 1892, England) succeeded Wordsworth as England's Poet Laureate in 1850. He is the chief representative of the Victorian Age in poetry. Much of his verse is based on mythological themes. He wrote a number of phrases that have become commonplaces of the English language, including: "better to have loved and lost" and "Their's not to reason why; their's but to do and die."

Flower in the crannied wall,
I pluck you out of the crannies;
Hold you here, root and all, in my hand,
Little flower but if I could understand.
What you are, root and all, and all in all,
I should know what God and man is.
Alfred Lord Tennyson

Poetry and religion are the same thing.
W.B. Yeats

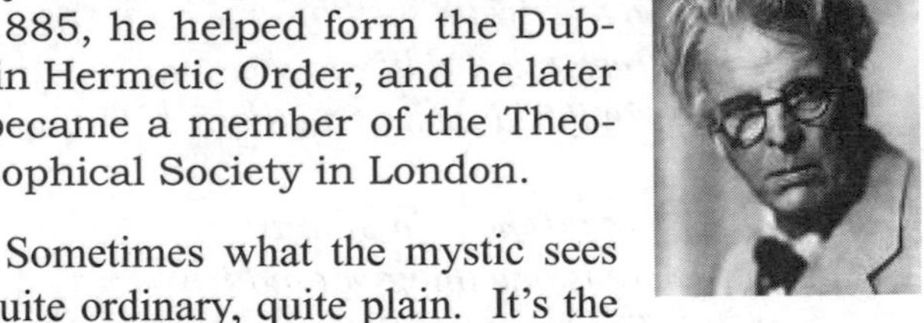

William Butler Yeats (1865 –1939, Ireland) was an Irish poet and dramatist who read extensively on mysticism and was especially influenced by Emanuel Swedenborg. In 1885, he helped form the Dublin Hermetic Order, and he later became a member of the Theosophical Society in London.

Sometimes what the mystic sees is quite ordinary, quite plain. It's the same thing that other eyes see; it's just that it's seen with different eyes. Here, for example, is a description of such a "seeing" experience by William Butler Yeats.

My fiftieth year had come and gone. I sat, a solitary man in a crowded London shop, an open book and empty cup on the marble top. While on the shop and street I gazed my body of a sudden blazed; and twenty minutes more or less it seemed, so great my happiness, that I was blessed and could bless.

Yeats experienced a moment of inexplicable delight in an otherwise quite ordinary experience. Yeats shifted from the mundane to another dimension where his delight seemed utterly boundless.

Rainer Maria Rilke (1875 –1926, Germany) is a mystic poet of the twentieth century whose images often focus on the difficulty of trying to express the ineffable in words. He thus created the 'object poem' that attempts to describe with clarity physical objects and the "silence of their concentrated reality." His poem "Neighbor God" is included in the *Liturgy of Hours*, and his poetry is often referenced in the writings of such contemporary spiritual teachers as Jack Kornfield.

Evening
The sky puts on the darkening blue coat
held for it by a row of ancient trees;
you watch: and the lands grow distant in your sight,
one journeying to heaven, one that falls;

and leave you, not at home in either one,
not quite so still and dark as the darkened houses,
not calling to eternity with the passion of what becomes a star each night, and rises;

and leave you (inexpressibly to unravel)
your life, with its immensity and fear,
so that, now bounded, now immeasurable,
it is alternately stone in you and star.

Zen has Haiku poems and paradoxical questions known as koans. A haiku (see below) is a 17-syllable verse form consisting of three metrical units of 5, 7 and 5 syllables.

Covered with the flowers,
Instantly I'd like to die
In this dream of ours!

In all the rain of May
There is one thing not hidden
The bridge at Seta Bay.

Harvest moon:
Around the point I wander
And the night is gone.

The first soft snow!
Enough to bend the leaves
Of the jonquil low.

Chapter 16

Mysticism, Humor, Simplicity, and the Heart

Mysticism and Humor

Comedy, Tragedy, and the Meaning of Life

The playwright Christopher Fry once told about a dream in which he said he was reading a huge book. He knew that when he reached the end he would find the meaning of life. When the last page came, it was uproariously funny. He awoke crying with laughter; then, as his mind returned to consciousness from the unconscious, the secret slipped out of his reach. What do you think he saw?

This world is sometimes too much with us, too serious, too overwhelming; and when it is, we need a different, higher, lighter, easier way of seeing. We need to look through the cracks in the cosmic egg to see the paradoxes, the ironies, and the incongruities of this world; and then we need to laugh. We need play, giggles, and belly laughs. We need humor to help us stay balanced, to deal with the insanity of the world, and to turn lightheartedness into enlightenment. For this reason, mystics are often wise fools.

Laughter is not only fun, it's sacred. With the right frame of mind and perspective, we can see irony, the absurd—the strange twists and turns the ego makes—and laugh at it. Humor is therapeutic. It reduces fear, anger, and resentment. Acknowledging our own misperceptions keeps us humble. Like all mysticism, joy, laughter, and delight abolish conventional division. Julian of Norwich (1342–1416) insisted that laughter be part of the Benedictine rule. There are reports from the fourteenth century of convents where the nuns danced themselves into rapture during the liturgy and the entire community lay dead-like on the floor or convulsed with laughter. When the Church in Rome got wind of what was happening, a ban was imposed on dancing and laughing in churches and the ban was not lifted until 1994!

Seriousness Is Foolishness

Problems often begin when we take things seriously. When we are serious, it is inevitable that we are judgmental. Anytime we trying to control a situation, things can get serious. To be serious, there is an insistence on having things done in the proper, "right' way. The worst state of health to be in is a *serious* condition. We laugh when we sense the difference between the way things are and the way serious people say they should be.

I love being asked many times, "Why do you laugh so much and make so many jokes? The Lord is all blissfulness. He is the reality behind all that exists. He is the goodness, the truth in everything. You are his incarnation. That is what is glorious. The nearer you are to Him, the less you will have occasion to cry or weep. The more we know of Him, the more misery vanishes.

Ramana Maharshi

A Texan traveled to England on vacation. While there, he attended a religious service and was amazed at how quiet it was. Then the Texan heard the minister say something he really liked and he shouted out "Amen!" Everyone in the church turned and stared. A little later the minister said something else he liked, and once again he shouted, "Amen!" This time the usher came over and admonished him, "You must not talk out loud." "But," protested the Texan, "I've got religion!" "Well," said the usher, "You did not get it here!"

Parables, Prayers, and Paradox

Jokes and parables have similarities. The word *parable* comes from the Greek *parabole*, meaning "to compare." A parable is a story that compares two or more ideas while pointing to something beyond the literal meaning, leaving us with a new way of seeing. Similarly, a humorous story, or joke, takes two or more ideas, compares them, and then provides an interesting *flip* ending called a "punch line." The punch line establishes the incongruity of the story, and we laugh. Jesus' parables are filled with irony, wit, hyperbole, and exaggeration. When he says, for example, "If your eye offends you pluck it out," he is using exaggeration. He does not mean that we should literally pluck out our eyes. We do, however, need to change the way we see.

Native American, Australian Aboriginal, and African tribal folk tales often include the story of some trickster or animal spirit who plays funny games with those who are too serious. One interesting, humorous mystical figure from the Middle Ages is **Nasruddin** (Nasreddin), an ironical Sufi figure. Many nations of the Near and Middle East (including Iran, Turkey and Afghanistan) claim him as their own. In China he is known as Afanti. Over time, he (like Lao Tzu) has become primarily a legendary figure, as all or most of the funny stories, anecdotes, and sayings attributed to Nasruddin are more than likely not actually from or about an actual historic figure. Most of Nasruddin sayings and stories are strange, yet ordinary; illogical, yet logical; rational, yet irrational; silly, yet witty; and simple, yet insightful and profound. Nasruddin stories serve as a means of releasing the pressures of society.

Dr. Elton Trueblood, author of *The Humor of Christ*, tells about reading the book of Matthew to his young son, when "...suddenly the boy began to laugh." His son laughed because he saw how preposterous it would be for a man to be so concerned about a speck in another person's eye that he was unaware that his own eye had a beam in it. The idea struck the boy as ludicrous.

Jesus' parables are filled with paradox—"the last shall be first and the first shall be last." Jesus asks ironical questions, "Do men gather grapes from thorns, or figs from thistles?" (Matthew 7:16) When he saw a great crowd gather about, he said, "Where the corpse is, there the vultures will gather." (Matthew 24:28)

Like Jesus; Abraham Lincoln, Mark Twain, Winston Churchill and Will Rogers were all story tellers. Lincoln was so good at telling funny stories that the *New York Herald* labeled him the "American Aesop." Lincoln once said, "They say that telling stories lowers the dignity of the presidential office, but I find that people are more easily influenced by a broad, humorous illustration than in any other way, and what the hypercritical few may think, I don't care." Lincoln, like Jesus, could turn a situation around by his ability to persuaded people to revaluate their views. His short parables could make even the seemingly most serious situation humorous. In a similar way, Zen stories catch us off guard and make us laugh—help us see anew. Zen stories are intended to produce an *"Ah ha!"* reaction or "Oh, now I see!" They are not designed to impart intellectual knowledge, but to jolt the ego.

Standup comedian Steve Bhaerman (Swami Beyondananda) says, "If there is a disease in our culture, it's irony deficiency. Now, seeing a doctor will not cure you of irony deficiency—but seeing a paradox will." Ego perception is upside down and backwards. Heaven is within us; yet we look for it in the external world. We think the material world is reality and Heaven is a fantasy when it's the other way around. We have to *flip* things over to see the truth. Similar to when we look in a mirror, it never occurs to us (unless we're wearing a name tag) that we are seeing everything backwards. So, paradoxically, we need to do a 180, to turn around, to see things straight—through the eyes of spirit and not through the eyes of the ego.

Laughter is the Jest Medicine

A merry heart doeth good like medicine.

Proverbs 17:22

Perhaps the best story of the healing power of humor is provided by **Norman Cousins** (1915–1990, USA) in his book *Anatomy of an Illness*. Cousins was a prominent political journalist, author, professor, and world peace advocate who was diagnosed with an incurable illness. For support he turned to good food, vitamins, and Marx Brothers and Candid Camera reruns. Cousins said that, "Ten minutes of genuine belly laugher had an anesthetic effect and could give me two hours of pain-free sleep."

After Cousins' experience, scientists began to study the healing power of humor. They knew it worked in practice; the question was—did it work in theory? They found that when we laugh, it releases endorphins, which are natural pain killers. Laughter lowers the blood pressure because when we laugh it causes our blood vessels to dilate—a lot better than having them die early.

Humor Gives Perspective

Many of the Nasruddin stories focus on the unreliability of perception. For example, someone shouts at Nasruddin who is standing on the other side of a river bank, "How do I get across?" "You are across," comes the answer. Humor is disarming. It opens up lines of communication and builds trust and rapport. It creates positive morale. It can even stop hostility and anger. It relieves pressure by providing a safety valve for the release of pain and emotions. It stimulates problem solving. It gently nudges the ego aside and stops over-burdening seriousness.

Humor is the healthy way of feeling
'distance' between one's self and one's problems,
a way of standing off and looking at one's
problems with perspective.

Dr. Rollo May

Rollo May, Ph.D. (1909–1969, USA) wrote the highly influential book *Love and Will.* According to May, the highest stage of life is the "Creative," the authentic adult at the existential phase, beyond ego. Such a person accepts destiny and faces anxiety with courage. May called upon people to rediscover the importance of caring, which he describes as the opposite of apathy. His first book, *The Meaning of Anxiety*, was based on his reading of Soren Kierkegaard.

Humorous stories can do more to enlighten questions of politics, philosophy and literature than any number of dull arguments.

Isaac Asimov

Here is a story told by economist John Kenneth Galbraith. During the Cuban missile crisis in 1961, the world was very tense and fearful that we might be on the verge of a nuclear war:

> A meeting was being held in Washington D.C., between Soviet and American delegates who had reached an impasse. Neither side was talking, and the delegates were sitting around with folded arms. Then a Russian delegate raised his hand and said, "Why don't we go around the room and everyone tell a joke? I'll go first." He said, "What is the difference between Communism and Capitalism? The answer is that under Communism, man exploits man; and under Capitalism, it's the other way around." An explosion of laughter came from inside the office building that might have prevented another explosion which would have had devastating consequence to this planet.

Dr. Victor Frankl, one of the few survivors of Auschwitz, in his book *Man's Search for Meaning* tells us that the inmates of Auschwitz had very little in the way of survival skills. A few, however, still had humor. Dr. Frankl says, "Humor was another of the soul's weapons in the fight for self-preservation. It is well known that humor, more than anything else in the human make-up, can afford aloofness and an ability to rise above any situation, even if only for a few seconds." Dr. Frankel discovered that when faced with an attempt to strip away their humanity, if people are able to maintain a sense of humor, there is a part of them that no one can get to. "Safety," says mystic Suzanne Segal, "can be found in even the most terrifying of moments, if you don't lose your sense of humor." Laughter, like changing a baby's diaper, may not permanently correct the problem, but it can make a situation more bearable.

Laughing at our problems somehow makes us bigger than the problems. Laughter helps us to remain defenseless. When we're defenseless it enables others to be defenseless. If we build castles, we must defend our castles. If we build egos, we have to defend our egos. What if there were no egos to defend? What if there was no one to get angry? When Jesus was standing in front of Pontius Pilate, Pilate said to him, "Don't you hear all the charges that have been made against you? Don't you have anything to say for yourself?" Jesus had no defense because no defense was needed. Don't take things personally. Don't be too serious. Stand back, look, laugh a little, and have some fun. Elizabeth Kubler-Ross, who studied death and dying, said people who live fulfilling lives approach death with an amazing sense of humor. If you can see life in the right light—it helps you to keep it light.

Laugh at your fears and replace them with peace. For fear lies not in reality, but in the minds of children who do not understand reality."

A Course in Miracles

Mysticism and Simplicity

Enlightenment is the simplest thing and the most profound thing at the same time.

Pema Chödrön (Contemporary Buddhist)

Pema Chödrön (1936 – Present, USA, Canada) is an ordained Buddhist nun in the lineage of Chogyam Trungpa. Noted for her approachable and down-to-earth teaching style, she is one of the most successful interpreters of Buddhism for Westerners. She is a prolific author and has conducted workshops, seminars, and meditation retreats throughout the world.

A scholar visited a Zen master and asked him, "What is the teaching of Zen?" The master recited a verse from the Dhammapada, "Do no wrong. Do only good," This is the teaching of all the Buddhas. "But," said the scholar, "a three-year-old child knows that." "A three-year-old may know it," the master said, "but an eighty-year-old may find it difficult to practice."

Physicists Isaac Newton, Albert Einstein, and Stephen Hawkins each discovered basic truths of physics by reducing everything to its most essential element by asking incredibly simple questions. Einstein once said, "Everything should be made as simple as possible. Any fool can make things bigger, more complex, and violent. It takes a touch of genius to move in the opposite direction." Einstein's insight into the nature of relativity came when he asked the simple question, "What would it be like if I could travel at the speed of light?" As mathematician Josiah Gibbs once expressed it: "The principal object of research in mathematics is to find the point from which the subject appears in its greatest simplicity."

Simplicity is the ultimate sophistication.

Leonardo Da Vinci

Jed Mc Kenna, a mysterious, contemporary mystic writes in *Spiritual Enlightenment: The Damnedest Thing*, "Enlightenment is truth-realization. Not only is truth simple, it's that which cannot be simpler—cannot be further reduced."

A Course in Miracles is sometimes said to be complex. There are over 1,300 pages, including 365 lessons, in the complete book. It takes a year to work though the Course; and when you get to the end, it says you are at the beginning. Yet, the Course is very simple. It says so several times. The Course says of itself that it is "very simple and direct" and then it adds,

"Simplicity is very difficult for twisted minds."

Bernard of Clairvaux said the primary characteristics of the soul are that it is simple, immortal, and free. According to Meister Eckhart, the soul simply is and God simply is. "It's in innocence and simplicity," he said, "that the soul is connected with God." In the early fifteenth century, Nicholas of Cusa reported a profound, revelatory experience in which he said he was shown that *God Is Simplicity Itself*. God, he said, can only be seen with an intellect that is completely simple. Over the eons, man's mind has become way too complex. Nicholas of Cusa said that 700 years ago, when life was arguably simpler than it is now. Today our minds are so full of soap operas, commercialism, religious doctrines, societal foolishness, and erroneous thoughts that we know of nothing except our own wheels spinning in a dream within a dream. Thoreau knew all kinds of things, he said, because his philosophy could be expressed in one word—*simplicity*. We can get to the truth only as we simplify, simplify, simplify. Thoreau said his life was so simple that he could keep his accounts on the nail of his thumb.

I am convinced that to maintain ourselves on this earth is not hardship, but a pastime, if we may live simply and wisely. I went to the woods because I wished to live deliberately to confront only the essential facts of life and to see if I could not learn what it had to teach and not when I came to die to discover that I had not lived.

. . . .

As you simplify your life, the laws of the universe will be simpler; solitude will not be solitude, poverty will not be poverty, nor weakness, weakness.

Henry David Thoreau

Dolores and I watched the PBS series *I Claudius* about the Roman Emperors of the first century: Augustus Caesar, Tiberius, Caligula, Claudius, and Nero. The opening show of this series, a story that might be called, "All about Lydia," tells of a complex web of lies, intrigue, and murder woven by Caesar's wife Lydia. With complete self-absorption and unbridled ambition, she saw to the poisoning of all of her stepchildren and even, it seems, Caesar himself. The stories of the succeeding emperors—Tiberius (Lydia's son), Caligula, Claudius, and Nero are complex dramas of intrigue, scheming, and murder. Nero even killed his mother because she tried to tell him what to do. All of the characters seemed trapped in a hell of their own making; there was such self-righteousness and unhappiness. Throughout the series, only the simpleton Claudius (though in fact he was not a simpleton) seemed to understand the entire tragedy. Likewise in the novel *Moby Dick*, only the first mate, Stub, seems to understand the drama, and he is described as "happy go lucky."

Innocence

The word *simple* comes from the Latin *simplic* meaning "the same or not divided." Simple means "free from guile and complication, innocent, modest, fundamental, unconditional and easy." Whoever or whatever is simple is straightforward, innocent, honest—humble and sincere. Jesus in the gospels asks that little children be brought to him "for as such, he said, are those in the Kingdom of Heaven" (Luke 18:16). Only through eyes of innocence can we see truth because innocence does not judge.

No guilt, no pride, no hate makes life simple.

Ramesh Balsekar

True strength is innocence, and innocence is wisdom because it is unaware of evil. There is nothing complicated, twisted, or convoluted about innocence. The last words of the pre-reformation reformer John Huss as he was being burned at the stake were *"O Holy Simplicity."*

John Huss (1371– 1415, Bohemia, now the Czech Republic) was a professor of theology at the University of Prague. Strongly influenced by John Wickliffe, Huss objected to the Pope's raising money to fight wars and the Church's selling of indulgences. For his "crimes," he was publicly strangled and, when not yet dead, burned at the stake. His followers, known as the Moravians or the Hussites, exist to this day. He was a hero to Martin Luther.

Mysticism and the Heart

In mysticism the will is united with the emotions in an impassioned desire to transcend the sensual world, in order that the self may be joined by love to the one eternal and ultimate "object of love."

Evelyn Underhill

Goethe said, "Mysticism is the scholarship of the heart." In Buddhist mysticism, mind and heart are frequently described in one word—*citta*—or "heart-mind." According to Buddhist philosophy, the heart is like a warm sun that generates within. It helps in the "cooking," the turning over of things. The mystic is a lover of life. It's easy to be a lover when you don't have your own "stuff" in the way. There is nothing that keeps the mystic from loving, so he or she can love God and everyone—infinitely.

There are many paths to enlightenment.
Be sure to take one with a heart.
Lao Tzu

Lao Tzu is the legendary founder of Taoism and the author of the *Tao Te Ching*. *Laozi* actually means "Old Man" or "Old Master." According to tradition, he lived during the sixth century B.C.E.. Scholars believe, however, that what we have recorded in the *Tao Te Ching* is a synthesis of ancient Chinese wisdom.

During the 1930s, Dr. Carl Jung visited some Indians in New Mexico. An old Indian told Jung he thought that white men were crazy. When Jung asked him why, the Indian said that he didn't know for sure, but he had heard that white men thought with their heads. Jung said, "You mean you don't think with your head?" And the Indian, pointing to his chest, said, "No, Indians think with their hearts." I told my mother, Milly, this story, and she said that she too thought from her heart. Having experienced her love, I know it was true.

If you could only love enough, You could be the most powerful person in the world.
Emmet Fox

Emmet Fox (1886–1951, Ireland, USA) was a mystic and spiritual leader of the early twentieth century. In 1931 he immigrated to the United States and became the minister of New York's Church of the Healing Christ. He was immensely popular as a speaker. His writings, especially *The Sermon on the Mount*, are popular in Alcoholics Anonymous.

In the middle of the eighteenth century, philosopher **Jean Jacques Rousseau** (1712–1778, Switzerland) observed that philosophy had left the role of the heart out of its "reasoning." Philosophy is after all a heady affair. Rousseau pointed out that the world was filled with debating, arguing, war and rumors of war, all of it being run by "the heads" of the church and the state. The mystic chooses both the heart and the head as a guiding force in life.

The best, most beautiful things in the world cannot be seen, or even touched.
They must be felt with the heart.
Helen Keller

Story Time

An eight-year-old girl in a Pennsylvania orphanage was shy and unattractive. Two previous asylums had her transferred, and now this director was seeking some pretext for getting rid of her. One day someone noticed the little girl writing a letter. An ironclad rule of the institution was that any communication from a child had to be approved before it was mailed. The next day, the director and her assistant watched the child steal out of the dormitory and slip down to the main gate. Just inside the gate was an old tree with roots showing above the ground. They followed and watched as the child hid the letter in one of the crevices of the root. She then scurried back to the dormitory. The director retrieved the note and tore it open. Without speaking, she passed the note to her assistant. It read. "Whoever finds this: I love you." What a great need there is for love in this world.

During my encounter with cancer, I saw clearly that love is the only thing that lasts—the only thing that is eternal—the only thing that matters. I had "understood" this truth before, but the encounter with death gave me an opportunity to look with fresh eyes. It was then clear that "Love is the only thing there is."

And now here is my secret,
a very simple secret;
it is only with the heart
that one can see rightly,
what is essential
is invisible to the eye.
Antoine de Saint-Exupéry

Antoine de Saint-Exupéry (1900–1944, France) was a writer and aviator, who, on his last reconnaissance flight, disappeared over the Mediterranean. His plane and bracelet were found under the sea many years later. His most famous book, *The Little Prince*, is a poetic tale in which he imagines himself stranded in the desert where he meets the little prince, a young boy from a tiny asteroid. It is a philosophical story that spoofs society and our many excesses.

Fall in love, and you know that all there is, **is** Love. Look at your mother, your child or your beloved and you may well know that all there is, is Love. When we know love, we know the eternal. When we seek only love, we know there is no other world than the world of God—the world of Love. God "knows" the world needs love.

The Second Commandment
Love Thy Neighbor as Thyself

There is no love but God's—God is the total, the Tao. The first commandment is to love God. The second, to love our neighbor, is like it. How are we going to love God? How do we love what we cannot see? A bridge is needed thus, the second commandment. The way to love God is to love those around us. We start in our own homes, with our own families, at our work, in our play and in each contact we make everyday. It is sometimes difficult to see past the mask to the spirit within, but mysticism asks us to do just that. Go beyond the mask to the reality of the Christ shining back our way.

Love cannot judge. As it is one itself,
it looks on all as one. Its meaning lies in oneness.
There is no love but God's, and all of love is His.
There is no other principle that rules where love is
not. Love is a law without an opposite.

A Course in Miracles

To love is to give: as we give love away, so we experience love coming back our way; just as, when we attack, we experience attack coming back our way. When we are no longer caught in distractions of the ego, it is much easier for love to flow freely from the self.

Love consists in desiring to give what is our own to
another and feeling his delight as our own.

Emanuel Swedenborg.

Emanuel Swedenborg (1688 –1772, Sweden), listened to an inner voice and wrote down what he heard. He experienced a simultaneous, dual consciousness of this

life and the afterlife. He is one of the most remarkable polymaths of all time. A philosopher and mystic, Swedenborg had a prolific career as an inventor and scientist. At age fifty-six, he entered into a spiritual phase, experiencing dreams and visions of a spiritual world where he talked with angels who guided his interpretation of the Scriptures. D.T. Suzuki referred to him as "the Buddha of the North." The Swedenborgian Church, now know as The New Church, continues to emphasize his teachings. (See www.newchurch.org)

For if Love is sharing, how can you find it except
through itself? Offer it and it will come to you
because it is drawn to itself.
But offer attack and love will remain hidden,
for it can live only in peace.

A Course in Miracles

Love is one; it has no separate parts and no degrees. We cannot love sometimes and hate at other times. We cannot love some people and withhold love from others. Mystical love is total and complete. As we love, love expands outwardly, like concentric circles created by a stone dropped in a pond. It touches everyone. When God's love fills the heart, it goes out to everyone, not just special "love" objects. We love those close in time and space—animals and nature, flowers, trees, and rocks. When we truly love, we know that all of humanity is us: our neighbor is our own self in another form, in a different shape. Human colors and sizes are just differences in the terrain, for the soul is colorless.

Going the Second Mile

Jesus suggests going a second mile—doing a little extra, learning a little more. We are to love others as ourselves, and we can't love others if we don't love ourselves. If we can't go the second mile for ourselves, how can we go the second mile for another? Here a little "willingness" is needed, a willingness to stretch out to the other, to refrain from judgment—to let things be what they are. In order to drop an addiction or let go of a negative thought, we have to stretch a little, go the second mile. It requires readiness, some effort, and a little willingness, but it is only a little willingness. Once we have given our lives over fully to the mystical, once we have given our lives over to love—love is all there is.

Success must come gently, with a great deal of effort
but with no stress or obsession.

Don Juan (in the Carlos Castaneda books)

How do we do something with great effort but with no stress or obsession? If we do something extra for ourselves, like meditating, eating correctly, saving money, exercising, etc., we make a little effort. We then find as we take care of ourselves, as we do good things for ourselves, we are loving ourselves. Going the second mile means not letting the ego take hold, not giving into temptation, to attack, to seeing the other as separate. We cannot love others without loving ourselves, and we cannot love ourselves without loving God because there is no love but God's.

Above, beyond, and transcending all things, there is divine love—an all-inclusive field, intrinsically true and ineffable. This love is timeless because it is forever. Love between man and woman is a deduction from a higher type of love. It is possible to speak of "love mysticism," as God reveals Himself in Love. The mystic is thus someone who is in love with God and feels loved by God. Love is surrender. It is the giving over of the self to love. Divine love always seeks the good of the other. The beloved is the soul, the Christ, God, Union, Completeness—the opposite of the ego. Similar to romantic love, in divine love there is a melting of self into the whole (which is no longer perceived as "other") along with the feeling of godliness and ecstasy.

True love is matchless in majesty; it has no parallel
in power and there is no darkness it cannot dispel.
It is the undying flame that has set all life aglow yet it
must be kindled and rekindled in the abysmal
darkness of selfish thoughts,
selfish words and selfish deeds.

Avatar Meher Baba

Meher Baba, (1894–1969, India) was an Indian guru of Persian descent who assumed a life of extreme simplicity. From 1925 to the end of his life, he maintained silence, communicating only with an alphabet board or by gesture. He spent long periods in seclusion, often fasting, but he interspersed these periods with travels, public gatherings, and works of charity. His tomb has become a shrine.

The soul is made of love and must ever strive to
return to love. Therefore, it can never find rest nor
happiness in other things. It must lose itself in love.
By its very nature it must seek God, who is love.

Mechthild Von Magdeburg

Divine Love

Spread love everywhere you go:
first of all in your own house.
Give love to your children, to your wife or husband,
to a next door neighbor. Let no one ever come to you
without leaving better and happier.
Be the living expression of God's kindness;
kindness in your face, kindness in your eyes, kindness
in your smile, kindness in your warm greeting.

Mother Teresa

Mother Teresa (1910–1997, Macedonia) was a Catholic nun who in 1950 founded the Missionaries of Charity. She won the Nobel Peace Prize in 1979 for her humanitarian work. She ministered to the needs of the poor, sick, orphaned, and dying in Calcutta, India, for over forty years.

When we fall in love, the beloved is all that we think about. Our only purpose is to fulfill the beloved to make him or her happy. We want to be with the beloved day and night. In this depth of romantic love, we may feel possessed by the beloved. When we fall in love, we become gentler, more loving, and less egoistic. This is the way St. Augustine describes his Love of God in his *Confessions*:

O Lord, do I love Thee.
Thou didst strike on my heart with Thy word and I
loved Thee. But what do I love when I love Thee?
Not the beauty of bodies nor the loveliness of
seasons, nor the radiance of the light around us,
so gladsome to our eyes, nor the sweet melodies of
songs of every kind, nor the fragrance of flowers and
ointments and spices, nor manna and honey,
nor limbs delectable for fleshly embraces.
I do not love these things when I love my God.
And yet I love a light and a voice and a fragrance
and a food and an embrace when I love my God,
who is a light, a voice, a fragrance, a food,
and an embrace to my inner man.
This it is that I love when I love my God.

Love is the most wonderful, expanding, and exciting experience. Each of us has a great desire to melt, merge, and fall back into oneness—the essence of being in love. I experienced falling in love with Judy Femmer, my high school sweetheart, as the most mystical, overwhelming, incredible, wonderful, and excruciatingly painful experience of my life up to that point. Falling in love is bigger than we are. It is out of our hands. It overwhelms us. It is beautiful, free, and flowing. Like a spring breeze, it brings fragrance and beauty. It brings joy and excitement. It shows us that we are not alone, that we are connected. God is the only thing which is real and God is Love.

Chapter 17

Going Deeper—Doing the Inner Work

We may come to mysticism through crash and burn, through illness or some other tragedy. Don't go this way, if you can avoid it. We may come to mysticism through meditation and contemplation. This is a good idea. We may come to mysticism "seemingly" accidentally or unexpectedly—when, for example, we get very relaxed. Good, but don't count on it. There is another way. It is the way most of us have to go. Gurdjieff and Ouspensky called their practice, "the work." The *Work* consists of regular application of spiritual discipline to become increasingly aware.

Self-disciplined begins with the mastery of your thoughts. If you don't control what you think, you can't control what you do. Simply, self-discipline enables you to think first and act afterward.

Napoleon Hill

Napoleon Hill (1883–1970, USA) was one of the earliest writers of personal-success literature. His most famous work, *Think and Grow Rich*, is one of the best-selling books of all time.

During the late 1970s, Vera Feldman, my then girlfriend, and I studied in New York City with a mystic named Eva Perrakos. Eva was a beautiful, vibrant woman with an intense intelligence. She and her husband, John Perrakos, M.D., were founders of Bioenergetics and later, Core Energetics. They called what they did *The Path Work*. You may know of the teachings of Byron Katie who calls what she does *The Work*.

You want salvation. You want to be happy. You want peace. You do not have them now because your mind is totally undisciplined.

From Lesson 19 of *A Course in Miracles*

A Course in Miracles consists of a Workshop, a Textbook and a Teacher's Manual. Obviously, we are trying to learn something. To learn something we have to engage in the inner transformational work that is done on ourselves. Mysticism is thus about being awake and responsible for absolutely everything that seems to come our way.

Enlightenment means taking full responsibility for your life.

William Blake

Working on ourselves requires a willingness to look at the dark places in our own psychic system. This is not

always fun but the results are wonderful. Success in the fulfilling of our destiny depends upon our willingness to practice steps that lead to this realization. When we begin to do this work we find that, as Dr. David Hawkins expresses it, *The life of the serious spiritual devotee becomes increasingly orchestrated by the Self rather than the ego/self.*

Travel at Your Own Risk

Sometimes when you're traveling, you'll see a sign which reads: *Travel at your own risk*. By posting such signs, the highway department not only warns us to be cautious but also absolves the state of responsibility in case of an accident. If a traveler comes to harm on the road, he cannot bring suit for damages. He is *traveling at his own risk*.

We each have our own lives to live. We are each the masters of our fate, the captains of our souls. Like it or not, we must accept responsibility for being here, in this incredible space at this incredible time. The more responsibility we assume, the freer and happier we are. The best way to assume full responsibility is to turn everything over to God.

Enlightenment demands that you take responsibility for your way of life.

Wayne Dyer

Self-Observation
Watching, Witnessing, and Willingess

A man hears of a guru who knows three secrets, the three most important things anyone can know. These secrets will enable him to master life and unlock the greatest mysteries of the universe. He travels over the most difficult of terrains, over many hills and through numerous valleys. After years of searching, he finds him. He explains to the guru how long it has taken him and all the difficulties he had to go through and would he please tell him the three secrets that will enable him to develop a mastery of life. The guru looks at him sternly and says, "*Very well then. 1. Pay attention! 2. Pay attention 3. Pay attention!*"

God is the only goal. We must then be vigilant for things of God and not the self. This is the way to fulfillment. Begin by "watching the mind." Watch projection, judgment and defensiveness. In order to see, we must stop projecting. Stopping projection is not like turning off a light switch. The first step is simply to be aware of how incredibly projective we are.

To enjoy good health, to bring true happiness to one's family, to bring peace to all, one must first discipline and control one's own mind. If a man can control his mind he can find the way to Enlightenment, and all wisdom and virtue will naturally come to him.

Buddha

Watching the mind is different than identifying with the mind. To watch the mind from a detached position is educational and non-stressful. It can be done with composure and serenity. Once we are "watching," we are not "wallowing." The very fact that we "see" the mind means we have begun to develop some control over the mind. We are no longer simply reactionary. When, for example, some difficulty comes up, it's a good idea to ask the question, What is this for? What purpose does it serve? And, how am I to respond? Shall I rely on my old buddies, *attack* and *defense* or is there a better way?

Spiritual devotion is a continuous inner lifestyle that incorporates constant watchful awareness.

Dr. David Hawkins

Several times in the Gospels, Jesus asks us to *Watch!*—be vigilant, alert, attentive and observant. (Matthew 24:42, 25:13, Mark 13:33-35 Luke 21:36, 14:38, etc.) I've heard preachers talk about these passages, saying what we should be watchful for is the devil and the enemies of God. God does not have enemies and darkness is not something outside of us. Watch for the nonsense from the tricky ego. There is no one here who has not experienced darkness, depression, guilt, fear, gloom, ignorance and unawareness. We all do stupid things and then beat ourselves up about it. It's called guilt, and we don't need it. We are easily induced into unconscious fantasy, sleep, and dreams. When so seduced we make mistakes. We do not realize how much we listen to our own idols. We are very vigilant for our own gods—the way we look, money and status. We can, however, also be just as vigilant against ego's demands as we are for them.

The Shadow

The darkness lurking within is described by Dr. Carl Jung as the shadow. The shadow is an unconscious complex containing the repressed aspects of consciousness. It is a ***knot*** in the psychic system, a place of unwitting reflexes, feelings and beliefs. We see these knots in slips of the tongue and behaviors that are "out of character" or hard to account for. The shadow represents traits we are ashamed of. Denial, projection, alcoholism, drug addiction, depression, anxiety, obsessive-compulsive behavior, laziness, tiredness and anger are all manifestations of shadowy material. We find the shadow in greed, envy, jealousy, the desire for prestige, aggressions, and similar "tormenting spirits," what native religions sometimes call demons or bad spirits. The shadow is everything we do not wish to acknowledge in ourselves though we recognize it clearly in others. The shadow is slippery. It is hard to catch. We think we've got a grasp on it and then we're seduced again. There is no way of knowing how deep the shadow goes until you've gone there.

Everyone carries a shadow, and the less it is embodied in the individual's conscious life, the blacker and denser it is. At all counts, it forms an unconscious snag, thwarting our most well-meant intentions.

Dr. Carl Jung

The shadow lives in the basement safely away from awareness. It surfaces when we "act out" or deny we're in trouble. We see it in over-spending, over-eating, or over-doing anything. The more unresolved issues are pushed underground the more energy it takes to keep them there—the more it drives us crazy. We spend an enormous amounts of energy denying truth.

Bringing Darkness to Light

It is important that we look at our dark side, lest we project our shadow onto others. As long as the shadowy tricks of the ego are acted out we will suffer.

Again and again have you attacked your brother, because you saw in him a shadow figure in your private world. The alertness of the ego to the errors of other egos is not the kind of vigilance the Holy Spirit would have you maintain.

A Course in Miracles

Bringing our dark and secret thoughts to Him, means being honest with ourselves. Until we bring the shadow to the light, we're at its mercy. Not till we are willing to look at darkness are we able to dissipate the shadow's energy and truly be able to help others.

Your ego is smarter than you are, way smarter, and if you don't recognize that and respect it, you stand very little chance against it.

Jed McKenna

You are not sufficiently vigilant against the demands of the ego to disengage yourself. This need not be.

A Course in Miracles

Trials, the Lessons of the Shadow

When a proud mother once announced to Mullah Nasruddin, "My son has finished his studies." Nasruddin replied, "No doubt God will send him more." A hero or heroine reaches mastery as a result of passing various tests and trials. Confronting our inner demons and nightmares enables the spiritual seeker to overcome doubt. Spiritual discipline means a willingness to engage in hard work. The return for such commitment is the magnificent awareness of truth. Zen Master Dogen said that a Zen Master's life is one continuous mistake.

According to Bernadette Roberts, in order to reveal the full strength of the soul's cementedness in God, there is need for tests and trials of all kinds. Only in this way can there arise the revelation of truth. Without tests and trials we can fall into a kind of sleep walking through the world. She says that trials alone are the vehicles of unity's revelation, so much so that the most terrible of human trials is the herald of the greatest of human revelations.

Cosmic Love is absolutely Ruthless and Highly Indifferent: it teaches its lessons whether you like/dislike them or not.

John Lilly

John Lilly (1915–2001, USA) was a medical researcher, writer, psychoanalyst, and good friend. He was a pioneering researcher into the nature of consciousness primarily interspecies communication between humans and dolphins. The inventor of the isolation tank, he was a part of the counterculture of scientists, mystics and thinkers of the 1960s and 70s who mixed of scientist and mystic. He wrote 19 books, including *The Center of the Cyclone, Man and Dolphin* and *The Mind of the Dolphin.*

Willingness, Practice, and Discipline

Freedom from ego requires perseverance, alertness, and a willingness to stay awake. It takes *willingness* to overcome the ego. Once we have demonstrated our willingness to face any problem, and be honest about our part in misperception, things change. Truth teachings are verified by anyone willing to engage in spiritual practices and discipline. Discipline helps us go deeper. Let's look at some principles that take "practice" deeper. These principles are not difficult. Their application may, however, "seem" difficult. It takes a certain amount of "willingness" and tenacity to make values come alive.

Shempa

One of the ways in which the shadow is manifest is in our getting caught in what in Buddhism is called *shempa.* The American Buddhist, Nun Pema Chödrön, talks about "Shempa" as a "hook." It's a place were we get stuck. It's the thing that grabs us, something that we get in our minds and we can't let go of it. It could be an idea, a person, or a thing. The hooks are the places where we are stuck, places we need to do our "work" in order to come to a more mature point of view. So it is that just when I think I've got life figured out, life slaps me with one more Shempa and says "try this one on for size."

If I see some defensiveness coming up; if I see attack thoughts arising; if I see some shempa coming up, I know—something has gone wrong with my thinking. Our brothers may indeed do hurtful things in the world. The question is how do I "see" what has been done? How do I respond? Do I hit back? Or, can I sit back? We cannot permit abuse but how do we respond lovingly—without being abusive ourselves? Those who test us are our best teachers.

Those who make you return, for whatever reason
to God's solitude, be grateful to them.
Worry about the others, who give you delicious
comforts that keep you from prayer.
Friends are enemies sometimes
and enemies' friends.

Rumi

Sri Aurobindo (1882–1950, India) a Hindu scholar, poet, and one of the leaders of the movement for the freedom of India from British rule developed a spiritual path he called integral yoga. He sought the development of a high level of spiritual consciousness which he called the Supermind. He describes the super mind this way,

The one aim of my yoga is an inner self-development by which each one who follows it can in time discover the One Self in all and evolve a higher consciousness than the mental, a spiritual and supramental consciousness which will transform and divinize human nature.

Sri Aurobindo

Watching Out

The following is a list of tricks of the ego to watch out for. If we can avoid being seduced by these tricksters and we can take things to a higher level, we'll be able to experience spiritual maturity and the development of mystical awareness.

A. Lying and Hiding

The two primary ego defenses are *denial* and *projection.* The first defense we learn to use as children is a form of denial called lying. What is the first thing that Adam does after "his eyes are opened" and he is able to distinguish between "good and evil?" He ***hides***

in the bushes. Denial is the most *subtle* and therefore the most tricky of the two defenses. It is sometimes easier to come to terms with our enemies (projections) than it is with ourselves (denial). Projection is “out there.” It’s “clear” why we are mad. We can probably come up with a list of reasons. It’s not always so clear when we are in denial; after all, *one of the qualities of denial is to deny being in denial*. Addicts of all sorts, consistently deny their addiction. We repress what we don’t want to look at. I ’m not saying that it’s necessary to dig up one’s dirty laundry and hang it up for the world to see. That would not be truly pleasant or helpful for the world or for ourselves. Being truthful and honest means being willing to take responsibility right now. It means looking at our projections and stopping our blaming.

The hero or heroine is called to go into the cave of unconsciousness to bring out what is hidden to the light. Watch carefully—be very honest. Lying separates us from others; and it cause depression. As Alcoholic Anonymous says, “We are as sick as our secrets.” What we hide is nothing, but we do not know that as long as we “cherish” our secret sins and hidden hates. Mysticism means awakening to the light. If we knew the light, we would be in the light and we would know nothing but light. We know more about darkness than light because that is where we have been hiding. It is important that, as we engage in spiritual discipline we try to be vigilant against the deceptions of the ego and not project our thoughts out on to the world in a destructive way. It is not enough to watch and witness, we must go further, recognize our part in the dreaming, and be willing to relinquish our role as guardian of our ego thought system. Escape from darkness involves two steps:

1. Know that darkness cannot hide.
2. That there is nothing you want to hide even if you could. This thought brings freedom.

When we are willing to hide nothing we enter into communication, peace and joy. What then should we do with our darkness? Know that:

1. **It is not necessary to be right.**
   It’s actually more refreshing to be wrong. If we admit that we’re wrong, we’re being honest. Speak the truth and then take a deep breath.
2. **Taking secret sins and hidden hates to God.**
   This means, being honest with ourselves.
3. **Take it to a comrade, companion, loving friend, therapist or fellow student.**
   Catharsis, getting it out, can be most refreshing. How nice it feels when we stop throwing up.

Alcoholics Anonymous works because people are given permission to say, “I’m an alcoholic” in a warm, trusting and accepting environment. Tell your mate, who already knows it, that you are an “egoacholic” and she/he might find that refreshing. Openness is always refreshing. Hiding is literally life-threatening.

Do I really need to go there?

When temptation arises to lie about even small things, an exaggeration perhaps, some embellishment or overstatement about how hard we work or how much money we spent ask, “Do I really need to go there?” If asked a question, answer as truthfully as possible. Why do we sometimes say, “I’ll be honest with you?” Does that mean the rest of the time they are not being honest? It’s important to feel clean. The soul by nature loves cleanliness. Cleanliness makes Heaven look beautiful. There are no dark spots or hidden places. Conscience is clear and we are free of the fear of hurting anyone.

B. Watch Judgment

We’ve been judging all our lives and we don’t just stop judgment—first just watch judgment happening—without saying anything. Not judging does not mean—not making simple judgments. “Am I having eggs or oatmeal for breakfast” or “What am I going to wear?” What we’re going to wear does not make much difference unless we’re into power dressing or sexy dressing, in which case, we are trying to manipulate the universe. Dress to be comfortable. Our concern is with judgments which involve condemnation, criticism and blame. We learn to observe without comment to another or to ourselves. Try fasting from judging. Just let it go. Just walk away. When “Shempa” comes up—think more than twice before speaking.

Look at the world
without adding anything to it.

C. Watch Complaining

Mr. Blackman goes to a psychiatrist. He says, “Doc, I have this terrible feeling that everybody’s trying to take advantage of me.” The psychiatrist says, “Relax, Mr. Blackman. It’s a common thing. Everybody thinks that people are trying to take advantage of them.” Mr. Blackman says, “Is that true Doc? It is such a relief to know that. Thank you. How much do I owe you?” The psychiatrist says: “How much have you got?”

When country singer, **Hank Williams** (1923–1953, USA) was asked where he got such good ideas for his songs, he said, *“Everybody feels good about feeling bad.”* Most country western songs are sad, "somebody done me wrong songs." The ego enjoys being mistreated, abandoned, and betrayed. It is proof that we are *innocent victims* of what other people (the world) has done to us. We can then feel "justified" in our attacks against others.

Story Time

A little boy wrote a story for his mother and gave it to her. The mother took the story and, noticing a mistake in grammar, she got a pen and fixed it. She noticed another error and still another error. Finally, she finished fixing the paper and gave it back to her little boy, who was in tears and he said:

"I didn't want you to fix it; I wanted you to like it."

Refuse to be a part of fearful dreams, whatever form they take, for you will lose identity in them.
A Course in Miracles

D. Watch for Anger and Attack Thoughts.

A student asked Master Zen Master Bankei "How can I cure my terrible temper?" "Show it to me," demanded Bankei, "I can't just show it to you like that because it comes on unexpectedly" explained the student. Bankei replied "Then it is not your true nature. If it were it would be with you at all time." Attack cannot occur without judgment and anger is never justified. The word is "never" not "sometimes." It does not mean we should never get angry; it just means if we do, something has gone wrong in our thinking somewhere and we need another way to see things. Attack in any form is "always" a mistake.

1. **Physical attack is an obvious mistake.**
   Only someone who lives in darkness could think that physical assault could result in their achieving what they want. War is never the answer!
2. **Verbal attack is a mistake.**
   We may get this strange idea that if we really tell someone off once and for all, they will get it and shape up. It never happens! It never happens because we're attacking another ego and they are going to perceive the attack not as "constructive criticism," but as an attack, and they will attack back in their minds even if they don't do it verbally or physically.
3. **Mental attack is also a mistake.**
   We have much more control over our minds than we think we do. Our task is to bring the mind in line with God. If I have a splinter in my finger and it is hurting me, I will "pluck" it out and throw it away. If a thought is hurting the mind, take it out and throw it away. Do not deny it or stuff it! Just "let it go." Any unforgiveness in the mind is hurting only one person and you know who that is.

If you perceive offense in a brother pluck the offense from your mind.
A Course in Miracles

E. Watch for Defensiveness

If someone walks up to you on the street and starts attacking your body, do everything in your power to stop them, for three reasons.

1. **You still believe you are a body.**
   Proof of that fact is that you are hanging out in one. As long as you are hanging out in a body, you will believe that it can be hurt. You would not want your body to be hurt or disabled, so you would do whatever you could to stop someone else from hurting it.
2. **Do not facilitate error in a brother.**
   Do not help someone make a mistake. If you let somebody beat you up, you are accessory to a crime. You would not want to be an accessory to a crime.
3. **We are not called upon to be martyrs.**
   To say do not defend means don't defend the silly ego. It is a silly ego and it is not who we are. Jesus is standing in front of Pontius Pilate. Pilate says to him, "Do you not hear all the accusations made against you? Don't you have anything to say for yourself?" And, he does not. If Jesus had come back at Pontius Pilate with, "Yes, I really am the Son of God and you're making a big mistake here," we might have questioned whether or not he was the Son of God.

We have two ears and one mouth, so we should listen more than we talk.
Zeno

Zeno (333 B.C.–264 B.C.) a Greek Stoic, said there was no power greater than the mind. People who adopted the Stoic philosophy are able to endure life's vicissitudes with calm and dignity. There are several qualities of Stoicism in Mysticism as Stoicism teaches self-control, flexibility, objectivity and freedom from negative and selfish emotions.

F. Listen Very Carefully!

What should we do if someone has a criticism of us? Listen! Listen very carefully! Ask, "Why is this person saying this? Are they absolutely crazy? Are they totally out of their minds? Or, is there maybe some tiny piece of "truth" in there that needs to be looked at? Maybe there is something I need to see. I can get angry and defensive. I can listen and see if maybe there is something I can do to make things better. Watch hiding or lying, judging, complaining, attacking and defending. Drop all such approaches and see what happens. A man who worked in construction in Alaska told me that he had been an alcoholic. One day when he once again was late for work, his boss started chewing him out. He was about to let the boss have it when he heard, "Shut up and Listen!" Holy Spirit gets through to each of us on our own level. He shut up, listened, joined AA and later became the foreman.

Watching Language: The Mystic's Miracle Diet

The following is a *suggested* way to refine *watching* even further by observing language. What do we do when we go on a diet? We cut out certain foods, or we cut back on the amount of food or both. If we put ourselves on a monetary diet, we cut back with our spending. Problems arise when we overdo, when we overspend, overeat, drink too much or "overplay" the severity of a situation. The solution is to cut back, to cut out, and to drop projective thinking—to say nothing. To see how projective we are, watch the words that come out of the mouth. Learn to cut out certain words and the thoughts behind them.

I have often repented of having spoken.
I have never repented of not having spoken.
Henry Suso

Every Word is a Projection

Every word is a projection, a statement, a declaration, an announcement, a proclamation, an assertion coming out of the void—made in the world. With words, we label, concretize, solidify, and make real. What is the first job given to Adam? He has to name things (Genesis 2:20). He begins by naming the animals. What is the first thing we learn in first grade? We learn "words." The first word I learned to read and you probably did too was, "Look." What is the first thing we do in a high school biology class? We begin by *labeling* the names of the parts of a flower and a frog. Then we learn how these parts work in connection with each other.

This universe, superimposed upon
Brahman, is nothing but a name.
Shankara (788? – 820?) Hindu Vedantis

Naming creates duality. It distinguishes the things that are named from the things that are unnamed. All such distinctions are imaginary because reality is not dual. It is one. The ego analyzes. Spirit accepts. The ego scrutinizes, dissects, and questions.

A True Story

A good friend, Tom Baker, a Course teacher in Virginia Beach, was once a Trappist monk and priest who later became a psychologist. Trappist monks do not talk—or do so as little as possible. Trappists "talk" in the sense that they sing their holy office several hours each day and they have learned sign language. They do not, however, talk about "frivolous" matters. Communication is kept to only that which is essential. Talking is an outward projective activity so they restrict talking to allow for inner reflection.

One day after four hours of continual chanting, thus inducing an altered state, Tom was out walking on the monastery grounds. He had not had a conversation with anyone for weeks. He was walking with one of those hoods that blocks vision to the right and the left. He was just looking down at the ground when, all of a sudden, the grass filled with light. He looked up and saw that the trees were all filled with light and there was a barn that also was filled with light. In that moment everything communicated with him. What it said was "we're happy just being," just being grass and just being trees. The grass is not worried that somebody might come along and mow it. It's just hanging out being grass.

Word Fasting

Jesus in the Gospels says that it's not what we put in our mouths that defiles us; it's what comes out of the mouth that defiles us. (Mark 7:15) I'm suggesting a "word fast" as a means of catching the tricky ego at play and thus avoiding falling into its clutches. Watch the words that come out of the mouth. The first few words are so obvious I should not have to mention them.

1. **Watch for profanity.** To damn a thing to hell is obviously a projection. Watch also the use of profanity for no reason at all as an adjective, say as we sometimes hear from teenagers.
2. **Watch for Name Calling.**
   Avoid the use of ***stupid***, ***insane***, ***ludicrous***, ***ridiculous***, ***idiotic***, and ***absurd***.
3. **Watch for *hate*, *fear*, *scary* and *afraid*.**
   Do you really "hate" something? One of my daughter's friends was talking about the way she "hated" her hair and how she "hated" the way she was dressed. Are we really "afraid" it might rain today?
4. **Watch for *want*, *need*, and *have to have*.**
   There are times of course when we may need to go to the grocery store or to stop for gas. Do we, however, really *need* or *have to have* some of the

things we may think we need? Byron Katie has a book called, *I Need Your Love. Is That True?* The development of mystical awareness leads away from needing, wanting or having to have anything.

5. **Watch for *disappointed*, *upset*, and *offended*.**
Do you ever say you are disappointed about something? There is only one way to be disappointed. First, you have to have an appointment. If you have an appointment you can be disappointed. You had some expectation about the way a situation was supposed to look, or unfold. It doesn't look that way. You get to be disappointed. Only an ego could be disappointed. Never tell a child you are disappointed in them. In the same way you can only be *disillusioned* if you had an *illusion* or *disenchanted* if you were first *enchanted*.

Did you ever say you were ***upset*** about something? What is it that is upset? Only an ego can be upset, and you are not an ego. To be upset, you must first have a set-up. You actually set it up, so you could be upset. Did you ever say that you are ***offended*** by something? If we are "offended," something pushes us "off the end." Only an ego can be offended. If you think you have been wronged or insulted—stop. No one can insult you, unless you think they can. Could Jesus be insulted? If you know the truth, all manner of evil can be said against you.

6. **Watch Judgmental Words**
During the years when I taught in Sing Sing prison (1982–1990), I noticed that one of the worst things a prisoner thought could happen to him was to have another individual "Dis" him—to disrespect him. "Hey, he ***dissed*** me man." Everybody needs respect.

I was listening to a popular speaker and she said something ***disgusted*** her. Consider the word disgusted. It is a highly judgmental word. Who are you to be "disgusted?" The choice to condemn, rather than to understand, leads to war. Did you ever say that something is ***appalling***, ***horrendous***, ***inexcusable*** or ***atrocious***? Is it really, or is our judgment about a thing keeping us from seeing? I was listening to someone who kept saying that something "irked" him. He kept saying, "It irks the hell out of me." To be irked means to be *irritated* or *annoyed*. Let us not underestimate the power of our own shadow. Even a minor stab of annoyance is a cloak drawn over deep anger.

7. **Watch for weasel words.**
These are a little more difficult to distinguish. They are "twists" on words and words with double meanings, quantifiers and qualifiers. We may use weasel words when we want to trick someone. There is a line in the Bible where Jesus says, we should let all of our answers be "Yes," or "No"—all else comes from evil. Weasel words may be used to avoid a straight-forward answer. They conceal the full picture and are used to manipulate. We say the company is "restructuring" rather than saying people are being fired. Weasel words include generalizations like "many people say...," "I heard that...," "There is evidence that...," "Popular wisdom has it that...," "the alleged thief..." Even the use of the word alleged makes it sound as though someone *is* a thief.

The Inner Voice of Reason

The mystic hears one voice—"the inner voice of reason." The inner voice of reason can be drowned out by the ego's voice of outrage. ***Outrage*** comes from the Anglo-French *ut-rage*, or *outer* or *uter*—like *other*. It's the *other* that's the problem. To be **outraged**, we must feel that either we or others have been injured or insulted. Yet we are called upon to teach that nothing they say can hurt us. If we do we are then also teaching ourselves that what is not of God has power over us. Does what I see make me outraged? Is there ever a time when we could be justifiable outraged? No, Nunca, Never! A mystic cannot be insulted. You cannot be insulted. Only an ego can be insulted. Anyone can say all manner of evil against us and it will have no effect on us if we know who we are in truth.

Our words, all of them, say a great deal. I was visiting with an amazing man, a professor who loves to play with ideas. It was wonderful to see the way his mind worked. He would start talking and then one thought would lead to another thought and he would say and "Oh, Oh, and then and then..." And then a little later the same thing would happen again. One of the phrases my friend used was, "What bugs me is." Why would anything "bug" us? A mystic is quite literally someone who cannot be "bugged."

I Have Learned a Great Secret
by Mary Baker Eddy

I have learned a great secret. I am going to tell you
what the secret is, and it is wonderful. It is this:
Not to see or hear or repeat any kind of imperfection.
It is seeing and hearing and repeating good only,
at all times and under all circumstances, and in spite
of everything that appears to the contrary.
I see perfection in myself in my friends, in my
so-called enemy, in my affairs and in world affairs.
The result has been simply marvelous.
Try it and you will find that
you will be seeing with God's eyes.

Not Having Buttons Which Can Be Pushed

You can't push a mystic's buttons, because the mystic does not have buttons which can be pushed. Not only are we not to judge, we don't have to get upset if others judge us. This is a real sign of spiritual development. Jesus going to the cross because of others' judgments of him is an extreme example. He was willing to be crucified to show us that it didn't mean anything. Sometimes we're tested big time—and we have to take it while placing no expectations on others. Expect nothing of others, and if love comes back your way enjoy it and keep giving your love away even if it goes unacknowledged.

Alexander Hamilton, the first Secretary of the Treasury of the United States, was killed over a word. The word was ***despicable***. Hamilton said that something Aaron Burr, the then Vice-President of the United States had done was despicable. What followed was like a conversation between two little boys. Aaron Burr asked him to take it back and Hamilton said, "No, I will not take it back." Then Burr said, "Okay, then, I'm challenging you to a duel." So they dueled in Weehawken, New Jersey, and Aaron Burr killed Alexander Hamilton over the word despicable.

I once heard an American historian say that he thought that of all the founding fathers, the one with the highest IQ was Alexander Hamilton. He devised the banking system we use to this day. He had sixty people working in his department when others had only five. He may have had the highest IQ, but he had a very low EQ (Emotional Quotient).

Better to trip with the feet than with the tongue.

Zeno

Mo Chao Bodhidharma, (early fifth century, B.C., China) the founder of Zen Buddhism, says, "Devise no words." In China, they call this state of mind mo chao—when we are not projecting words. Mo means "serene or silent" and chao means "reflection" or "awareness." It is a mirror-like quality that just reflects—just sees—just receives—just loves. Watch carefully and see what is being said. Are these words coming from ego or Spirit? Remember our words constantly give us away.

A wise old owl sat on an oak.
The more she saw
the less she spoke.
The less she spoke
the more she heard.
Why aren't we more like
that wise old bird?

Be careful of your thoughts,
for your thoughts inspire your words.
Be careful of your words,
for your words precede your actions.
Be careful of your actions,
for your actions become your habits.
Be careful of your habits,
for your habits build your character.
Be careful of your character,
for your character decides your destiny.

Chinese proverb

Mysticism and Forgiveness

The most important aspect of spiritual development centers on how we treat our brothers, our sisters, and ourselves. Mysticism requires a reversal in thinking—a complete undoing of projective seeing. The main mechanism of reversal is forgiveness and the world is much in need of our forgiveness.

A Sad Story Time

A boy named Pocho and his father got into a disagreement in Madrid, Spain, and the boy ran away. The father felt badly for the way he treated the boy so he put an ad in bold type on the back of the local paper. It read. "Dear Pocho. All is forgiven. Meet me in front of the main post office at 12 Noon Saturday. I love you—your Papa." The next Saturday at 12 noon, standing in front of the main post office in Madrid were more than one hundred young boys named Pocho.

What is Forgiveness?

If a man cannot forget,
he will never amount to much.

Soren Kierkegaard

Much of what we often call forgiveness is not forgiveness. We may say "I forgive you." Have we? Have we let it go to the point where our grievance no longer affects us? People sometimes say, "I can forgive, but I can't forget." If you can't forget, you haven't forgiven. Forgiveness is empty unless it includes correction of misperception. Without a reversal in thinking, it is still judgment, not healing.

I can forgive, but I cannot forget, is only another way of saying, I will not forgive. Forgiveness ought to be like a cancelled note—torn in two, and burned up, so that it never can be shown against one.
Henry Ward Beecher

Henry Ward Beecher (1813–1887, USA) was a bright, influential preacher and prominent American liberal Congregationalist, social reformer and abolitionist. He counted among his admirers, Abraham Lincoln, Mark Twain and Walt Whitman.

Forgiveness is impossible for the ego. The ego version of forgiveness is not forgiveness. It is judgment masquerading as forgiveness. We cannot seek out sin, provide testimony to its reality—and then say we are going to overlook it. The ego's idea of forgiveness is to have us see error clearly first, then try to overlook it. We cannot, however, overlook what we make real.

A Sunday School teacher asked one of the boys in her class what we must do before we can be forgiven of sin. She was expecting the boy to say that we must first repent. But he carried it back one step further. "First," he said, "you must sin."

Testifying to the reality of sin makes us blind and forgiveness impossible. Someone once said, "No one forgets where the hatchet is buried." Each of us can probably think of times when something we thought was long forgotten and well buried in the past is much the topic of conversation: "Remember in 1993, when you lost all our money on that lousy investment?" It has not been forgotten so it has not been forgiven. In the story of the woman taken in adultery (and in the story of the woman anointing the feet of Jesus), the disciples are surprised that Jesus does not see the woman as someone with an unsavory reputation. He saw who she really was, not a sinner, but, like himself, a child of God.

We are forgiven as we forgive.

In the Lord's Prayer we say, "Forgive us our debts, **as** we forgive our debtors." This statement is a simple acknowledgement of a basic metaphysical law of the universe. As we *give* so do we *receive* and as we *forgive* so are we *forgiven*. As we forgive, the truth about ourselves returns to our minds. As we offer salvation to others—so are we saved. Since the illusions about ourselves and the world are one, all forgiveness is a gift we give ourselves. As giving is a preface to receiving and judging is a preface to being judged, so forgiveness prefaces being forgiven. If our brother merits pardon, we then learn that forgiveness is our right as much as theirs. The only person we can ever forgive is ourselves, for having made a judgment in the first place.

In judging others and ourselves, we make our fears real and ignore the peace of God. We make hell real. We value that which is valueless. We find the world full of sickness, sadness, and despair. We fear the future and promote the idea of hell. God cannot forgive sin because God does not condemn. In order to have forgiveness, first we must have condemnation. There is no forgiveness in Heaven because it's not needed. Mystics demonstrate knowledge of Heaven by showing others that their attacks have no effect. Not being affected by "sin," we dissolve its cause.

The ego lives in time, constantly rehearsing the past and projecting the future. If there is no past, then there is nothing to hang onto. There is nothing to project. There is just this moment. As a country western song once expressed it: *There is no future in the past*. When Henry David Thoreau was on his death bed, one of his aunts asked him if he had made his peace with God, and he replied: "We never argued." The problem lies in thinking there is an argument.

When you bury a mad dog,
don't leave his tail above ground.
Charles Spurgeon

Charles Spurgeon (1834–1892, England) was a British Baptist clergyman. Called "The Prince of Preachers," he was a contemporary of Henry Ward Beecher in the United States and highly influential among Reformed Christians of different denominations.

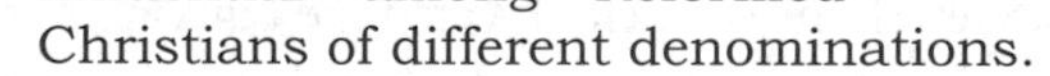

Hold on to nothing.

Forgiveness must be radical—total—complete; otherwise we're still attached. There is nothing to forgive, unless we think there is. As we forgive by not condemning, we are freed of suffering. In this process we ourselves are healed. As we give, we receive; as we forgive (by not making the error real), so are we forgiven. As we forgive, so do we remember Heaven.

Self Forgiveness

As sin is an idea you taught yourself, forgiveness must be learned by you as well, but from a Teacher other than yourself, who represents the other Self in you. Through Him you learn how to forgive the self you think you made, and let it disappear. Thus you return your mind as one to Him Who is your Self, and Who can never sin.

A Course in Miracles

There is really no one to forgive but ourselves and what we forgive ourselves for is our own misperceptions. We are only capable of forgiving ourselves from a higher plane. We cannot forgive from the ego's perspective. The ego doesn't even know how to forgive. True forgiveness is always prefaced by Self-realization. The mystic forgives everyone, everything. To be free, we must do whatever we can to remove the t(error)ist hiding within, however cleverly cloaked.

The soul that would preserve its peace, when another's sin is brought to mind, must fly from it, looking to God for help against it. To consider the sins of other people will produce a thick film over the eyes of our soul, and prevent us for the time being from seeing the 'fair beauty of the Lord'

Julian of Norwich

Julian of Norwich (1342–1413, England) is one of the best remembered mystics. The name "Julian" comes from the church, St. Julian of Norwich, where she occupied a cell as an anchoress (one who lives in seclusion). At the age of thirty, suffering from a severe illness and thinking she was about to die, she had a series of visions which were the sources of her major work, *Sixteen Revelations of Divine Love*, the first book written by a woman in English.

Suddenly, I realized... ***"It really is like this, in reality there is not a single thing!"*** *With this single thought, all* ***entanglements*** *were broken.*
Suddenly, it was as if a load of a hundred pounds had fallen to the ground in an instant.
It was as if a flash of lightning had penetrated the body and pierced the intelligence.

A.H. Almaas

A.H. Almaas (1944 – Present, Kuwait) developed the Diamond approach to wisdom. He says that we cannot achieve enlightenment unless our life is free of all *entanglements, embroilments*, and *perplexities*. If I'm living in a "soap opera," I'm not going to find peace of mind till I've cleared up all the difficulties with my fellow beings. If my mind is preoccupied with unforgiveness and grievances, I cannot have a mystic's state of mind.

Chapter 18

Self Fulfillment and Authentic Maturity

The vision of truth is not self-denial,
but rather self-fulfillment.
Evelyn Underhill

Completeness—Wholeness—Integration

A mystical experience or even many mystical experiences do not make someone a mystic. Being a mystic requires the integration of experience into an ongoing, deepening, contemplative awareness. Though we may reach a plateau of peace and maintain a high level of stability until we leave the body, there will be more tests ahead. As we go though future trials, will we maintain our peace or will we be pulled off course? It is possible to attain a level where there are no broken relationships; a place of truth and integrity; free of guilt, shame, and fear; a joyous state. We attain this plateau realizing that we already have what we need and that continuing to search is like looking for our glasses while they are resting on our nose.

Enlightenment is not about becoming divine.
It's about becoming more fully human.
It is the end of ignorance.
Lama Surya Das

Lama Surya Das (1950 – Present, USA) is an American-born Lama in the Tibetan Buddhist tradition. He is a poet, spiritual activist and author of several books on Buddhism. Born Jeffrey Miller in 1950, on Long Island, an honors graduate of the University at Buffalo, New York, Lama Surya Das spent many years studying in India and Tibet.

What is Enlightenment?

What would it be like to have no worries, no anxiety, no problems—no major concerns? What would it be like to hold no grievance, no hurt feelings, no unforgiveness or condemnation? What would it be like to be forever calm, patient, and serene? What would it be like to be free of judgment? What would it be like to experience the love of God flowing from the heart to everyone you met every day? What if there were no fears of death—no sense of limitation? What if you knew you were not a body? What would it be like to know eternity? What would it be like to know God?

The spiritual journey does not consist of arriving at a new destination where we gain something we did not have. It consists in the dissipation of ignorance concerning ourselves. Enlightenment comes in emergence from immaturity. We are not called upon to be angels; we are called upon to be mature human beings. *A Course in Miracles* repeatedly refers to us as little children. It never refers to us as adults. Jed McKenna speaks about our moving from Human Childhood, an ego state, to Human Adulthood. According to mystic Bernadette Roberts, author of *The Path to No Self*, "a mystic is an authentically, mature human being."

"Egoless" does not mean "less" than personal
it means "more than personal."
Ken Wilbur

The Empty or Whole Mind

John White, author of *What Is Enlightenment?* says that "Enlightenment is realization of the truth of Being." In enlightenment, the path, the goal, the journey, and the teaching become one. Enlightenment is being in a continuous, meditative state. It is living wonderfully, delightfully—meaningfully. Enlightenment is the surrender of duality. Wei Wu Wei refers to enlightenment as "whole-mind." Enlightenment is peace of mind; or, as Ramesh Belsekar says, it is an empty mind. Empty mind does not mean there are no thoughts. It means there are no distractions. The empty mind is like a calm body of water reflecting the brilliance of the moon. Nothing can take away our peace of mind. When the mind is empty, it is open. Like a mirror, an empty mind reflects without attachment. Free of the *busy* mind, we realize the *undisturbed* mind. Obsessive, compulsive, neurotic thinking is no longer. The world is what it is. An open mind is free. A closed mind lives in a prison. Addictions and grievances are prison houses of the mind. When the mind is still the universe surrenders.

All we see in darkness are shadows and illusions. In darkness, we believe there is much to fear. To be enlightened means to see in light. To see in light is to know truth. When we no longer see darkness we are enlightened. Spiritual sight, or true vision, brings light. The peace of enlightenment comes in letting go—nothing happens. The most profound element of enlightenment is simplicity. We do not have to manipulate anything. We do not have to have anything above and beyond the present.

When peace comes at last to those who wrestle with
temptation and fight against the giving in to sin;
when the light comes at last into the mind given to
contemplation; or when the goal is finally achieved
by anyone, it always comes with just one happy
realization; "I need do nothing."
A Course in Miracles

According to the modern mystic Wayne Teasdale, there are many transformative, contemplative, mystical stages of awareness and subtle forms of consciousness. According to Teasdale, there is a transpersonal awareness characterized by impersonal infinite mind. There are also angelic realms with numerous degrees of perfection and beyond that, Divine consciousness which is infinite awareness, compassion, love, and sensitivity in an eternal now. (See: *The Mystic Heart*, New World Library)

G.W.F. Hegel, Pierre Teilhard de Chardin, and Dr. David Hawkins each speak of our moving from perfection to perfection. Once a state of perfection is reached, the new state becomes the potential that eventually collapses into the next new state. The universe is infinite. What does infinite mean? There is no beginning and ending—there is no before and no after. There just is.

Delight in the Present Moment

If we achieve freedom from the ego, what then? As long as the body continues in time, there will be another minute. What do we do in the next minute? Though a mystic might have any occupation, mystics are often multi-talented, self-taught seekers. They are often polymaths and renaissance-type folk: musicians, poets, artists, writers, teachers, therapists, gardeners, and sculptors—crafts people of all sorts. They are simply folks who have learned how to stop, look, listen, and see deeply. Free from the tyranny of the ego and its "special" needs, we can just love. Enlightenment unfolds as we awaken from unhappy dreams and ego dramas. We can then embrace the world knowing it is an illusion. Free of judgment, everything has a fresh, "expectant shine." It's wonderful just "being." As Vilama Thaker says it, "As a lover of life, how can I stay out of life?"

Vimala Thakar (1920 – Present, India) is an Indian teacher and a student of Jiddu Krishnamurti. She teaches balancing inner spiritual development with outward social development. An active traveler and lecturer during the 60s and 70s she now lives at Mount Abu, Rajastan, India.

Alive, alert, and attentive, we are free to enjoy whatever presents itself—nature, relationships, exercise, dancing, laughing, playing music, singing, work, food, sexuality, reading, or any creative act. Mysticism includes Stoicism and Epicureanism. Physical appetites may be of little consequence. When it comes to sexuality, for example, the mystic might enjoy sharing life in this way or live without it with equanimity. In the same way—an apple eaten in a conscious, contemplative state is as delicious and as satisfying as a multi-course meal. A mystic might live alone or with others with equal composure. There is no need to avoid, mitigate, dull, or dilute life. Present in each moment, the mystic delights in the now.

Appreciation and Mindfulness

According to Franklin-Merrell Wolff, a mystic is anything but an ascetic because "He who has realized Spiritual Gold enjoys more, not less." Buddhism speaks of mindfullness or prayer-fullness. Of what are we mind "full?" Mind is full of the present. There is no place else to be. There is no place else to go. There is no fearful dreaming—no lingering guilt or haunting fear. All we need, we have. Present in the moment, we savor the moment, whatever it is. Mysticism sharpens focus as we do whatever needs doing. We are then attentive drivers, good typists, cooks, dishwashers, cleaners, mothers, fathers, brothers, sisters, employers and employees.

Events occur in the world which elicit a response. We may receive unwanted news. Though she knows there is no death, because a mystic loves deeply, she will mourn as much as anyone the loss of a parent, spouse, child, friend, or pet. Mourning is a part of spiritual growth. Embrace the pain. If you are going through hell—keep going. Time is a physician and grief is medicine and a necessary part of our letting go of the world. Though the immediacy of our loving is gone, that which is eternal can never be lost. It is natural to weep over that which has been our delight. Mysticism is, if anything, natural.

All of the things that people typically have
trouble with—money, food, sex, relationships, desire—
they want their saints to be without. "Egoless sages"
are "above that" is what people want.

Ken Wilbur

The Mystic Gourmet

Let's take one thing we all do several times a day, one thing we all enjoy—eating. Having dinner one evening with a friend, I noticed he was wolfing down his food, only occasionally looking up from his plate. Notice the way dogs eat. Often, in just one or two gulps, it's gone. They then look up at you begging for more and you think, "You could have savored that a little longer." Eating is a very physical activity and it's easy for it to become compulsive and thus overdone. The following is a suggestion only. Remember there are no laws, no rules or required ways of behaving for the mystic. Or, the only law there is is the law of love—but even this law we do not follow out of compulsion—we follow it because it's the best way.

Ten Suggestions for Conscious Eating

1. Before eating, look at the surroundings and those you are with.
2. Say a prayer of thanks aloud or to yourself.
3. Be thankful for the people you are with, the food, the cook or cooks, and the ambiance.

4. How does the food look—good?
5. Be patient, wait. Let others begin first.
6. Notice the mouthfeel.
   (Yes, there is such a word.)
   Is it—sweet, salty, sour, or bitter?
7. Eat slowly. Savor each bite.
   Relish in it. Delight in it. Notice the aroma, the fragrance, and the temperature.
8. If the cook is present, thank the cook.
   Or, thank those who prepared the meal.
9. Eat slowly. Put the fork down frequently perhaps even between each bite.
10. With friends or family, this is a time for relating—talking. How are the people with you? How are they doing? What was their day like? What are they thinking and feeling?

Detached Involvement and a Rest Most Busy

The mystic mind is calm, detached and involved, relaxed and alert. Relations are harmonious. Why wouldn't they be? There is no need for projection, reproof, argumentation or re-organization.

When faced with the ups and downs of life, still the
mind remains unshaken, not lamenting,
not generating defilements, always feeling secure.
This is the greatest happiness.

Buddhist Sutra Nipata

Having realized oneself as the Self is to become selfless. When there is no ego needing things to happen; when there is no need to change the world, we can love as God does—without conditions. The enlightened mind is a place of peace and ordered activity. It is according to Walter Hilton, a *rest most busy*. The mystic is alive, alert, attentive, yet also passive, quiet, and serene.

Selfishness is of the ego, but Self-fullness is of spirit
because that is how God created it.

A Course in Miracles

According to Tich Nhat Hanh, the seven factors of enlightenment are mindfulness, investigation of mental objects, energy, joy, tranquility, concentration, and equanimity. Bring awareness to all activities: working, shopping, exercising, singing, or dancing. We do what we do for the joy of doing it, with whomever, wherever we are. One of my favorite mystics is a philosophy professor who loves to wind surf; another is a musician, another is an airline attendant; another is a therapist; yet another is an accountant. They each embrace life and the other people in it in fullness.

When there is no ego needing things to happen; when there is no need to change the world, we can just be and love as God does—without conditions. According to Walter Hilton, enlightenment is a symptom of growth, or a living process. Spirit is overcome by a heavenly peace; but it is the peace of ordered activity, not idleness—*It is a rest most busy.* The mystic is alive, alert, attentive and yet passive, quiet and serene. The insanity of this world does not upset the mystic.

Walter Hilton (1340–1396, England) was a priest and canon of an Augustinian Priory. *His Scale of Perfection* is the first exhaustive work on mystical theology in the English language. It is a guidebook for the journey to "contemplation in perfect love of God".

Humility

Entering into Self is coming home. It is a returning to who we already are in our primordial condition; who we are from time immemorial. Along with the validation of Self there comes deep humility. In greatness we realize our small wonderful part in the larger scheme of God's universe.

I am a very little soul, who can offer
Only very little things to the Lord.

St. Thérèse de Lisieux

Saint Thérèse de Lisieux (1873–1897, France) was a Catholic nun who is now recognized as a Doctor of the Church. She is also known as "The Little Flower of Jesus." She is especially remembered for her spiritual memoir *L'histoire d'une âme* (The Story of a Soul). It was a religious best-seller in the early part of the 20th Century.

We come nearest to the great
when we are great in humility.

Rabindranath Tagore

Humility and grace are natural states for the mystics. If we are not in a state of grace, we are out of our natural environment. Spirit is in a constant state of grace. Our reality is Spirit, therefore we are each in a state of grace forever. The perception of God's grace, coupled with an acute awareness of her own state, formed the heart of Madame Gurion's autobiography. She thus could say, "My earnest wish is to paint in true colors the goodness of God to me, and the depth of my own ingratitude."

[It is] beyond the senses, beyond the understanding,
beyond all expression. It is the pure unitary
consciousness, wherein awareness of the world
and of multiplicity is completely obliterated.
It is ineffable peace. It is the Supreme Good.
It is One without a second. It is the Self.

Mandukya Upanishad

Wonder, Awe and Reverence.

Concepts create idols.
Only wonder comprehends anything.
People kill one another over idols.
Wonder makes us fall to our knees.

St. Gregory of Nyssa

St. Gregory of Nyssa (335–394, Greece) was a Christian bishop and the younger brother of St. Basil the Great. Gregory and his two brothers, Basil and Peter, are known as the Cappadocian Fathers. They tried to show that Christian philosophy was better than Greek philosophy. He is a major figure in *apophatic mysticism* which says it is easier to say what God is not than what God is. God is not limited. God is not hate, or fear or guilt, etc.

Wonder is evoked by the experience of an event inexplicable by the laws of the world. Confronted with the divine, we can only say, "Awe" like *Amen* or *Om*; it is the most basic of sounds and a deep release. In moments of awe, there are feelings of respect and veneration, honesty, and gratitude. In awe we behold what is and, like God after creation, say, "How very good it is." In wonder we praise God without words. It is said of the shepherds on the hillside, at the time of the birth of Jesus, that when the angels appeared to them, they were filled with awe. All they could do was look! It is an incredible thing to be a human being, and the more awake we are, the more incredible.

Freedom, Happiness, Joy, and Bliss

No one has ever been a lukewarm,
Indifferent, or unhappy mystic.

C.F. E. Spurgeon

True happiness is in the pursuit of the highest
good which is God. God sees everything.

Boethius

Nothing makes us happier than doing God's will. Doing God's will is what we want to do because it is our own will. Realizing identity with Reality brings freedom from suffering and death. St. Francis of Assisi embodied joy, as did Mother Theresa, Rumi, Kabir and Whitman. Words cannot express the jubilation of the mystic. Nothing is more exciting than "being." It is okay to have a good time in the universe. Salvation is a joyful event. Hinduism sees the world as something of a playground. The joyous antics of Hindu gods and goddesses exemplify this attitude. As Katherine Hepburn once observed, "I never lose sight of the fact that just being is fun." It is possible in every moment to be "in love" with the universe. Once we know God, we are free. Sorrow has ended and birth and death are no more.

We are born to be happy, to be abundantly supplied
with every good thing. To have fun in living,
to consciously unite with the Divine Power
that is around us and with us,
and to grow and expand forever.

Ernest Holmes

I have been delivered from this ego and self-will—
alive or dead, what an affliction! But alive or dead,
I have no homeland other than God's Bounty.

Rumi

Mysticism leaves us happy and free. Responsibility is not a burden. Enlightenment exists in freedom. We are all eternal. God has been, is and will be, taking care.

Joy is what happens to us when we allow
ourselves to recognize how good things really are.

Marianne Williamson

Marianne Williamson (1952 – Present, USA) is an author, spiritual activist, lecturer and founder of the Peace Alliance, a grass roots campaign to establish a Department of Peace. Her debut work *A Return to Love* was a *New York Times* bestseller in 1992. She is also a friend. We met in 1973 when she came to rent a room from my then girlfriend Edie Cadenhead in New York City.

Enthusiasm

Enthusiasm means "to be inspired"—the quality of having God within. It comes from the Greek *en* and *Theos*, or *God*. Enthusiasm is being *in God*. Being in God is the opposite of being in ego. In the seventeenth and eighteenth centuries, *enthusiasm* was religion experienced through an opening to the Divine. From this perspective, creed and dogmas are traps and restraints.

Why wait for Heaven?
Those who seek the light are merely covering
their eyes. The light is in them now.
Enlightenment is but a recognition,
not a change at all.

A Course in Miracles

Actually, no one can say "I am enlightened" because there is no "I" to be enlightened. While there is no "I" to be enlightened, it is fair to say that here, at the beginning of the twenty-first century, there are a growing number of mystics. Mysticism is becoming mainstream. Being the perennial philosophy it's always been, its time is coming round again. The more I travel, the more folks I meet, the more it seems clear that many people are ready for the undiluted truth of God. Every now and then someone will claim enlightenment. You may think you are the Christ—because you are but don't let it go to your head. When that happens, the subtle ego can take over and what was blissful becomes a downer.

Perhaps someone is enlightened, who am I to judge? As we have seen, judging is not the province of the mystic. Knowledge, fame, and power, however, are powerful intoxicants. Intoxicants can make people feel invincible. As contemporary author, Steven King says, "When beer takes over people do bad things." Intoxicants are toxic, and history shows that intoxication with power, or thinking that one is right can easily usurp wisdom, derail sanity and the potential for enlightenment. This often happens in hero mythology as it does, for example, with the villain Darth Vader of *Star Wars*.

If you think you are enlightened,
go and spend a week with your parents.
Ram Dass

The Brighter the Light, the Darker the Shadow

You may achieve a profound insight into the nature of the psyche. Some are called to share this information. Some of them are brilliant. Specialness—"thinking that we are someone"—takes us off track. Start believing your own press release and you're in trouble. Feeling we are blessed; feeling we know what "Christ Consciousness" or "Buddahood" is all about, can also bring omnipotence, and with it, the subtle slip-shod ego thought that we no longer have a shadow. If everything is working just right and you think you cannot make a mistake—beware.

To exist is to change, to change is to mature,
to mature is to go on creating oneself endlessly.
Henri Bergson

A Caution—The Illusion of Knowing

Enlightenment is an extraordinary experience. It involves a leap to an entirely new state of being. Having made the jump, it can be a precarious position. If you think you've arrived—you've probably got work to do. Without attention, spiritual insight turns into ego-aggrandizement. During the 1970s, 80s and 90s a number of gurus took heavy falls. How many of us know how much "stuff" may yet lie hidden in the cellars of the unconscious? Claiming perfection is risky business. Jesus got crucified for it as did the Islamic Sufi mystic Al Hallaj. Like Jesus, he was tried and executed for claiming that God had come to dwell in him.

Enlightenment does exist.
It is possible to awaken.
Unbounded freedom and joy, oneness with the Divine, awakening into a state of timeless grace—these experiences are more common than you know and not far away. There is one further truth, however: They don't last...
after the honeymoon comes the marriage.
Jack Kornfield
in *After the Ecstasy, the Laundry*, Introduction

Take an enlightened master from India, plop him down in Kansas give him a $2,000 a month mortgage, 3 kids, a dog and cat, a wife who nags, a boring job and an angry boss, insurance bills, credit card bills, taxes, and more, and see how long enlightenment lasts. If you think you are enlightened, try raising a teenager.

Contemporary mystic Andrew Cohen writes, "I started to notice that many of the individuals who'd had an identical *experience* to my own—in terms of its overwhelming intensity and apparently life-changing revelatory power, remained, as they say in the vernacular, not completely 'cooked,' or 'finished,'... In other words, it became clear over time that in most cases, the profound surrender of the ego or separate self-sense to God, or that unspeakable mystery, had not authentically occurred."

Andrew Cohen (1955 – Present, USA), is an American guru and spiritual teacher, author, and musician who has developed a path of transformation which he calls Evolutionary Enlightenment. He is the publisher of *What is Enlightenment?* magazine.

The longer I've lived, the more "stuff" I discover that I left buried somewhere which I may still need to look at. I think I'm beyond judgment and then make a judgment. I think I'm beyond anger and then I discover some annoyance and realize—I'm not there yet. The ego often plays the role of "sneaky Pete," slipping in the back door when we aren't looking. Fools do indeed rush in where angels fear to tread. In order to reveal the full strength of the soul's cementedness in God there is need of continual tests and trials of every kind. In this way all the sloth is burned off and we are left clean and whole.

Trials alone are the vehicles of unity's revelation, so much so that the most terrible of human trials is the herald of the greatest of human revelations.
Bernadette Roberts, *The Path to No Self*

God Is

There is a wonderful story about one of Helen Schucman's visionary dreams. She saw herself entering a cave in a bleak, windswept seacoast. In the cave she found an old parchment scroll. She picked it up and began to unroll the scroll. In the center were the words. "God is." She could also see on either sides the beginning of little letters. Then she heard a voice which said, "If you unroll the scroll to the left you will be able to see into the past, and if you unroll the scroll to the right you will be able to see into the future."

The little letters on the sides were beginning to become clearer and she was tempted to look more closely. Then she quickly rolled the scroll up to everything except the middle part which said, "God Is." She said, "I'm not interested in the past or the future. I'll stop with this." Then she heard the voice say, "Thank you. You made it this time." Helen was given a test and she passed it. How many time does temptation come our way, we make a choice and no one says "Thank you!" To dig up the past or project into the future is not to be contented and at home, the place where "God Is."

We can barely see the ego by ourselves and we need the honest critique of friends. Listen to them! Freedom from ego requires perseverance and a readiness to stay awake and attentive. I would not want to claim enlightenment unless it could be done with complete assurance that I was "there." Jesus did it. He could afford to, because it was real. He also got hung on a cross for it. Fortunately, it was all part of the plan.

...a man without a self is not about to stand up
and say, "I have no sin." He cannot say this because
the truth of the matter is "he has no I."
When there is no "who" anymore, the question
of who sins or does not sin is a contradiction.

Bernadette Roberts

To exist is to change, to change is to mature,
to mature is to go on creating oneself endlessly.

Henri Bergson

Henri-Louis Bergson (1859–1941, France) was a major philosopher, evolutionist and friend of William James. He won the Nobel Prize for literature in 1927. He is best known for his book *Creative Evolution.*

Characteristics of a Mystic and a Mystical Path

Whatever discipline or path we choose: Sufism, *A Course in Miracles*, Buddhism, Taoism, Gnosticism, Yoga, Mystical Christianity, the Kabala, any of the thousands of forms, or simply our own unique inner paths—all mystical paths reflect one universal, perennial path. This path has certain characteristics.

Mysticism has no requirements.

Mysticism makes no demands. There is no pledge to sign. There are no rules or regulations. There is no organization for mystics, no pledges, no dues. There are no magic formulas, no mysteries, no secrets, no oaths, no rites, no rituals, no dogmas, and no creeds. Relax, take a deep breath. God makes no demands.

Mysticism does not proselytize.

Mysticism is not about converting or being in competition with any thought system. There is no missionary effort and no saving of lost souls because there are no lost souls. There are those who know and those who have temporarily forgotten. Some folks remember God now, and others will be remembering. For the enlightened few—God's kingdom has come. For the seeker it's—*Thy Kingdom Come.*

Mysticism brings purpose and meaning and enables the completion of our destiny.

Mysticism does not have an agenda. Mysticism is a matter of "listening" and doing God's will without demanding that our will be done. The mystic sees the insanity of the world, and then chooses not to play the game. Truth is truth and needs no proof. Truth does not cause anything. Truth is everything. Revelation replaces the illusion of a separate, individual ego.

A Mystic is happy to help.

Having much, it is easy to share. The mystic lives for, and with, God and neighbor. When God loves us, God loves God. The mystic gains everything and loses nothing. It is one of the pleasant obligations of the awakened to help awaken those who sleep. If someone asks for help, the mystic helps. See a need, respond to the need. Mysticism is a place of "balance," so one also learns to help without being taken advantage of.

Mysticism is inclusive.

Mysticism is interfaith and not against anything. There are no opposites and no enemies. There is no need to castigate or make wrong. This does not mean that others might not behave in hurtful ways. There is no reason, however, to attack those who see differently than we do. Mysticism identifies with the all—mankind, nature, animals, the earth, music, the mind, the heart.

Mysticism attracts without persuasiveness.

Mysticism disregards glamorization. There is no hierarchy in mysticism. No one is special. We are all equal here. There is no pomp and pageantry. Though a mystic might be a monk or brother, a priest or minister, mystics, on the whole do not wear special clothing. Everyone is respected. We are all just people here.

There is no guilt in mysticism and no fear.

Life is eternal, and there is nothing to be afraid of. At death, only the illusory shell, the body and the false ego self is lost. In this loss there is freedom. The best thing about dying is that prison doors are open and the body no longer places a hold on spirit. This is the message of resurrection.

Mystics appreciate silence and autonomy.

Mystics are not loners, yet it easy to be alone. They also mix well with others. They want to know how others are doing and their appreciation of people and things is fresh. They often have a few strong intimate relationships that are profound, deeply loving, and long-lasting.

Mysticism is realistic and responsible.

Mystics accept themselves, other people, and the natural world for what it is. They get on with life and "let others be." Mystics are good time managers, preferring to do it now, rather than delaying, tabling, or waiting. Living in the now also enables focus and flow.

Mysticism is simple.

It is so simple that it is easily missed, misinterpreted or misunderstood. The mystical lies hidden in most "ordinary" experiences and the most obvious of spots. It lies quietly in the heart.

Mysticism is creative.

Mysticism naturally finds creative expression in a myriad of forms. Even ordinary things are interesting, including that which others might pass over as ordinary.

Mysticism is fun.

Mystics are spontaneous. Mystics like to play, easily see irony, and laugh frequently. In possession of the moment—the moment is everything.

Mysticism is grateful.

Gratitude is a fundamental quality of mysticism. What an incredible thing it is to be a child of God. What an incredible thing it is to *be*!

Mysticism is an affirmation of life.

All there is is life. Mysticism is thus appreciative and compassionate and aware of an intrinsic beauty.

Mysticism is patient.

Mysticism is tolerant, uncomplaining, tranquil, and serene.

Mystics are not special.

Everyone is ordained by God and everyone will one day realize the truth of God.

Mysticism is free.

As a dew-drop slips from the leaf into the river, and the river slips into the ocean, so the mystic slips into the All. Now the mystic is the ocean.

Mysticism just is. "Is-ness" is wonderful.

Appendix

An Appendix is an Addition.

As one of my mentors, Rabbi Joseph Gelberman says,

Not instead of but in addition to.

I've quoted so many different individuals throughout this text that it might be helpful to add a timeline on the history and evolution of mysticism. The next several pages could easily develop into another book. Perhaps someday they will. There seems to be a call for it. We'll see. Remember, mysticism as a manifestation of eternity stays the same. It does not evolve. It is itself a constant.

In time, mysticism is something we discover, not something we create. As different individuals come to an awakening in different epochs and ages, their approaches are inevitably dissimilar to, yet the same as, those of other times and places. The thoughts of these great men and women have colored the whole of humanity. St. Augustine for example (C. 400), among the earliest of the Christian theologian mystics, strongly influenced the works of many of the mystics who came after him. Philosophical thinking usually develops in a *response* to or *reaction* to previous thought.

The History of Philosophy and the Philosophy of History

By studying the history of philosophy, we can see how thought has evolved, devolved, and then evolved again in a new way. History tells a story about how things have been and therefore very likely the way they are going to go. All theological and philosophic thinking comes in response to the thought that preceded it. Each philosopher looks back to those who have gone before. They then have something to say about what was good or true or "right on" in that thinking. They then add their insights. Religion is in a constant state of flux and changes in time. Liberal periods are followed by more conservative times, and the conservative times are followed by times of liberation. Major changes also take place when one religion "invades" another religion, as Catholicism changed when it came in contact with the native religions of Central and South America. Although Catholicism won out, it had to go though many adaptations.

The Protestant Reformation was a direct response to growing corruption in the Catholic Church. It developed in many different directions. One was the creation of the Protestant Church, which in turn split into literally thousands of different denominations, politics, and interpretations. Another development was the growth of esoteric philosophies like the Freemasons, the Rosicrucians, and the Order of the Golden Dawn. At the same time, there was a new emphasis on mysticism outside of the realms of any form of organized religion or revelations in science. The sexual liberalism of sixteenth century Europe was in part a response to the heavy-handedness of the Catholic Church, and Puritanism developed in direct response to the sixteenth century's sexual liberalism. When things change they often take a wild swing in the opposite direction.

To be *against* is to be in ego. We cannot "fight" against crime or "stamp out" evil. While murderers should not be allowed to continue to murder or other criminals to commit crimes, the way we truly change things is to provide a better, clearer example. The Church's method of dealing with what it did not like was to stamp it out, to kill it completely and utterly. This process inevitably makes opposition stronger. Mystics listen to what people have to say—without telling them what to do. Had the church engaged in its own reformation, history obviously would have been different. This following history is a reporting of what happened in time and how it affected the whole of what we call spirituality.

Time, Texts and Teachers

A Short History of the Evolution of Mysticism, Philosophy and Religion

History would not exist if the same errors
were not being repeated in the present.
A Course in Miracles

The story of the interplay between spirit and ego is fascinating. "Truth" is indeed stranger than fiction. And yet what is the truth? Is mythology the truth? Is history the truth? Is the ego's story the truth? Is history the record of a disaster or a story of promise? The extravagances of the ego are inestimable. As I watched the airplanes fly into the twin towers in New York City, the first thought that went through my mind was a line from the Course which says, "Never underestimate the insanity of the ego." The ego is quite insane and can do insane things like flying airplanes into skyscrapers, possibly screaming "Vengeance is mine!"

Much of history is one battle after another, one tribe killing another tribe, one emperor squeezing out another emperor, one pope stepping on another pope, one class suppressing another, one nation taking over another nation. What we have is one soap-opera after another; we need only look at our own nation and the situation in the Middle East. The story of brother against brother is the oldest story in the Bible, next to creation itself. As soon as we've got a body, we've got an ego; we've got competition and we've got trouble right here in River City. (From *The Music Man* in case you did not remember).

As long as the ego is in charge, it plays itself out in acts of anger and aggression. This scenario will continue till there is no more need for time. As Ralph Waldo Emerson expressed it, "History is one damn thing after the other." Or, as English historian Edward Gibbon, author of *The Decline and Fall of the Roman Empire* said, "History is little more than the register of the crimes, follies, and misfortunes of mankind." Spirit remains constant, while ego tries and fails, redevelops and then tries and fails again. Every time the ego fails, Spirit lovingly picks up the pieces. Mankind, hopefully, gains a better perspective, and we move forward once again, *trying* to remember not to repeat the mistakes of the past. Then we run into something we don't like; ego takes a hold, and we have another power play, another assassination, another political upheaval and another war.

In 1841, during the progressive period of industrialization and colonization, Ralph Waldo Emerson published a series of essays in which he sets out a transcendentalist approach to history where the "innate Humanity" that is common to all of mankind is seen as operating throughout the ages in the shaping of events.

There is one mind common to all individual men.
Of the works of this mind history is the record.
The creation of a thousand forests is in one acorn,
and Egypt, Greece, Rome, Gaul, Britain, America,
lie folded already in the first man. Epoch after epoch,
camp, kingdom, empire, republic, democracy, are
merely the application of this manifold spirit to the
manifold world.

Emerson hoped for a broad and deep viewing of history, one that would demonstrate the evolution of humanity to a higher ideal. Following Darwin, Wallace, and the other creative force philosophers of the nineteenth and twentieth centuries; Schelling, Huxley, Bergson, and Pierre Teilhard de Chardin each held out hope for the positive evolution of man. Sir Alister Hardy, who did extensive research on mysticism, wrote *The Divine Flame*, a book on *The Evolution of Religion*. We see this evolution now in the decline of Catholicism and main-line Protestantism, the growth of Buddhism (perhaps the world's most peaceful religion), and the growing interest in more open mystical, interfaith, New Thought, and holistic perspectives.

Religious Freedom and Personal Religion

A comparison can be seen between the Inquisition and the political police of the Roman Catholic Church and the Holocaust and the Gestapo. During the Inquisition, the priests in charge did anything they wanted to get a confession, as did the Gestapo. One difference between the Inquisition and the Holocaust, however, is that the Inquisition lasted for 650 years (1184–1834), while the Holocaust lasted a much shorter period. Like the black plague, the Inquisition went likes waves from one country to another; as it was beginning to dissipate in one country, after a while it was renewed in yet another.

The history of the Church is an autocratic story of the suppression of freedom, while mysticism is the granting or discovering of freedom, not the loss of it. Pope Innocent III (1161–1226, pope from 1198–1226) is thought to have been responsible for the death of more than two million people. Under his orders, Jews and Islamic people were given a choice—convert or die. Those whose faith and will were strong died.

As long as we live in time, we can make use of this wonderful tool called "time" for spiritual growth. Although living in time, the mystic experiences "collapses" of time—when receiving an insight and suddenly coming to a more enlightening perspective. Such collapses of time bring the mystic into the center of Now. When we reach the mystic's perspective and are centered in the Now, we see that we already have everything we need. There is no need for war. We know that when we freely share, we all prosper.

His-story

History is all about people. Indeed, there are those who say that there is no history as such, just biographies. History can, after all, be understood as "his-story" or "her-story." In any event, it's about the personalities of different individuals and how for good or ill they affected the whole of mankind. What matters historically and otherwise is what kind of people they were. Were they kind and benevolent, or were they selfish, arrogant, and egotistical? History is about people with power. It's also about creative, loving, and adventurous people. It's about people of genius, like Michelangelo and Albert Einstein. It's about people who make discoveries. It's about people with drive. It's about megalomaniacs, like Genghis Kahn and Hitler, and deeply spiritual mystics, like St. Francis of Assisi, Gandhi, and Martin Luther King, Jr.

Don't Miss It for the World

A study of history shows that the ego repeatedly implodes. As Jesus in the Gospels expresses it, "What good does it do to gain the whole world and lose your own soul?" We cannot lose our souls, but we can lose our awareness of them. The more "fascinated" we are with the world, the more we buy into game playing, the more we lose awareness of our souls, the more empty life becomes. The lives of such dictators as Hitler, Mussolini, Hannibal, Attila the Hun, Napoleon, and Genghis Kahn all came to unpleasant ends. Alexander the Great, the first and perhaps the toughest of the batch, sought to make the whole world his, and he nearly succeeded. He never lost a battle and killed hundreds of thousands. Although other conquerors would outdo him, Alexander killed more people than anyone in history up to that time. Then when he was just 33 years old, he was himself killed, historians think, probably by malaria. A tiny mosquito did him in. Those who seek to dominate history and to make the world theirs, lose out time and time again. In the last temptation of Jesus, the devil takes him to a high mountain, shows him all the kingdoms of the world, and tells him that he can have them all if he will kneel down and worship him—the ego. After each of the tyrants died their kingdoms were divided among their generals. Eventually, these kingdoms too disappeared. Every time the ego fails, Spirit breaks through again like a Phoenix rising out of the ashes.

The tyrant dies and his rule is over,
The martyr dies and his rule begins.
Soren Kierkegaard

St. Francis & Genghis Kahn

Let's consider two contemporaries of the twelfth century who died one year apart: Saint Francis of Assisi in Italy (1182–1226) and Genghis Kahn (1166–1227) in Mongolia. Genghis Kahn is an example of the ego out of control. When Genghis Kahn raided a town or village, he killed everyone: men, women, children and even animals. Only one person, usually a cleric (someone who could write), would be left alive to tell the tale of how horrible were the acts of Genghis Kahn. On the other hand, St. Francis has been called the best example of Jesus since Jesus. Although (like Alexander the Great) Genghis Kahn sought to make the whole world his and nearly succeeded, St. Francis was not interested in owning anything—he loved everything—and was thereby incredibly rich. Spirit does not battle because there is no battle. Thinking there is a battle gets us into trouble. Televangelists tell us there is a fight going on with the devil, and we need to get an army of Christian solders. A headline in the newspaper one day said *"Musicians for Peace Face Hostile Take Over."* Think about that! Spirit simply loves, waits for the ego to fail, and then cleans up the mess. Time and time again, Spirit breaks though the darkness. Time and again, the ego becomes power hungry and then fails. Every time the ego fails, a little more love comes through. As Mahatma Gandhi was to say:

When I despair, I remember that all through history
the ways of truth and love have always won.
There have been tyrants, and murderers,
and for a time they can seem invincible,
but in the end they always fail.
Think of it... always!

A Short Chronology

The subsequent list is far from comprehensive. Neither is the list of all of the following individual mystics. Some of them no doubt saw further and were able to live more peacefully than others. This list also includes a few people who are not thought of as mystics, although they made a contribution to the understanding of the psychology of man and thus to mysticism. Aristotle, Galileo, Henry VIII, Mark Twain, Thomas Paine, Thomas Jefferson, Shelly, Voltaire, Nietzsche, and Sigmund Freud, for example, are not thought of as mystics; yet they each play an important role in the development of spirituality. Mark Twain saw the non-reality of this world, and Sigmund Freud helped us understand the nature of this thing we call an ego. Henry VIII helped transform the church, and men like Thomas Jefferson and Thomas Paine gave us a country with freedom of religion. I'm including a few tidbits along the way, a note about what else is happening in time, in scientific discoveries, world exploration, developments in literature and art, etc. The following are those thinkers who have had the greatest influence on me. Another writer might have a different list, though no doubt there would be many overlaps.

The Greatest Scriptural Texts

In the beginning was the Word.
And the Word was with God
and the Word was God.
John 1:1

Fundamental Eastern Texts
Hinduism: One of Our Oldest Religions

Our oldest scriptures are songs and poems. It's true for the *Vedas* from Hinduism, the *Psalms* from Judaism, and the *Iliad* and the *Odyssey* from Ancient Greece. Mythology plays an important role in helping us understand the basic cosmology of a religion. *Cosmology* comes from the Greek *kosmos*, meaning "world or universe," and *ology*, meaning "the study of." Cosmology is concerned with man's place in the cosmos and the interrelatedness of all things. Eastern texts are more cosmological than Western texts. Eastern texts focus on questions concerning *balance* and *harmony*. Western texts are more history driven and focus more on law.

B.C.E. (Before the Common Era)

Akhenaton, a Pharaoh of Egypt who reigned from 1353 to 1336 B.C.E., tries to introduce the idea of monotheism into Egyptian culture. His wife Nefertiti was made world-famous by the discovery of her beautiful sculpted and painted statue.

Humanity's oldest scriptures are the ***Vedas*** and the ***Upanishads***. They concern themselves with cosmological questions. It is generally believed they were composed in India between 1,500-500 B.C.E.; some scholars, however, think they were written as early as 1,800 B.C.E. The one underlying theme of these scriptures is the inner realization of the identity of Atman (Self) and Brahman (Universal Consciousness).

In this very being of yours,
You do not perceive the True;
But there in fact it is. In that which is the subtlest
essence of your own being, all that exists has its Self.
An invisible and subtle essence is the Spirit of the
whole universe. That is the True,
that is the Self, and thou art That.
From the *Chandogya Upanishad*

The *Vedas* and the *Upanishads* explain the philosophy of ***Vedanta***, the world's oldest and most basic philosophy. Based on the *Vedas*, Vedanta is a combination of the word *Vedas*, which means "knowledge" of our divine nature and *anta*, which means "the end of" or "the goal of." Vedanta is a search for the Self knowledge that is also the knowledge of God. Vedanta affirms the oneness of existence, the divinity of the soul, and the harmony of religion. Its application is relevant to all countries, cultures, and tribal backgrounds. Many of the mystics profiled in this book were or are strongly influenced by Vedanta.

In 1,000–500 B.C.E. India, we find the composition of the ***Mahabharata*** which contains the ***Bhagavad Gita***, "The Song of God," the Bible of India. Attributed to the legendary sage Vyas, *The Bhagavad Gita* is a dialogue between Arjuna, a warrior on the battlefield, and Krishna, his chariot driver, an incarnation of God. It symbolizes a dialogue between a man and his indwelling Spirit, or Self.

Hinduism as I know it entirely satisfies my soul, fills
my whole being... When doubts haunt me, when
disappointments stare me in the face, and when I see
not one ray of light on the horizon, I turn to the
Bhagavad Gita, and find a verse to comfort me.
Mahatma Gandhi

In Hinduism there is nothing like the obligatory monotheism of the West. ("Thou shalt have no other Gods.") Also, Hinduism has for the most part not tried to proselytize itself. It does not "compete" for the souls of other people because it's important to purify one's own soul.

The Axail Age. Though scholars are not sure why, an interesting event occurs around 500 B.C.E. During this time, several of the world's major religions appear. First Zoroaster starts Zoroastrianism in Persia; then in India, Mahavira starts Jainism, and Buddha begins Buddhism; in China, Lao-Tzu begins Taoism, and Confucius begins Confucianism; in Ancient Greece, it's the time of the great Pythagoras, the other Pre-Socratic Philosopher; and then Socrates, Plato, and Aristotle. It is also the time of the development of monotheism in Judaism. Each of these theologies took the old religions from the past and transformed them into a more transcendental approach to the supreme. This theme is played out time and again throughout the course of history.

In China B.C.E.

700–500 B.C.E. The Classic Chinese books the ***I Ching*** and the ***Tao Te Ching*** written around 600 B.C.E. describe a cosmology that centers on the balance of opposites, the evolution of events as a process, and the acceptance of the inevitability of change. Sixth century, B.C.E. ***Lao Tzu***, is the legendary author of the ***Tao Te Ching***. Tao is the highest, omnipresent order of the universe. A life following Tao is a life lived in accordance with nature.

Confucius (551–479 B.C.E.) is not a mystic as much as he is a socialist and a legalist. His many sayings recorded in the ***Analects*** are basic to the whole of Chinese Philosophy. *Jen* or human-heartedness is the highest virtue. *Li* (order) is the path to attaining *Jen*.

We might think of Taoism and Confucianism as representative of left-brain and right-brain thinking. Taoism says: lie back, relax, and follow the natural flow of things. Confucianism, on the other hand, is analytical, logical, and rational. It says there is a proper direction that things should follow. When it comes to sex, Taoism says it is part of nature. Confucianism, however, speaks of "right" relationships, and everything is run by *Li*—Law.

The ***Tripitaka*** is the canon of the Buddhist scriptures. *Tripitaka* means "the three baskets or containers." The most mystical part of the *Tripitaka* is the ***Dhammapada***, or the *Treasury of Truth*, consisting of 423 verses attributed to the Buddha in the course of his forty-five-year teaching ministry. An important aspect of Buddhism is the experience of "awakening." *Buddha* is a title, not a proper name, and means "one who is awake." Whenever you see a quote attributed to Buddha, there is a very good chance it is not from Buddha, although it probably is from a Buddhist.

In the West B.C.E.

The Bible is a compilation of writings comprised of 66 books written over a period of 1,600 years by 40 or more people. The Old Testament contains 39 books written from approximately 1,500 to 400 B.C. The New Testament contains 27 books written from approximately 40 to 100 A.D. Mark, the first gospel to be written, dates from around 70 A.D. The Bible has been an important inspirational tool for billions of people. Sitting at my desk, I can reach out and pick up the ostrich leather bound red-letter edition of the King James Version of the Bible with concordance and subject index my mother Milly gave me for my thirteenth birthday. I loved it then and love it still. Like a lot of scriptures, the Bible is a mixed bag. In places like the Sermon on the Mount and the other many sayings of Jesus, I am convinced that we are reading the word of God. Much of the story of King David, however, reads like a soap opera. God of the Old Testament is not always a nice guy; He is anthropomorphic, angry, and jealous—"Thou shalt have no other Gods before me." He kills whoever displeases him. He slays the Egyptians, and destroys Sodom and Gomorra. He brings plagues, fires, and pestilence. As the British novelist, Virginia Woolf (1882–1941) expressed it, *"I read the Book of Job last night. I don't think God comes out well."*

In Judaism

The area of Jewish thought that discusses cosmology is found in the ***Kabbalah***, meaning "to be receptive or to accept." A mystic is "receptive," rather than "projective." Traditionally, the *Kabbalah* is not taught until the age of forty, when students have completed their education in the books of the law—the ***Torah*** and the ***Talmud***—and are old enough to understand more esoteric teachings. According to ancient Judaism, scripture can be understood on different levels with a higher, or deeper, level being available to those who have received proper training. The Talmud is a recording of various rabbinic discussions pertaining to Jewish laws, moral code, traditions, and history. It is composed of the *Mishnah* from around the year 200, the earliest written collection of Jewish oral law, and the *Gemara* from about 500, a discussion of the Mishnah and related other rabbinical writings.

The Ancient Greeks

The Mystery Religions

1,800 B.C.E.–400 A.D. The Eleusinian, Dionysian, Orphic, and Mithraic Mysteries developed first in Greece and then Italy. *Mystery* comes from the Latin *mysterium*, meaning "secret rite or doctrine." Someone who follows a Mystery is a *mystes*, "one who has been initiated," from *myein* "to close, shut." Only initiates are allowed to observe and participate in rituals. Mystery religions are characterized by their lack of orthodoxy and scripture. The meaning of 'mystery' is preserved in the expression 'mystery play'.

The Pre-Socratics

Socrates is such an important figure in Western philosophy that those before him are called Pre-Socratics. With Socrates, we now have a new concept of the philosopher as "a lover of wisdom." It is an exciting time with many developments of *techne* "news skills," from which we get the word "technology."

C. 585 **Thales** is thought of as *the first rational philosopher*. He believed that "There are Gods in all things." A joke was once made about him by a servant girl because Thales, walking along looking up into the night sky, fell into a well. Mystics are thus people with "their heads in the air." His students were Anaximander and Pythagoras.

580–490 B.C.E. **Pythagoras** (Italy) founded the religious movement called Pythagoreanism, which emphasizes a mystical relationship between numbers, nature, and soul. He is best known for the discoveries of the Pythagorean Theorem and that music is mathematical.

540–480 B.C.E **Heraclites** was the first to create a philosophical system. He influenced Socrates and Plato. "All that we see when awake is death."

515–450 B.C.E **Parmenides** said that all that exists is unchanging. Change is an illusion. Being, or "is-ness," is the fullness of existence. Parmenides loved paradoxes.

C. 490–430 B.C.E **Zeno of Elea** was a disciple of Parmenides. Reality is one. Like Parmenides and most mystics, he too loved paradoxes.

490–420 B.C.E. **Protagoras of Abdera** said that man is the measure of all things. What is true is dependent upon the mind that is making the judgment.

C. 460–370 B.C.E. **Hippocrates** is the most famous physician of the ancient world.

C. 350–275 B.C.E. **Euclid** was a great mathematician. All mathematics can be expressed in lines, areas or solids. Space is infinite.

The pre-Socratics got us thinking about the nature of reality. They all place a great importance on unity of being and believe there is something behind everything—this "something" is in charge of the cosmos. Also, there is a turning away from mythology to an understanding of order unrelated to what happens with the gods.

469–399 B.C.E. **Socrates**, the teacher of Plato, was influenced by Pythagoras and Heraclites. He was a man of reason who obeys divine guidance. Short, stocky, jovial, balding with a pudgy nose, he develops the "Socratic" method of teaching—asking leading questions that draw out the right answer. He was so gentle, so kind that all of his students loved him. Charged with atheism and corrupting the youth, he was condemned to death.

428–347 B.C.E. **Plato**, along with Socrates and Aristotle, laid the foundation for Western philosophy. The goal of the intellect is the discovery of eternal, immutable forms or "ideas." There are some who believe that nothing new has been said since Plato.

384–322 B.C.E. **Aristotle**, a student of Plato, developed his own school. Human inquiry is guided by its end, which is a particular good. He believed that the world, the cosmos, and all things are "alive." He was also a tremendous influence on later mystics.

341–270 B.C.E. **Epicurus** was interested in mental tranquility, or *ataraxia*—the state of being detached from the cares of the world and at peace with oneself. Today, however, an epicure is considered to be someone who enjoys fine food and drink.

Stoicism and Deism

333–264 B.C.E. **Zeno** is thought of as the first of the Stoic philosophers. Stoicism teaches self-control, resilience, and detachment from negative and selfish emotions. Indifference to distractions allows for clear thinking, which improves spiritual well-being. Stoicism was an important influence on many later mystics, including Seneca and Marcus Arelius.

C. 4–65 a.d. **Seneca** was a Roman Stoic philosopher, statesman, dramatist, and humorist of the Silver Age of Latin literature. The teacher of Nero, Seneca was killed by Nero during a fit of his insanity.

55–135 A.D. **Epictetus** was a Greek Stoic philosopher and deist best remember for saying, "We are disturbed not by events, but by the views which we take of them."

Deism says that the existence and nature of God must be derived from reason and personal experience, rather than from scripture or the testimony of other people. What organized religions see as divine revelation and holy books, deists see as interpretations made by others. While deists believe in God, they may or may not participate in "organized religion." Often, they do not.

161–180 A.D. **Marcus Aurelius** was a Roman emperor, stoic philosopher, deist, and one of the five "good" Emperors. The universe is governed by reason, which is God. Human happiness is a life lived in accordance with reason. The bad acts of others do not harm us. We are harmed only by our own "ideas" about those acts. All things happen as they should.

The First Century and Beyond

4 B.C.–29 A.D. **Jesus'** (Israel) teachings became the foundation for Christianity. Jesus was a mystic. He "saw" into the beyond and talks about it. The whole of his message that theologians agree to tell us about concerns the Kingdom of Heaven. God is his Father and Heaven his home. We are all strangers here, but it is possible to know Heaven even in this world. If we love God, we will be able to see God. When we love the world, all we see is the world. We cannot serve two masters; we cannot follow ego and spirit.

14 **Caesar Augustus** died. His wife Lyvia killed off (poisons) Caesar's children from his previous marriage and eventually poisons Augustus so her son Tiberius can become Emperor. Caesar's dying words are, *"Did I play my part well in this tragedy?"* He seemed to have known that it was all a dreadful game.

35–107 **Ignatius of Antioch** was a Christocentric mystic. For him Christ's death and resurrection took on a mystical significance.

64 **Rome caught fire** and burned for six days. Emperor Nero, needing a scapegoat, blamed the Christians. A reign of terror followed including the murder of Nero's old teacher, Seneca. Christians literally went underground into the catacombs for their worship.

64 **St. Peter**, the disciple of Jesus, was crucified upside down in Rome.

69–155 **St. Polycar** had a mystical vision that foretold his martyrdom by fire.

105–165 **Justin Martyr**, influenced by Pythagoras, Plato, Aristotle, and Stoicism, used Greek philosophy as a steppingstone to Christian theology.

Neo-Platonism

205–270 **Plotinus** is considered the father of Neo-Platonism which is based on the teachings of Plato. It is a form of idealistic monism—all is one. The Soul is real; the body is not. There is a World Soul, which is the Mind. Above the intellect is the One. The concept of the One is more clearly defined than it was by Plato. Upon death of the body, the soul returns to the Monad or One.

185–254 **Origen** in Palestine was a student of Plotinus. God is the Ground of Being; unknowable except to Spirit. God has communicated through the Logos, the word made manifest in Jesus, Moses, and the Greek Philosophers. Though each individual soul has fallen, we will ultimately return to God through the Logos, or Christ.

232–305 **Porphyry** compiled Plotinus' *Enneads*, and wrote a *Life of Plotinus*. Strongly anti-Christian, he is an important figure in the history of Christian mysticism.

257 Rome issued an edict forbidding Christianity.

272 Roman Emperor **Lucius Aurelianus** burned the great library at Alexandria. Many of the books were moved. The Christians finish the job of the library's destruction in 391. One of the saddest events in history – tens of thousands of books are lost.

296–373 **St. Ananasius**, Bishop of Alexandria, wrote *Life of Anthony*. He influenced later Eastern Orthodox mysticism.

263–339 **Eusebius of Caesarea**, the bishop of Caesarea in Palestine, is called the father of church history because he recorded the history of the early church. He compiled his version of the New Testament, and Emperor Constantine had him make 50 copies. Although none of the copies survived, we know his version of the New Testament was in use during the Middle Ages and is different from what we use today.

The Gnostic Gospels

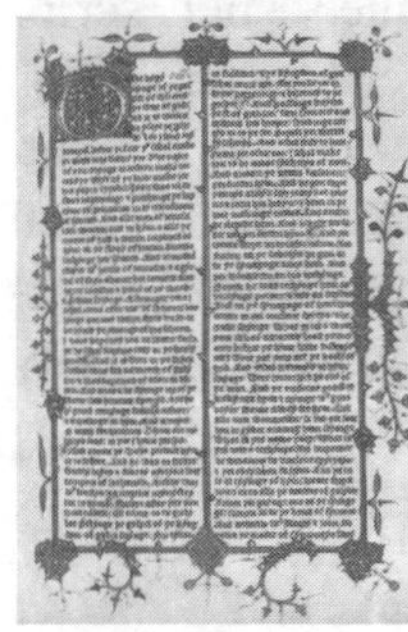

The Gospels of the Bible focus mainly on the body and the world, while the Gnostic Gospels are more concerned with the mind and the heart. For the Gnostics, as for the Hindus and the Buddhists, the material world is an illusion. People fall asleep and are seduced into thinking the world is real. According to the Gnostics, there is a deeper wisdom revealed by Jesus that can lead us out of this illusory world. We have to be able to "see," or "know," the non-material world in order to attain it.

The word *Gnostic* comes from *gnosis*, which means "knowledge." The Gnostics say we can be privy to a knowledge about the divine, hence the name. Until 1945 our knowledge of the Gnostic Gospels was limited to criticism from the early Church Fathers who wrote against them. Most of the Gnostic Gospels were discovered in 1945 in Nag Hammadi in Upper Egypt, when an Arab peasant happened upon the scrolls in a series of caves. While Orthodox Jews and Christians say that a chasm separates humanity from its creator (God is wholly other and must be worshipped and honored), the Gnostic Gospels see God as Self-evident. Self-knowledge is also knowledge of God; the Self and the divine are one and the same. There is no separation.

Jesus in the Gnostic Gospels speaks of *illusion* and *enlightenment*, not *sin* and *repentance*. Instead of coming to save us from sin, Jesus comes as a guide to provide access to mystical knowledge and thereby salvation. When the disciple attains enlightenment, Jesus no longer serves as spiritual master, for the two become one. Included in the Gnostic Gospels are *The Gospel of Thomas*, *The Secret Book of James*, *The Gospel of Mary*, *The Gospel of Truth*, *The Act of Peter*, *The Gospel of Judas*, and many more. (The best book on this topic is *The Gnostic Gospels* by Elaine Pagels.)

The Desert Fathers and The Beginning of Christian Monasticism

The Desert Fathers were early Christian hermits, ascetics, and monks who lived in the desert of Egypt and Israel beginning in the third century. They were mostly Christians fleeing the persecution of the Roman Empire. They observed strict self-discipline as did their contemporaries, the hermits in India.

251–356 **St. Anthony** is the most famous of the Desert Fathers and the Father of Monasticism. His long periods of fasting produce incredible hallucinations and visions.

The Beginning of The Holy Roman Catholic Church

280–337 **Constantine**, the Roman emperor, adopts Christianity. In 313 he made Christianity the state religion. A number of other older Roman cults and religions remain active. Constantine is responsible for the creation of the institutional church and had Eusebius draw up a list of books to be included in the Bible. After this, more mystics fled to the desert seeking spirituality through hermitage (living alone) and in monasteries, thus avoiding as much as possible the politics of institutions.

347–395 **Theodosius**, the Emperor of Rome after Constantine, in 391 made Christianity "the official religion of Rome. All pagan rituals were banned. ***The Nicene Creed***, a statement of correct belief, was made binding on all subjects. Things were tightening up. There was a right way to do things to be a true Christian. This leads to war with the non-Christians. Theodosius also stops the Olympic Games, which have been going on since 776 B.C.E. They did not resume until the nineteenth century.

367 **New Testament Codified.** The letters of Paul, along with Matthew, Mark, Luke, and John, were chosen as "the" gospels, and the Gnostic gospels were rejected. We then had an official Bible.

354–430 **St. Augustine** (North Africa) was Bishop of Hippo. Only eternity is real. Everything else is a fleeting fantasy. He influenced many of the mystics who follow him. He is so significant we can talk of Augustian mysticism.

335–394 **Gregory of Nyssa** (Greece), a Christian bishop and saint, argued for the infinity of God.

404 **St. Jerome** translated the Bible from Greek into Latin. Known as the ***Vulgate***, it became "the" Bible of the Catholic Church. Even though only priests and lawyers can read Latin, it was the language of the church. People could not understand what the priests were saying during mass, which made mass all the more "mysterious." The use of Latin only in the mass continued until 1965!

480–524 **Boethius** in Italy is either the last of the Roman philosophers and/or the first of the medieval scholastics, though he is closer in time to Rome. He took on the ambitious project of translating the works of Plato and Aristotle and then tried to reconcile the differences between them. His major contribution was his preservation of Aristotle for the Middle Ages. *"True happiness is in the pursuit of the highest good which is God. God sees everything."*

Beginning of the Dark Ages also the Medieval, or Middle Ages, the Age of the Barbarians

This period has been called "a thousand years without a bath." The idea of a dark age was created by the Italian scholar Francesco Petrarch in the 1330s as a criticism of the character of late Latin literature. After the fall of Rome in 467 until about 1000, there is very little progress in philosophy, literature, and art. The oxcart that passes the house the day you are born looks like the oxcart that passes the house the day you die. The Church dominates the lives of the people in Europe, controlling almost all aspects of society: professions people hold, who they can marry, how they dress, even what they eat and how they die.

Buddhism in China and Tibet

526 **Bodhidharma** is credited as the founder of Zen Buddhism. He emphasized practice and empirical understanding, particularly as realized in mediation, or ***zazen*** (sitting Zen), for the attainment of awakening. He de-emphasized the study of sacred texts in favor of direct experience through meditation.

638–713 **Hui-Neng** was a Zen Buddhist monastic who advocated a direct approach to Buddhist practice or "Sudden Enlightenment."

645 **Buddhism reached Tibet** and was developed into its own "form" known as Tibetan Buddhism.

646 Third and final burning of the great library at Alexandria, Egypt.

Hinduism in India

788–820 In India, **Shankara** was the most famous Advaita (Non-dual) philosopher of Vedanta. His mysticism is one of reason without dogma or ritualism. Vedanta is non-dualistic. There is only one energy, one force, one God, one song, one dance, one Universe.

Islamic Mysticism

The sayings of Muhammad are a treasure of wisdom, not only for Muslims but for all of mankind.

Mahatma Gandhi

570–632 **Muhammad** began Islam. ***The Koran***, or ***The Quran***, the holy book of Islam, means to "collect" to "tie together" to "read" or "recite." *The Koran* recorded the revelations given to Muhammad written down by people around him from 610 to 632 A.D. The Koran's description of heaven is more cosmological than that of Judaism and Christianity. As God does not have a form, geometric art better expresses the infinite than pictures of people with personalities.

Sufism is the school of mystical philosophy in Islam based on the pursuit of spiritual truth. A Sufi is on a journey to the Truth. Those who are absorbed in the material world do not perceive the infinite. There are many Sufi traditions or lineages. Each one honors the truth in all religions, not just Islam. Sufism is a path of heart, and Sufis have an intense passion for the divine. Their scripture is the poetry of Rumi, Hafiz, and other Persian Poets. There is a strong and vigorous American Sufi movement. Although Sufism is certainly an important mystical branch of Islam and while the Kabbalah and Hassidism are important mystical branches of Judaism, they are not the only mystical branches within either religion.

Important Medieval Sufi's

922 **al Hallaj**, a Muslim mystic, claimed, as did Jesus, that he and God are one. Since this is thought to be sacrilege he was tortured and publicly crucified (in some accounts he was beheaded and his hands and feet were cut off) for "theological errors which threaten the security of the state."

971–1034 **Sirhindi** (India) said the world is not the same as the Divine Being, but has a reality of its own.

980–1037 **Avicenna** (Persia, now Iran) was a Muslim polymath, physician, philosopher, poet, physicist, and theologian. Like Benjamin Franklin, he was an *autodidact*, a self-taught or self-directed learner.

980–1050 **Mulla Sara** (Persia, now Iran) believed that there is a unity of Being. Becoming is a spiritual journey from the less perfect to the more perfect.

? – 1111 **Al Ghazali** was an Aristotelian philosopher who argued for a mystical knowledge going beyond reason. The mystical vision of truth is the only way to achieve certainty.

1126–1198 **Averroes** said esoteric questions of faith should not be discussed in public.

1165–1240 **Ibn Arabi** claimed it is possible to reach perfection. The real cannot be known dualistically as an object by a subject. He wrote over 300 works.

1207–1273 **Jalaluddi Rumi**, (Afghanistan), is the most widely read poet in the world today.

The 5th - 9th Century Ireland

C. 433 **Saint Patrick** was a Christian missionary and the patron saint of Ireland. Born in Roman Britain, he was captured by Irish raiders and taken as a slave to Ireland. He escaped and returned to his family where he entered the clergy. He later returned to Ireland as a missionary.

800–877 **Johannes Scotus Eriugena** was an Irish theologian and neo-Platonist influenced by Plotinus, Augustine, and *Pseudo-Dionysius*. He translated Pseudo-Dionysius from Greek into Latin. Humans are a microcosm of the universe; that which is shared, the essence of all things, is God. Reason and revelation are sources of truth. God and the Universe are identical and creation is timeless. The Catholic Church was very upset with him. He was, however, lucky. The Inquisition had not yet begun, so neither he nor his books were burned.

11th Century Europe

The church is still the most dominant part of societal life in Europe. There are few other interests: little in culture, music, theater or any of the other arts. The preaching of "sin, guilt and fear" is a major tool of the church for keeping people "in line," along with an emphasis on teaching the eternal fires of hell.

1033 **One Thousand years since the death of Jesus** many people thought it was the time of the Apocalypse. They were convinced that Jesus was going to return again.

Beginning of the Cathedrals and Universities

A major development is the beginning of the building of cathedrals San Marco in Spain and Notre Dame in Paris. It is also the time of the starting of universities.

1160–1345 **Notre Dame** was built in Paris.

1216–1272 **Henry III**, king of England, built Westminster Abbey.

1054 The Catholic Church splits between Greek Eastern and Latin Roman Papacy

Known as the great schism of 1054, the church has become too large, and different traditions are developing in Rome and Constantinople. While the Roman church rules with a heavy hand, things are more relaxed in the East where the laity has a greater part in church administration.

1077 There was a **Battle of Church and State** in Northern Italy over the question of who will appoint bishops. **Pope Gregory VII** excommunicated **Henry IV**, Emperor of Germany. Henry kneels in the snow and begs for forgiveness. He was forgiven. After he regained his power, Henry drove Gregory VII into exile.

Scholasticism, St. Anselm, Peter Abelard, Albertus Magnus, and Thomas Aquinas

C. 1050–1350 ***Scholasticism*** is the term used to refer to the medieval thought practiced in Christianity. It was an attempt to bring classical Greek philosophy into Christian doctrine. It is grounded in Aristotle's logic and used the dialectic of asking questions and then arriving at logical answers.

1093–1109 **St. Anselm**, Archbishop of Canterbury, England, is the last of the Neo-Platonists. He came up with the ***ontological*** argument for the existence of God. The argument implies the actual existence of God. That is, if we can conceive of God, then God exists; or if something is perfect, it must exist. Nonexistence would be a sign of imperfection.

1079–1142 **Peter Abelard** (France) wrote *The Story of My Misfortune* based on *Augustine's Confession*. He is famous for his love affair with Heloise for which he was castrated by Heloise's uncle. He spent the rest of his life in a monastery absorbed in study. Abelard renounced aristocracy in favor of the pursuit of scholasticism. He argued that the dialectic was the road to truth and helped move scholasticism out of the monasteries and into the universities. He and Heloise, who became a nun, remained in contact through their love letters.

1084 **Pope Gregory** insisted all clergy have to be celibate. Priests are to stop *concubinage* (the practice of taking mistresses). Married priests were forced to abandon their wives and families. From this time forward, priests must repress all sexual desires. We're in trouble now.

1085–1148 **William of St. Thierry** (France) was a Trappist contemporary of Bernard of Clairvaux and a student of Augustine. He emphasized love-mysticism.

1090–1153 **St. Bernard of Clairvaux** (France), also a Cistercian (Trappist) monk, was the voice of conservatism during the Renaissance and an opponent of the rising interests in scholasticism.

1098–1179 **Hildegard of Bingen** (Germany) was an early speculative mystic influenced by Augustine. She was greatly respected in her time for her writings, her music, and her art.

The Crusades

1096 **Pope Urban II began the Peasants' Crusade.** Anyone who would go to Jerusalem and kill the Turks would upon their own death receive immediate entrance into Heaven. God has given them special dispensation to overlook the sixth commandment, "Thou shalt not kill." Although the Muslims were in control, Jerusalem was open to Jews and Christians who wished to visit and live there. The Koran shares its history with Judaism and says that Jesus is a prophet. The crusades were thus political, economical, and power-based. A major concern was the opening of the "Silk Road" to China.

The head of the Crusade, **Duke Gottfried of Leon**, took 60,000 people with him. People sold everything they had to join the Crusade. They were promised as much booty as they can carry back. An army of 60,000 needs a lot of supplies. Thus they plundered the countryside on the way to Jerusalem. They were on a "Holy War" so it was justified. The taking of Jerusalem was a slaughter. Muslims tried to protect the Jews without success. Everyone was killed (not just Muslims): Jews and Christians—women and children. There were piles of heads; and soldiers walking in pools of blood as deep as their ankles (some reports say as deep as their knees). With no supplies and starving to death, soldiers ate the dead; roasting children on spits like pigs. All done in the name of God, but it sounds like hell.

1147–1149 **The 2nd Crusade** was another slaughter. On the way to the Holy Land, soldiers sacked Zara, a Christian city, just for the booty.

1189–1199 **The 3rd Crusade**, Richard I (The Lionhearted), King of England, took a crusade to the Holy Land. He spent less time in England than any other king. Six more Crusades would follow, each promoted by different Popes.

1212 **The Children's Crusade** had 30,000 children and adults from France and 7,000 from Germany. They never made it to Jerusalem. Most died of starvation or disease; the remainder were sold into slavery.

The Cathars, Beghard, and the Beguines

During the time of the Crusades, the land teemed with deserted women whose husbands and sons had gone off to fight in the Crusades. People outside of the direct influence of the Church or those who felt disenfranchised by the Church begin their own spiritual communities without asking permission from Rome. Two mystical sects developed during this time.

The Cathars, a religious sect with Gnostic leanings, appear in France in the eleventh through the thirteenth centuries. The Cathars believe in living a life of simplicity, and they see the Church as having betrayed the original purity of Jesus' message. They are opposed to priests, and they protested the moral, spiritual, and political corruption of the Church. The Church declares them heretical. Pope Innocent III launches the *Albigensian Crusade* to destroy all Cathars. Innocent III offers the lands of the Cathars to any French nobleman willing to take up arms and kill them. The Cathars, a peaceful people, have no defenses. More than 200,000 die in the resultant blood bath.

Beghards and **Beguines** are religious communities of the thirteenth and fourteenth centuries who also live without vows, creeds or special clothing. They are influenced by the *Cathars* and the *Brethren of the Free Spirit*. They view everything as an all-encompassing immanent God. The Beguines, a group of women, devote themselves to prayer and good works, in particular helping the poor. At the beginning of the thirteenth century some of them grouped together in community, thus forming the first Beguinage. They are condemned as heretics, but not destroyed as were the Cathars before them.

Beginning of the Inquisition

1184 **The Church started "Trial by Ordeal."** Inquisitors were to stamp out all signs of wickedness. People could be tortured simply for saying they did not believe in some aspect of theology; for example, saying that Mary was not a virgin.

12th and 13th Century, Jewish Mysticism

1135–1204 **Moses Maimonides** (Spain, Egypt) was a great philosopher and the foremost intellectual figure of medieval Judaism. He tried to combine philosophy and traditional Jewish law. He was also influenced by Muslim philosophy.

1240–1291 **Abraham ben Samuel Abulafia** was one of the founders of the Spanish Kabbalah.

1250–1305 **Moses ben Shem Tob de Leon** wrote *The Zohar* (The Book of Splendor) and was perhaps the most significant writer of the most important Kabbalist document.

13th Century The next 200 years are referred to as **The High Middle Ages**.

Italian Catholic Mystics—The Franciscans

1182–1226 **St. Francis of Assisi** began the Franciscan Order, which emphasized self-renunciation and poverty. St. Francis was a nature mystic. He saw God in all living things. The complete opposite of his contemporary Genghis Kahn, St Francis taught that no one (none of God's creatures) is to be harmed in the slightest way.

? – 1262 **Aegidius of Assisi** was a companion of St. Francis of Assisi. St. Francis called him, "the knight of our round table."

1217–1274 **St. Bonaventure** (France), a Franciscan monk influenced by Aristotle and Augustine, was one of the architects of the philosophical, theological, and the mystical side of the Franciscan Order.

Scholastics and other Italian Mystics/Scholars

1206–1280 **Albertus Magnus** was influenced by Augustine and Pseudo-Dionysius. In the tradition of Pythagoras, he emphasized the unity of science and mysticism. He was the teacher of Thomas Aquinas.

1225–1275 **St. Thomas Aquinas**, a Father of the Catholic Church, was influenced by Aristotle, Augustine, Pseudo-Dionysius, Eriugena, and Albertus Magnus. He had a profound mystical experience six months before he died, after which, he said that all of his writings were as "so much straw." His writings become the main theology of Catholicism.

1347–1380 **St. Catherine of Siena**, a Catholic nun, spent three years in hermit-like seclusion. There, she said, she found the desert and solitude in the midst of people.

13th Century, Buddhism in Japan

1173–1232 **Myoe** said moral action is a means for gaining enlightenment. Nature is to be read as language.

1200–1253 **Dogen Zenji** was a Buddhist teacher of Zazen (sitting Zen). The moment one realizes *shinjin*, one's birth in the Pure Land is settled.

1222–1282 **Nichiren** said the Buddha nature exists equally within all beings, and Buddhahood is obtainable for all.

Rome Reinstates the Inquisition

1231 **Pope Gregory IX reinstates *The Papal Inquisition*.** The idea that you can kill, stamp-out or destroy evil continues to be a major emphasis in the Church. Hundreds of thousands are brutally tortured until they willingly confess to anything. They are then killed in an attempt to destroy evil. The Church confiscates land taken from the heretics and is now the owner of a third of all Europe. The monasteries are getting wealthy from donations and from renting land to peasants. People pay the monks to pray for them because they do not have time to pray for themselves.

1302 **Papal bull** declare supreme papal authority.

14th Century, End of the Middle Ages and Beginning of the Renaissance

Slowly, now throughout the sixteenth century, we find the beginning of cultural and artistic developments. There is a revival of interest in Ancient Greece and classical culture, the beginning of modern science, and world exploration. There is a new emphasis on individualism and secularism. We find the first houses built with chimneys and the first use of glass in windows.

1305–1375 With a majority of French cardinals, the papacy is moved to Avignon in France for 70 years. This period is later referred to as *the Babylonian captivity of the church*.

13th through 15th Century, Rhineland Mystics in Germany

Rhineland mysticism is a Christian mystical movement prominent in Germany and an important precursor to the Reformation. The Rhineland is the land on both sides of the river Rhine in the west of Germany which abuts boundaries with France, Luxembourg, Belgium, and the Netherlands.

C. 1200s **Hadewijch**, a female Dutch poet and mystic, wrote about her visions. Her poetry followed the form used by the trouvères of her time. Rather than romantic love, however, she sang of the love of God. Probably involved in the Beguine movement, she was not a nun as she traveled and lived in several places. She was a precursor to the Rhineland mystic Jan van Ruysbroeck, who adopted many of her ideas.

1210–1285 **Mechthild of Magdeburg** was a mystic and a Cistercian nun who experienced a complete disrobing of the ego. Her book *The Flowing Light of the Godhead* describes, with passion, her many visions. In 1230 she also became a Beguine, and lived a life of prayer and mortification under the guidance of Dominican priests. Her criticism of church dignitaries aroused hostility.

1260–1326 **Meister Eckhart** was a Neo-Platonist influenced by Pseudo-Dionysius. He is ***the best known of the pre-Reformation mystics***. His sermons were in German; his writings were in Latin. A member of the Dominican Order, he held senior ecclesiastical and teaching posts all over Europe. Brought before the Inquisition, he died before the end of his trial. After his death, his teachings were repudiated by the Catholic Church. He was consequently "Meister" Eckhart, not Saint Eckhart.

1293–1381 **Jan Van Ruysbroeck** (Flemish), influenced by Eckhart and Hadewijch, outlined the stages of the mystical life.

1295–1366 **Heinrich Seuse** (or Suso) was a Dominican mystic. Suso and Johannes Tauler were friends and students of Meister Eckhart. Eckhart, Suso, and Tauler formed the center of the Rhineland School. As a troubadour and poet of divine wisdom, Suso explored with emotional intensity the spiritual truths of Eckhart's mystical philosophy. He wrote *The Little Book of Truth.*

1300–1361 **Johannes Tauler** was also a Dominican influenced by Eckhart and Mechthild of Magdeburg and part of the community that produced the *Theologia Germanica.*

1380–1471 **Thomas à Kempis** was an Augustinian monk influenced by Eckhart. He stressed the practice of simple piety and asceticism. His book, *The Imitation of Christ* was the second most popular book in sales next to *Pilgrim's Progress* until the nineteenth century.

1400–1464 **Nicholas of Cusa**, a philosopher and Christian mystic, was also influenced by Plotinus, Pseudo-Dionysius, and Eckhart. He had a profound, visionary and revelatory experience of the "incomprehensible" and paradoxical nature of God. Like Meister Eckhart, *"God,"* he said, *"is simplicity itself."* God can only be seen by an individual whose intellect has become simple. Man's mind is too complex, filled with religious suppressions, and many erroneous thoughts.

14th Century, Italy

1265–1321 **Alighieri Dante** was a poet and author of *The Inferno* and *The Divine Comedy*. Love, he said, is the movement of the spirit and the primordial energy of the universe. In mystical love, the psyche desires union with God, which is the harmony of the will of the soul and the will of God. The Catholic Church confiscated Dante's property and put him in prison. While there, he wrote *The Inferno*, where he describes the various levels leading into hell. He was the first to describe hell in such vivid detail. You will not find this imagery in the Bible, not even in *Revelations.*

1370–1378 **Pope Gregory XI** faced increasing restlessness. The more agitated people were in the lands the farthest away from Rome and therefore were the most difficult to control. Vigorous measures were revived against the heresies that have broken out in Germany and England. He was the first to declare that Mary Magdalene was a prostitute, although there is no biblical evidence. 600 years later, in 1969, the Church, realizing there is no basis for this assertion, retracted the statement.

14th Century, English and Swedish Mystics

1285–1347 **William of Ockham** (England), Oxford University, was influenced by Aristotle, Aquinas, and John Scotus. He taught *Nominalism*, the idea that the universal is found in the particular. He also developed the idea know as *Ockham's razor*. We should cut away any elaborate hierarchy of ideas to get to the truth. What we need is simplicity. Excommunicated by the Pope, he spent the remainder of his life in exile.

1300–1349 **Richard Rolle** emphasized the physicality and sensual nature of mystical awareness.

1303–1373 **St. Bridget of Sweden** became the founder of the Bridgettine Order.

1342–1413 **Julian of Norwich** was a visionary, religious writer, and anchoress.

1320–1384 **John Wycliffe** translated the Bible into English. He was a pre-Reformation reformer. He questioned the use of relics, the selling of indulgences, and the idea of papacy infallible. The Bible, he said, contains all that is needed for salvation. The Scriptures should be read by everyone, not just by the clerics. The papacy was created by men and not by God. For his beliefs, he was expelled from his teaching position at Oxford. Forty-four years after his death, the Pope orders his bones exhumed and burned as a heretic. Intense persecution followed, stamping out his followers and his teachings. It will be 200 years before Martin Luther resurrects the reforms of which Wycliffe dreamed. The Bible was reprinted in England again in the early part of the sixteenth century by William Tyndale, who met the same fate as Wycliff. Finally, in the seventeenth century, the King James Version survived and became a classic.

1371–1415 **John Huss** (Prague) was a Professor of Theology at the University of Prague. Strongly influenced by Wycliffe, Huss objected to the Pope's raising money to fight a war by the selling of indulgences, and he too questioned the authority of the Pope. He was burned at the stake. His followers, known as the Moravians, exist to this day. He was a hero to Martin Luther.

1347–1350 **The Black Death** (The Plague) swept through Europe killing 40 percent of the population in just three years. 80,000 people died in London alone. According to the book of Revelations, the Plague is the second horseman of the Apocalypse, and many people believed it was the end of the world. Many believed they were being punished for their sins. People did whatever their priests told them to do to be saved. There was thus a movement back to the Church.

1340? – 1396 **Walter Hilton** wrote the first exhaustive work on mystical theology in English.

Two Anonymous Mystical Texts

1350–1400 The ***Theologia Germanica*** became available. The authors are unknown. They probably kept quiet to avoid the same fate as Wycliff and Huss. The book strongly influenced Martin Luther. In 1375, an important mystical writing by an unknown author appeared in England. ***The Cloud of Unknowing*** was written for a young person beginning a life devoted to contemplation as a monk or a solitary. It advocates an apophatic mysticism: an approach to an interior life that seeks to find the Holy beyond words or mental images. The seeker puts all mental concepts beneath a "cloud of forgetting" in the mind and single-heartedly seeks to love the Divine.

15th Century Europe

1401–1468 **Johannes Guttenberg** (German), not a mystic, invented movable type and the printing press. In 1445, he printed the first book ever printed in the West—the *Bible*. Since more people were able read than before and there was more general knowledge about what was going on with the papacy, there was a growing call for reformation. Martin Luther's *The 95 Theses* printed in 1518, would become the first major best-seller.

1412–1431 **Joan of Arc** or **Jeanne d'Arc** was a heroine of France. She was tried and burned at the stake for heresy when she was only nineteen. Five hundred years later, she was canonized as a saint. Joan said she had visions from God telling her to save France, so King Charles VII sent her to the siege of Orleans. Joan overcame the dismissive attitude of her veteran commanders and secured victory in only nine days. Wounded during an attempt to recapture Paris, she was captured and tried by a politically motivated court. The heroine of her country at the age of seventeen, at nineteen she was dead.

1450–1750 **Witch Hunting in Europe and America** lasted 300 years. Everyone was suspect, especially old women who knew how to use herbs and could heal with prayers. Taken by the Inquisition, the suspects' bodies were examined to see if there were moles or warts that would not bleed. After being examined, they were burned at the stake.

15th Century Italian Renaissance

1447–1510 **St. Catherine of Genoa** (Italy) was abused by her husband, and her traumas led her into mystical experiences through suffering. She argues that "purgatory" is a stage on the mystical path, the final purification of the effects of self-love.

Archetypes of the Renaissance

1452–1519 **Leonardo da Vinci** (Italy) was an advanced polymath, artist, scientist, and inventor. He painted the famed *Last Supper* and perhaps the finest painting of the High Renaissance, the *Mona Lisa*.

1475–1564 **Michelangelo** (Italy) was a painter, sculptor, poet, and engineer. His contributions to humanity cannot be overlooked. He is often thought of as the archetypal Renaissance man.

15th and 16th Century—the Church in Rome

Power corrupts and absolute power corrupts absolutely. Although there was no one in whom the light had gone out completely, it seemed very weak in the papacy in Rome at this time. The ego seemed to have full control.

1414–1484 **Pope Sixtus IV** was one of the most corrupt popes of all time. He taxed brothels and murdered whomever he wanted to, including several members of the Medici family. He sold indulgences to get extra money and openly accepted bribes from corrupt priests in order to keep them in power.

1431–1503 **Pope Alexander VI** had several mistresses and innumerable illegitimate children. He actively killed those he did not like and poisoned cardinals who opposed him. He built up a Vatican army and engaged in war. He was "accidentally" killed by some of his own poisons of which were intended for one of his cardinals.

1513–1521 (Reign) **Pope Leo X** was one of the Medici Popes. Not a religious man, he loved to throw elaborate parties and actively promoted enjoyment of all the sensual delights and extravagances. He once spent 1/7 of his predecessor's reserves on a single ceremony. He also spent huge sums to fix up St. Peter's, driving the papacy into debt. To get out of debt, he promoted the sale of indulgences because it was so lucrative. He was pope when Luther nailed his *The 95 Theses* on the church door in Wittenberg.

1571 **Pope Pius V** ordered the drawing up of an index of books to be censored. More repression followed.

15th and 16th Century India and the Birth of Sikhism.

1440–1518 **Kabir** (India) was one of the poet saints of India. He became a disciple of the Hindu ascetic Ramananda. He saw all of humanity as one. Some believe him to be the precursor of Nanak. Kabir, however, did not like to be classified as Hindu, Muslim or Sufi, and he had a strong aversion to established religions.

1469–1539 **Nanak** (India) was the founder of Sikhism and the first of the ten Sikh Gurus. He is also honored by Hindus.

Sikhism comes from the word *Sikh*, meaning "disciple" or "learner." The fifth largest religion in the world, Sikhism advocates the quest for salvation through disciplined, personal meditation on the name of God. God is not anthropomorphic. God is the universe itself. The Sikhs follow the teachings of their enlightened leaders, as well as the holy scripture—the *Guru Grantah Sahib*. Most Sikhs live in the state of Pujab in India. A number of them also live in North America.

5th Through 17th Century European Esoteric and Mystical Philosophers

By the fifteenth century, it is clear that those engaged in personal spiritual pursuits cannot talk of their spiritual adventures in public without reprisals. If they speak up, they are tortured and burned at the stake. It thus becomes necessary to go underground and be more secretive about spiritual studies. During this time, there is a renewed interest in alchemy, freemasons, and other explorations termed "esoteric." This is also the time of the formation in Europe of the various guilds and associations of craftspeople in particular trades.

Esoteric knowledge is thought to be known only to an enlightened few and is thus contrasted with **exoteric** knowledge which is well-known, or public. Esoteric knowledge is the study of a deeper spiritual reality that extends beyond reason and the physical sciences. That which is esoteric is not so much hidden as it is unknown.

The Rosicrucian Order is an esoteric order envisioned as a "College of Invisibles" aiming to give assistance in humanity's spiritual development. Although Rosicrucians themselves claim to go back to ancient times, there is now a renewed interest in esoteric philosophy, particularly among German Protestants. Between 1607 and 1616, three anonymous documents are published in Europe: *Fama Fraternitatis Rosae Crucis*, *Confessio Fraternitatis*, and *Chymical Wedding of Christian Rosenkreutz anno 1459*. The author, or authors, did not want to reveal their names for fear of reprisal.

This was also the time of the development of **Freemasonry**, a fraternal organization also claiming ancient origins. The various lodges share moral and metaphysical ideals, including belief in a Supreme Being. Freemasonry uses the metaphors of operative stonemasons' tools and implements against a symbolic backdrop to convey *"a system of morality veiled in allegory and illustrated by symbols."* The Catholic Church, not surprisingly, opposed the masons and threatens to excommunicate any Catholic who becomes a mason.

The following two esoterics were doctors and alchemists who were successful in treating the black plague without themselves getting the plague.

1493–1541 **Paracelsus** (Switzerland) was a speculative mystic more interested in medical alchemy, astronomy, and natural philosophy than pure mysticism.

1503–1566 **Nostradamus** (Michael de Nostredame, France) was an apothecary and seer who published collections of now famous prophecies.

1575–1624 **Jacob Boehm** (Germany) was a shoemaker mystic and one of the first "non Catholic" mystics. He was influenced by Eckhart, the Kabbalah, Valentine Weigel, Renaissance alchemy, and Paracelsus. Though his works were censored, he was a prolific writer. His major work was *Aurora* of 1612.

1688–1772 **Emanuel Swedenborg** (Sweden) was a polymath and one of the most incredibly prolific Renaissance men and esoteric mystics of all time.

Non-Catholic Christian Mystics And the Protestant Reformation in Europe

1483–1546 **Martin Luther** (Germany) started the Protestant Reformation in 1517 and is therefore very important in the evolution of religion. While he was influenced by mystics like Augustine and the *Theologica Germanica* and while he had mystical experiences himself, Luther had an antipathy toward mysticism. He was interested in changing the world, and he still does. Luther succeeded in reformation when for centuries others failed because Northern German Princes also disillusioned with the Church, protected Luther.

1484–1531 **Huldrych Zwingli** (Switzerland) was a humanistic scholar, the leader of the Protestant Reformation in Switzerland, and founder of the Swiss Reformed Church.

1488–1525 **Thomas Müntzer** (Germany), an early Protestant reformer mystic, was burned at the stake.

1509–1654 **John Calvin** (Switzerland) started the Presbyterian Church. He believed in predestination; some are to be saved, others condemned. He promoted the doctrine of original sin. He was not a mystic.

The Spanish Catholic School

While there is a great deal of corruption in the papacy in Rome, that doesn't mean that the whole church is corrupt. There are those who continue to strive to know God, often living in the monasteries.

1491–1556 **Saint Ignatius of Loyola** was the founder of the Society of Jesus (the Jesuits), a religious order of the Catholic Church. He was the compiler of the *Spiritual Exercises* and an active fighter against the Protestant Reformation. He was the impetus for the Catholic Counter-Reformation.

1515–1582 **St. Teresa of Avila** was a Carmelite nun influenced by Augustine and a powerful reformer of the Carmelite order. She formed the Discalced (Barefoot) Carmelites along with St. John of the Cross. She described seven stages of the mystical journey. God dwells in the soul. She was easily one of the most important female Catholic Mystics of the sixteenth century.

1541–1591 **St. John of the Cross** was a student of St. Terese, a mystic, and a poet celebrated for his deep love for God. He subjected mysticism to intellectual analysis. Suffering, he said, is "epistemology." We learn from it. His famous book is the *Dark Night of the Soul*.

C. 1550, Beginning of Modern Science and the Baroque Period in Art and Architecture.

Baroque is an extravagant style of art characterized by curving lines, gilt, and gold, sometimes becoming excessively decorated and overly complicated.

Science, Mysticism and the Church

Just as the explorers want to know more about the world, the mystics want to know more about Heaven. The more we know, the more we become mystified by what we know. Why time? Why space? Why is there anything at all? The more we find out, the more we realize we don't know. Still we continue to explore. Mysticism continually moves us away from what we think of as the center to a new center. That new center is even more "centered," more grounded, more sure, and yet it is not the end. So we move to another "deeper" center, only to find again that it is not the center. What is the center? Is it just something nebulous, something ephemeral? The Church says the earth is the center, and Rome is the center of the earth.

1401–1464 **Nicholas of Cusa** (Germany) was a cardinal of the Roman Catholic Church, a mathematician, astronomer, and philosopher generally thought of as one of the greatest polymaths of the fifteenth century. He had an experience at sea that led to his writing about mysticism. He was a great influence on Giordano Bruno and Galileo. He taught that the universe is infinite and, like Kepler, he predicted the elliptical orbits of the planets.

1548–1600 **Giordano Bruno** (Italy) was one of the most important philosophers of the Renaissance. He advocated nature mysticism with a scientific component. According to Bruno, there are an infinite number of worlds, and these worlds could be inhabited by intelligent beings. On Feb. 17, 1600, he was burned at the stake. Bags of gun powder were hung around his neck, and he was gagged so that onlookers will not be seduced by his sacrilegious lies.

1571–1630 **Johannes Kepler** (Germany) was an astronomer who discovered that the planets move in elliptical, not circular, orbits. God, he said, did not create a meaningless universe.

1564–1642 **Galileo** (Italy) was one of the first "real" scientists. That is, he would postulate a theory and then did experiments to see if it was true. If it was true, he then drew up proofs as to why it was true. In 1608, the telescope was invented in Holland. Galileo immediately made his own telescope and turned it to the heavens. Copernicus, he said, is right; the earth is not the center of the universe. Brought before the Inquisition, he was forced to recant his teachings and live out his years under house arrest. It was that or death. He is thought of as the greatest scientist prior to Newton.

1642–1727 **Isaac Newton** (England) was born the same year that Galileo died. Newton was a loner, genius, and sensitive person who was obsessed with sin. He had no friends and few people liked him. He never married. Made a professor at age 26, he described gravity, worked out the laws of motion and light, and invented calculus at the same time as Leibniz in Germany. As a "secret" alchemist, he had no time for anything but study. He was in fact "possessed" by his work, often working 18–24 hours at a time alone without interruption. His main exercise was pacing back and forth in his room, thinking.

The Humanists

1466–1536 **Desiderius Erasmus** (The Netherlands and Switzerland) was a Humanist. Although he remained a Roman Catholic throughout his lifetime, he was critical of the excesses of the Church. His calls for moderation in the Church were, however, drowned out by the rallying call of the Protestant Reformation. We should imitate the life of Jesus, the highest example of morality. He was a friend of Sir Thomas More in England.

178–1535 **Sir Thomas More** (England) was a lawyer, author, statesman, and leading humanist scholar. More coined the word "utopia" as an ideal, imaginary land. He is remembered for his refusal to accept King Henry VIII's claim to be supreme head of the Church of England, a decision which led to his beheading for treason.

16th Century England and the Church

1491–1547 **Henry VIII** was king from 1509–1547. When the pope refused to grant him an annulment, Henry VIII closed the monasteries in England, seized their gold, silver and jewels, and made himself head of the Church in England, thus starting the Protestant Reformation in England. He died a Catholic.

1516–1558 **Mary Tudor**, or **Bloody Mary**, queen from 1547–1558, was the eldest child of Henry VIII and a staunch Catholic in a then religiously divided country. She utilized the methodology of the Church and burned 300 Protestant heretics at the stake in an effort to bring England back to Catholicism. Her attempts at stamping out Protestantism simply made it stronger. She had two false pregnancies and felt that God was punishing her for not killing enough heretics.

1558–1602 **Elizabeth I** was queen in England. The daughter to Henry VIII and Anne Boleyn, she never married nor had any children. Elizabeth was a Protestant, but she was tolerant of Catholicism. Her main goal was peace, which she believed came with freedom of religion. Elizabeth died at seventy years of age after a successful forty-four year reign. Under her reign, England flourished culturally with playwrights like Shakespeare and economically with conquest of much of the world through sea power.

1564–1616 **William Shakespeare** is probably the most famous playwright of all time. With a mystical point of view, his plays show an incredible depth of understanding of the nature of the insane ego.

1561–1626 **Francis Bacon** was a polymath, philosopher, lawyer, statesman, and a central thinker of the English Renaissance. As an Anglican, Bacon believed the universe has a Mind. "A little philosophy inclineth man's mind to atheism, but depth in philosophy bringeth men's minds about to religion."

1611 **King James Version of the Bible** was published in England. It was dedicated to King James. John Wycliff tried publishing the Bible in English in the 1300s and William Tyndale in the 1500s. This time the Protestants were in charge, and no one was killed.

1564 **Ivan the Terrible** (Russia) began the Inquisition in Russia, devising such new, and more horrible ways, of torturing and killing, such as roasting people alive over open pits. Deeply disturbed, he killed 60,000 people in one day. He killed his own son, an event which seemed to drive him even more insane.

1572 **St. Bartholomew's Day massacre** (France). Thousands of (estimates run from 10,000 to 100,000) French Protestants (Huguenots) were massacred by a Catholic mob in Paris and then throughout France with the compliance of Catherine de Medici, the king's mother.

1618 **Start of the Thirty Year War** Protestants revolted against Catholic oppression; Denmark, Sweden, and France invaded Germany.

17th Century England

1605–1682 **Sir Thomas Browne** was an author and philosopher. He said the visible world is only a vague picture of reality.

1608–1674 **John Milton** wrote *Paradise Lost* (1667), widely considered the greatest epic poem in English. After the death of his two wives and his two children, he became blind. He was miserable, and in his misery he wrote *Paradise Lost*. It was, in a way, a continuation of Dante's *Inferno*. Now the devil is elevated to the level of a warlord.

Non-Catholic Christian Mystics in England

1624–1691 **George Fox** was the founder of the Quakers. God is experienced by every person through the presence of the indwelling Spirit. Everyone is equal and should be respected, for God is in everyone. Worship takes place in the soul. There should be no hierarchy and no clergy.

1644–1718 **William Penn** helped George Fox found the Quakers. He is best known as the founder of Pennsylvania.

1628–1688 **John Bunyan** is the author of *Pilgrim's Progress*, which discusses, in allegory, the journey of the soul. He was jailed for twelve years for preaching without a license. While in prison, he wrote *Pilgrim's Progress*, the most widely read book, next to the Bible, until the beginning of the twentieth century.

1686–1761 **William Law**, a student of Jacob Boehme, wrote *A Serious Call to a Devout and Holy Life*.

17th Century French Mystics

1567–1622 **St. Francis de Sales** is known for his writings on spiritual direction and spiritual formation. His book *The Devout Life* is a classic of French spirituality.

1611–1691 **Brother Lawrence** was a true mystic and lay brother of the Carmelites.

1623–1662 **Blaise Pascal** was a mathematician, physicist, and religious philosopher. Often sickly, after a near-death experience, he had an intense religious vision; then, like William Blake, he was subject to states of rapture.

The Beginning of Rationalism

Rationalism is the belief that reason and logic are the primary sources of knowledge and truth.

1596–1650 **Rene Descartes** (France) is known as "the father of modern philosophy." He is remembered for his *Cogito Ergo Sum* "I think therefore I am." Knowledge comes from logical rational deduction. Mind and matter are two clearly distinct substances.

1638–1715 **Nicolas Malbranche** tried to combine Descartes and Augustine. *"We see all things in God."*

1646–1716 **Gottfried Wilhelm Leibniz** (Germany) was a philosopher and metaphysician who discovered calculus at the same time as Newton. His most important contribution was to blend inner life with rationality. God has created the best of all possible worlds. Man, having freewill, "mucks it up" by not doing God's will.

15th–17th Century England and America

Puritanism develops in England by those who were seeking "purity of worship" and strict obedience to the scriptures. Puritanism refers to a type of religious belief, rather than a particular religious sect. Since the Puritans are Protestants who see the Church of England as just another hierarchical system, they must now try to extirpate themselves from the Church of England, just as the Church of England extirpated itself from Catholicism. They want to get back to the Bible. Worship is to be very simple, with no fancy rituals, vestments, or singing. Everything is to be simple and straightforward.

17th Century Cambridge Platonists

The Cambridge Platonists react to the dogmatism of the Puritans, which they feel leaves God uninvolved with the majority of mankind.

1614–1687 **Henry More** was a liberal theologian fascinated by Neo-Platonism and the *Theologia Germanica*.

He coined the term "spissitude" to describe a fourth spatial dimension in which he believed the spiritual realm exists.

1617–1688 **Ralph Cudworth**, a metaphysician, wrote *The True Intellectual System of the Universe*. He believed there is an ancient wisdom, the knowledge of which is the knowledge of God.

17th and 18th Century Jewish Mysticism

1632–1677 **Baruch Spinoza** (the Netherlands) has been called "the world's most sensible mystic." Spinoza, along with Descartes in France and Leibniz in Germany, was the greatest of the rationalists. For Spinoza, the intellectual love of God frees man from desire and confers immortality. He had no followers, but his freethinking religious view helped pave the way for The Enlightenment. He is considered the founder of modern biblical criticism. There is only one infinite, divine substance comprising all of reality.

1698–1760 **The Baal Shem Tov** (Ukraine) founded Jewish Hasidism. He said the whole universe, mind and matter, are a manifestation of the Divine Being, and he placed an emphasis on bringing joy and dancing, not just study, back into community.

1730–1797 **Menahem Nahum**, Ukraine, Hasidic.

1665 **Beginning of the Trappist Order** (France) in reaction to the relaxation of religious practices in the monasteries. The reform was led by the Abbot at La Trappe, France. Trappists take an inner silent, mystical approach and only speak when necessary. Idle talk is strongly discouraged. Meals are usually taken in contemplative silence.

1665 **Great Plague** in London kills 75,000.

1666 **The Great Fire in London** burned for four days and destroyed 4/5ths of London. The fire stoppped the plague by killing the rats.

17th Century Religion in America

America is a hodge-podge of religions: Puritans and Congregationalists in New England, Quakers in Pennsylvania, Catholics in Maryland, and Dutch Reformists in New York. Episcopalians, Baptists, and others can be found almost everywhere. The Methodists and Unitarians won't show up until the eighteenth century.

1619 A Dutch ship brought the first African slaves to British North America.

1620 **The Pilgrims**, after a three-month voyage in the Mayflower, arrived at Plymouth Rock. It was the height of Puritanism in New England: the belief in strict religious discipline and simplified, non-ritualistic worship.

1631 **Roger Williams**, after being kicked out of Massachusetts for his "diverse, new, and dangerous opinions," established Rhode Island as a place for freedom of religion. No one should have to worship against his or her will.

1663–1728 **Cotton Mather**, a Puritan minister, published 469 works on ethics, religion, and the evils of witchcraft. He was not a mystic.

1692 **The Salem Witch Trials.** Based on the hysteria of three teenage girls, twenty-four women were burned at the stake.

1703–1758 **Jonathan Edwards**, a Calvinist, preached hellfire and damnation and said that human suffering is the result of original sin. Only the elect will be saved.

18th Century in the West

Beginning of the Enlightenment in Europe

The Enlightenment emphasizes reason and science in philosophy and the study of human culture and the natural world. The Enlightenment is an important prelude to American transcendentalism, Unitarianism, and New Thought. Benjamin Franklin is one of the most outstanding examples of the Enlightenment.

British Empiricism, Deism, and Religion in 18th Century America

Empiricism is the idea that the knowledge we get through observation and experience is more reliable than knowledge we get from reason and intuition alone. Mysticism says that knowledge from experience, reason, the senses, the heart, intuition, inspiration, and imagination are all important.

1632–1704 **John Locke** (England) described human understanding in empirical terms. All knowledge comes from experience. There are no innate ideas. The mind begins at birth as a *tabula rasa*—a "blank slate." Locke was a deist.

1706–1790 **Benjamin Franklin** was a deist, a Freemason, and a true Renaissance man. He was a self-made, self-educated, elder statesman of the American Revolution, the oldest signer of the Declaration of Independence, a scientist, diplomat, author, printer, publisher, philosopher, philanthropist, and publisher of *Poor Richard's Almanac*. After he discovered deism, Franklin became disillusioned with organized religion. Like most Enlightenment intellectuals, Franklin saw virtue, morality, and faith as something a person can have with or without religion.

1732–1799 **George Washington** was an Episcopalian, Freemason, deist and of course, the first president of the United States.

1743–1826 **Thomas Jefferson** was, like Washington, an Episcopalian and a deist. The third president of the United States, he wrote the Declaration of Independence. Freedom of religion must be absolute.

1737–1809 **Thomas Payne** was an American Revolutionary leader, a deist, and the author of *Common Sense*, a bestseller with over 500,000 copies, a respectable number even in the twenty-first century. *Common Sense* is an important prelude to the American Revolution.

1751–1836 **James Madison**, the fourth president of the United States and a deist, is considered to be the Father of the U.S. Constitution

1758–1831 **James Monroe**, the fifth president of the United States, was a Freemason and a deist.

New Denominations

1703–1791 **John and Charles Wesley** (England and USA) founded the *Methodist* Church. Originally a group for studying the "methodological" of the scriptures, Methodism's becoming a church was resisted by Charles Wesley to the very end. On his deathbed he was still saying: "Don't do it."

1788–1886 **Alexander Campbell** in 1832 founded the *Disciples of Christ* (Christian Church). He presented a rationalistic Christianity based on the New Testament. At one time, the seventieth largest denomination in the US, the Disciples of Christ Church lost fifty percent of its membership during the last half of the twentieth century.

1830 Aug. 29 **Joseph Smith** founded the Church of the Latter Day Saints of Jesus Christ. *The Book of Mormons* is based on engraved gold plates that he found and translated. They then disappeared. He, along with Brigham Young, advocated polygamy.

1801–1877 **Brigham Young**, a Mormon Church leader, settled Salt Lake City in 1847.

18th Century in the East

1703–1762 **Sha Wali Allah** (India) The understanding of religious injunctions requires going to the higher level of idea, the World of Images.

1720–1781 **Ramprasad Sen** was a Bengali songwriter and singer of Hindu devotional songs. Devoted to the goddess Kali, his life is the subject of many mystical stories.

From Eastern Orthodox Monks

The ***Philokalia***, an anthology of mystical philosophy, appears in the eighteenth century. *Philokalia* comes from the Greek meaning "the love of good things." The *philokalia* is the love of the beautiful, the exalted, and the excellent. The writing comes from a variety of monks from the fourth to the fifteenth centuries. The authors are striving for purification of the mind and spiritual perfection. Next to the Bible, the *Philokalia* is the most admired and widely read example of mysticism from Eastern Orthodox Christianity. It is featured in another much shorter Russian book called *The Way of the Pilgrim*.

18th Century French Mystics and Philosophers

1712–1778 **Jean-Jacque Rousseau** (Switzerland and France) wrote *Discourse sur Les Sciences et Las Arts*. According to Rousseau, society has corrupted mankind's natural instincts and freedom. Philosophy needs to take the heart (love) and emotion into consideration, not just the intellect and senses.

1713–1784 **Denis Diderot**, an atheist, edited the massive 17 volume first real encyclopedia.

1734–1815 **Franz Anton Mesmer** "discovered" Mesmerism, or hypnosis. It became "the rage." Everyone wanted to try it. A new emphasis was placed on the power of the mind. P.P. Quimby in the U.S. would take up Mesmerism, which would lead to mind healing. It is also grounding for what would develop as *New Thought* with Christian Science (Mary Baker Eddy), Religious Science, and Science of Mind.

1743–1803 **Louis Claude de Saint-Marin** was a preacher of mysticism drawing on the Kabbalah, Boehme, and Swedenborg. He was the first to translate the writings of Boehme from German into French. In England he met and worked with the English mystic William Law. His books were placed upon the Catholic Index of Forbidden Books. His admirers formed the *Friends of St Martin*, later known as Martinists. They were influential in the founding of the Hermetic Order of the Golden Dawn.

1798–1857 **August Comte** founded Philosophical Positivism and Sociology which he saw as a religion of humanity.

1729–1781 **Gotthold Ephraim Lessing** (Germany) was a deist, poet, philosopher, writer, and representative of the Enlightenment known for his wit and his ability to see irony. Truth is not something solid or something that can be owned. We are always approaching the truth.

18th Century, English Metaphysical, Romantic and Victorian Poet/Mystics

1757–1827 **William Blake** was a true mystic. He wrote *The Marriage of Heaven and Hell*. For Blake, imagination is the Divine Being in every person. Imagination supersedes reason. Rationalism is limited to time, space, and causality. Orthodox religions enslave humankind with a system of controls. In Heaven there is no division or need for controls.

1759–1796 **Robert Burns** (Scotland) was the National Poet of Scotland. He was a Freemason and a major figure in the Romantic Movement.

1770–1850 **William Wordsworth's** most important collection, *Lyrical Ballads*, was published jointly with Samuel Taylor Coleridge in 1798. He was a friend of Emerson and Thomas Carlyle.

1772–1834 **Samuel Taylor Coleridge** was a poet, critic, and leader of the Romantic Movement. His best known poem is *The Rime of the Ancient Mariner*.

1785–1863 **Jacob Grimm**, mythologist and philologist, with his twin brother wrote *Grimm's Fairy Tales*. Fairytales are a wonderful way of discussing the soul's journey without saying that is what you are doing.

1795–1881 **Thomas Carlyle** (Scotland) was an essayist and historian. "A well-written life is almost as rare as a well-spent one." He was a religious non-Christian and a friend of Emerson, Wordsworth, and Coleridge.

1809–1892 **Alfred Tennyson** is often regarded as the chief representative of the Victorian Age in poetry.

1802–1885 **Victor-Marie Hugo** (France) was one of the most influential exponents of the Romantic Movement in France. His best-known works are *Les Miserables* and *The Hunchback of Notre-Dame*. His books were consistently placed on the Pope's list of "forbidden books." He believed Catholic dogma to be outdated and dying. The authoritative nature of the Church will, he said, one day lead to its demise. People will still believe in God and the Soul. A deeply religious man, he believed strongly in prayer.

1799 **The Rosetta Stone** was discovered in Egypt, making it possible for the first time to translate and read Egyptian hieroglyphics.

18th and 19th Century German Idealism

According to **idealism**, the properties we discover in matter depend on the way objects appear to us as perceivers. We are the determiners of the world we see. The world is as we make it, nothing more than that. German Idealism leads in part to transcendentalism.

1724–1804 **Immanuel Kant** (Prussia, now part of Russia) was one of the most influential thinkers of the Enlightenment. His theory of *Transcendental Idealism* says that our experience of things is about how they appear to us, not about how they are in and of themselves. The mind, said Kant, surrounds things with space and time. The world is not an objective fact apart from us; it is a product of the law of our understanding. Kant was a Lutheran and a deist.

1749–1832 **Johann Wolfgang von Goethe**, although not a German Idealist in the same philosophical sense as those who come after him, he was a man of letters and a great polymath. He is best known for his dramatic poem *Faust*. Never satisfied with any organized religion, his spiritual perspective evolved along the lines of deism, pantheism, humanism, and mysticism. Goethe influenced Rudolf Steiner, Darwin, Hegel, Schopenhauer, Nietzsche, and Jung.

1762–1814 **J.G. Fichte** said the essence of Kant's philosophy is that the subject, or ego, is the fundamental matter for inquiry. Instead of human knowledge being derived from empirical knowledge, it's the other way around—the empirical world is the creation of the knowing mind. The *ding-an-sich* (thing in itself) does not exist. The world is "absolute ego."

1770–1831 **G.W.F Hegel** rivals Kant as the greatest of the Idealist philosophers. There is only one absolute reality—God. It is possible to know God through a process of dialectics.

1775–1854 **Frederick Von Schelling** said nature and consciousness are expressions of absolute reality.

1788–1860 **Arthur Schopenhauer** was a student of Plato, Kant, and Fichte and the first western philosopher to study *Vedanta*. The world, he said, "is my representation." Only through denial of irrational unconscious will can one obtain wisdom. He wrote *The World as Will and Idea*. Will is an expression of absolute reality.

1844–1900 **Frederick Nietzsche** had little patience for logic and proofs about the ultimate nature of things. Flashes of insight, aphoristic expressions, and proclamations characterize his work. "Every philosophy is a foreground philosophy. Every philosophy 'conceals' a philosophy."

Founding of the Bahai Faith

1817–1892 **Baháulláh** (Persia, Iran) founded Baháí, a new religion. Although its roots come from Shiite Islam and Sufism, Bahai was, at the time, a wholly new religion. Bahai is often hated in the Islamic world due to its claim that Baháulláh succeeded Mohammed. Now we have an argument about who is the greatest. Bahai is open to and respects all other world religions. It is now a worldwide religion with about 6 million followers.

19th Century Esoteric/Mystical Philosophy

1831–1891 **Madam Blavatasky** (Russia and USA) is the author of *The Secret Doctrine* and was the founder of the Theosophical Society.

1847–1933 **Annie Wood Besant** was an author, theosophist, women's rights activist, writer, and orator. After reading *The Secret Doctrine* by H.P. Blavatasky, she embraced theosophy and in 1907 became the president of the Theosophical Society. In 1909 she and Charles Lester Leadbeater discovered Jiddu Krishnamurti whom they saw as the incarnation of Christ. Krishnamurti and Besant developed a close attachment, and he thereafter addressed Besant as "amma," or mother.

1895–1986 **Jiddu Krishnamurti** (India and USA) was a philosopher, author, and lecturer. In 1929 Krishnamurti disbanded *The Order of the Star of the East* founded to support him. He taught the pursuit of freedom from the ego. At age 90 he addressed the United Nations on the subject of peace, and he was awarded the 1984 UN Peace Medal.

1861–1925 **Rudolf Steiner** (Austria) was another polymath and Renaissance man. Influenced by Fichte, Schelling, Kant, Hegel, and Nietzsche, he built the Goetheanum Arts Center in Dornach, Switzerland. He founded the Waldorf Education Movement and biodynamic agriculture. He significantly influenced Albert Schweitzer.

1866–1949 **G.I. Gurdjieff** was a Greek-Armenian spiritual philosopher, and traveler. His teachings might be summed up by the title of his writings: *Life is Real Only Then, When 'I Am'* and *All and Everything*.

19th Century Hindu Mystics and Guru's

1836–1886 **Ramakrishna** taught the Vedanta system of non-dualism. He sought to also experience the mysticism of Christianity and Islam and concluded that the goal of all religion is the same—to embody the divine.

1863–1902 **Swami Vivekananda** was the chief disciple of *Ramakrishna*, a major figure in the history of the Hindu reform movements, and one of the most influential teachers of Vedanta and yoga. He is the first known Hindu sage to come to the West.

19th Century Transcendentalism in America

Transcendentalism is based on a belief in the supremacy of insight and intuition over logic and reason, the essential unity of all creation, and the innate goodness of man.

1780–1842 **William Ellery Channing** was the founder of the Unitarians in the U.S. His religion and thought were among the chief influences on the New England transcendentalists.

1799–1888 **Amos Bronson Alcott** was a writer and the founder of the Concord Summer School of Philosophy and Literature in 1879.

1803–1880 **Ralph Waldo Emerson**, influenced by William Ellery Channing, is often thought of as the greatest of the transcendentalist mystics. The natural world is coursed through with the immanent flow of a deity, a "world soul," in and above the world. His main student was Henry David Thoreau.

1817–1862 **Henry David Thoreau** was a devout nature mystic. He wrote *Walden*, clearly a favorite of many mystics. Thoreau went alone to the woods to live deliberately, to confront the essential facts of life, and not, when it comes time to die, find he had not lived.

1810–1850 **Margaret Fuller** was a journalist, freethinker, women's rights activist, and friend of Emerson.

1811–1896 **Harriet Beecher Stowe** wrote *Uncle Tom's Cabin*, which raised American awareness about the conditions in the segregated South. Henry Ward Beecher was her uncle.

1813–1887 **Henry Ward Beecher** was a brilliant preacher in Brooklyn, NY. He did not believe in hell, and he defended evolution.

1819–1892 **Walt Whitman** was a poet, mystic, and essayist. He is known for his free verse, best exemplified in *Leaves of Grass*. He was an "extroverted" mystic—he was out there in the world.

1830–1886 **Emily Dickinson** was a poet and mystic who lived an introverted and hermetic life, spending much of her time alone in her room. She was influenced by Emerson and Thoreau. Of her 1,800 poems, only eight were published in her lifetime. She is, along with Walt Whitman, regarded as the exemplary American poet of the nineteenth century.

1832–1880 **Louisa May Alcott**, novelist and daughter of Amos Bronson Alcott (above), is best known for the novel *Little Women* published in 1868.

1836 **The Transcendental Club** was started in Boston, Massachusetts, by Ralph Waldo Emerson, Amos Bronson Alcott, William Ellery Channing, Theodore Parker, Margaret Fuller, and others. The club was a meeting-place for thinkers and an organizing ground for their dissatisfaction with American culture and society, in particular the intellectualism at Harvard and in the Unitarian Church.

19th Century Mystics Worldwide

1798–1863 **Eugene Delacroix** (France) was perhaps the most important of the French Romantic painters.

1802–1876 **Harriett Martineau** (England) was a Unitarian, prolific writer, and philosopher.

1807–1882 **Henry Wadsworth Longfellow** (USA) was an American poet best remembered for *The Song of Hiawatha* and *Paul Revere's Ride*.

1809–1849 **Edgar Allen Poe** (USA), a poet and storywriter, is called "America's most famous man of letters." Orphaned in 1811, he married his 13 year old cousin, Virginia. He is best known for his poem "The Raven," published in 1845, for which he was paid $15. He lived his whole life in poverty.

1813–1855 **Soren Kierkegaard** (Denmark) is regarded as the father of Existentialism, which claims that individual human beings create the meanings of their own lives. It is a reaction against more traditional philosophies like rationalism and empiricism. He wanted only his name and the words *"The Individual Thinker"* on his gravestone.

1820–1903 **Herbert Spencer** (England) proposed evolution before Darwin and "survival of the fittest." Darwin gave him credit. Darwin was the one who did the work of science.

1828–1910 **Leo Tolstoy**, a Russian mystic and Christian anarchist (one who believes the only source of authority is God), was a vegetarian, moral thinker, and one of the greatest novelists of all time.

1828–1889 **St. Sharbal** (Lebanon) was a hermit much respected for his piety. His grave is now a site of pilgrimage.

1835–1910 **Mark Twain**, born Samuel Clemens (USA), a Presbyterian by heritage and a deist at heart, he liked to make fun of Presbyterian theology. On his 67th birthday he said, "But we were good boys... we didn't break the Sabbath often—once a week perhaps." A great humorist and social critic, he saw the "non-reality" of "The Gilded Age."

1839–1914 **Charles Sanders Pierce** (USA) was a pragmatist. Beliefs are established habits of action. Knowledge is derived from activity. A person learns to drive a car by driving a car, not by reading a book. Likewise, a person learns to love by being a lover.

1840–1926 **Claude Monet** (France) was an impressionistic artist and nature mystic.

1843–1879 **Saint Bernadette** (France) experienced visions of the Virgin Mary. In 1943, a movie was made about her life called *The Song of Bernadette*.

1844–1889 **Gerard Manley Hopkins** (England) was a mystical poet, Jesuit priest and scholar.

1848–1887 **Richard Jeffries** (England) was a nature mystic and author of *The Story of My Heart*.

1853–1890 **Vincent van Gogh** (Dutch) originally planned on being a preacher. He was a mystical and brilliant painter verging on madness.

1873–1897 **Saint Therese de Lisieux** (France) wrote *The Story of a Soul*, a best-seller in the early twentieth century.

1875–1965 **Albert Schweitzer, M.D., OM**, was an Alsatian theologian, musician, philosopher, and physician. He disputed the traditional Christian view of Jesus. Jesus is, he said, a prophet who expects the imminent end of the world. He received the 1952 Nobel Peace Prize for his philosophy of "reverence for life." He founded and sustained the Lambaréné Hospital in Gabon, West Central Africa.

1887–1985 **Marc Chagall** was a Russian artist. "Great art picks up where nature ends."

20th Century Hindu Mystics and Gurus

1861–1941 **Rabindranath Tagore** was a poet influenced by the mysticism of the Vedic sages, the Upanishads, and the Bhakti-Sufi mystic Kabir. In 1913, he became the first "non-Westerner" to receive the Nobel Prize for literature.

1869–1948 **Mahatma Gandhi**, "the father of India," remained a Hindu his entire life. Well known for his nonviolent resistance, he practiced simplicity, vegetarianism, celibacy, and was an exemplary mystic.

1879–1950 **Ramana Maharshi** taught self-enquiry. When a student would come to him and ask a question, he would respond with, "Who wants to know?"

1882–1950 **Sri Aurobindo** was a Hindu nationalist, scholar, poet, mystic, and evolutionary. He developed a spiritual path he called Integral Yoga. *A Life Divine* is not world denial; it includes active participation in life.

1884–1963 **Swami Ramdas**, a student of Ramana Maharshi, is considered by many as a master teacher, philosopher, and guru.

1893–1952 **Paramahansa Yogananda** was the founder of the Self-Realization Fellowship. He taught the need for direct experience of mystical truth. "The true basis of religion is not belief, but intuitive experience. Intuition is the soul's power of knowing God. To know what religion is really all about, one must know God." His *Autobiography of a Yogi* is still a bestseller.

1894–1969 **Meher Baba** was an Indian guru of Persian descent who spent long periods of fasting in seclusion. From 1925 to the end of his life, he communicated only with an alphabet board.

1896–1981 **Anandamayi Ma** (Bangladesh) said she became completely empty with no sense of "I am." She is, she said, "nobody."

1897–1981 **Maharaja Nisargadatta** said our true nature is perpetually free, peaceful awareness. This awareness is different from the personal, individual consciousness that is related to the body. He influenced Wei Wu Wei and Jed McKenna.

1889–1964 **Jwaharlal Nehru** said no state will willingly give up its power unless effective pressures are brought to bear. The use of nonviolent non-cooperation is the way to freedom.

1908–1982 **Swami Muktananda**'s message is honor your Self, worship your Self, and see God in each other. God dwells in everyone.

1931–1990 **Osho** or **Bhagwan Shree Rajneesh** was a guru with an interfaith perspective. Born into a Jain family, he did not want to be thought of as a Jain or a Hindu. A great intellect, he said his main teaching was through his jokes.

19th and 20th Century and the New Thought Movement in the USA and England

The New Thought Movement was inspired by transcendentalism. It now comprises several denominations: Unity, Religious Science, Divine Science, Interfaith, and more. According to New Thought, an Immanent Mind is the primary basis of all interconnected reality. God as all powerful spirit is the totality of real things. True human self-hood is divine. Divine thought is a force for good.

Sickness originates in the mind, and 'right thinking' has a healing effect.

1802–1866 **Phineas Parkhurst Quimby** based his work on Mesmer and the idea of the Mind as the most important element. Christian Science, Religious Science and Unity are all influenced by his thought.

1821–1910 **Mary Baker Eddy** was the founder of *Christian Science*. Basing her works on P.P. Quimby, Mary Baker Eddy later repudiated her dependency on him. Christian Science grew so fast, initially Mark Twain predicted that by the middle of the twentieth century everyone would be a Christian Scientist. The polity of Christian Science, however, became rigid, doing everything to the letter of the law. Lacking ministers and any opportunity for innovation, Christian Science has been dying for the past fifty years or more. Unlike Religious Science, it is not "open at the top."

1837–1902 **Richard Maurice Bucke** (Canada) was a psychologist and the author of *Cosmic Consciousness*. He was a friend and admirer of Walt Whitman.

1842–1910 **William James** was a philosopher and pragmatist. He taught the first class in psychology at Harvard in 1885. He said of himself that he is not a mystic, but he longed to be one.

1845–1932 **Myrtle Fillmore** co-founded Unity Church with Charles Fillmore in 1889. Her major works are *The Prayer of Faith* and the collection *Healing Letters*.

1854–1931 **Charles Fillmore** was co-founder of Unity in 1889 with his wife, Myrtle. He is sometimes referred to as "the Missouri Mystic."

1847–1916 **Thomas Troward** (England) helped usher in the New Thought movement.

1856–1915 **Elbert Hubbard** was a practical mystic, theosophist, and Rosicrucian who founded the Roycroft Crafts Guild in East Aurora, NY.

1862–1932 **William Walker Atkinson** was an attorney, publisher, and author. His 1906 book *Thought Vibration or the Law of Attraction* inspired the thinking of the 2006 book and movie *The Secret*.

1866–1954 **Horatio W. Dresser** interpreted the work of P.P. Quimby and the New Thought Movement.

1875–1941 **Evelyn Underhill** (England) was a mystics, novelist, pacifist, and metaphysical poet. In 1911, she wrote an outstanding book on mysticism simply titled *Mysticism*.

1877–1945 **Edgar Cayce**, known as "the sleeping prophet," is the founder of the Association for Research and Enlightenment.

1879–1950 **Dr. Bob Smith** was co-founder with Bill Wilson of Alcoholics Anonymous. There are interesting similarities between Alcoholics Anonymous and *A Course in Miracles*, as both place emphasis on the individuals' accepting responsibility for their decision-making, eliminating the need for projection.

1896–1971 **Bill Wilson** was the co-founder with Dr. Bob Smith of Alcoholic Anonymous.

1886–1951 **Emmet Fox** was an Irish American author of *The Sermon on the Mount*, next to "The Big Book," an important document for Alcoholics Anonymous.

1887–1960 **Ernest Holmes** was the founder of Religious Science and author of *The Science of Mind*.

1892–1964 **Joel Goldsmith** was a non-denominational teacher of "practical mysticism" and author of *The Infinite Way*.

1897–1985 **Franklin Merrell-Wolf** was a true mystic, who said that awareness transcends the intellect. His main student was Dr. John Lilly.

1904–1971 **Mildred Mann** founded the Society of Pragmatic Mysticism in New York City. Her book, *Become What You Believe* is influential among New Thought practitioners, especially "the Seven Steps in Demonstration."

1912–2003 **James Dillet Freeman** was an American-Indian poet and Unity minister.

1914 **The International New Thought Alliance** was founded in London, England.

19th and 20th Century Psychology and Mysticism

1856–1939 **Sigmund Freud, M.D.** (Austria), was not a mystic, but he made great strides in understanding the ego and the nature of man's unconscious mind. Interestingly, his last three books were on religion.

1875–1961 **Carl Gustav Jung, Ph.D.** (Switzerland), was the founder of analytical psychology. Jung was one of the first to bring an in-depth psychological exploration of the mystical dimension. He was a true mystic willing to look at his own darkness in order to dispel its energy.

1902–1994 **Erik Erickson, Ph.D.**, was a Jewish German developmental psychologist.

1905–1997 **Viktor Emil Frankl, M.D. Ph.D.** was an Austrian neurologist and psychiatrist, Holocaust survivor, and author of the bestselling *Man's Search for Meaning*.

1909–1981 **Helen Schucman, Ph.D.**, was a professor, research psychologist, and scribe of *A Course in Miracles*.

1923–1988 **William Thetford, Ph.D.** was a psychologist and collaborator with Helen Schucman in the production of *A Course in Miracles*.

1909–1969 **Rollo May, Ph.D.** (USA), wrote the highly influential book *Love and Will*.

1914–1995 **Dr. Thomas Hora** was the founder of *meta-psychiatry*, which attempts to integrate principles from metaphysics, spirituality, and psychology.

1915–2001 **Dr. John Lilly, M.D.** was an explorer of reality including interspecies communication.

1927–1989 **Ronald David Laing** (Scotland) studied the experience of psychosis. He is associated with the anti-psychiatry movement and, like many of his contemporaries, was critical of psychiatry. Some forms of insanity come from the inability to handle society's norms and other "insanities" of the world.

1945–1997 **Susan Segal**, author of *Collision with the Infinite*, offered a cosmic interpretation of reality.

20th Century and Contemporary Buddhism

1870–1966 **D.T. Suzuki** (Japan, USA) brought Zen Buddhism to the West. Many of the Zen centers in North America are based on his work.

1905–1989 **Kalu Rinpoche** was a Buddhist meditation master, scholar, teacher, and one of the first Tibetan masters to teach in the West.

1928–1990 **Dainin Katagiri** (Japan, USA) was head of the Minnesota Zen Meditation Center.

1926 – Present **Thich Nhat Hanh** (Vietnam, France) coined the term "Engaged Buddhism" in his book *Vietnam: Lotus in a Sea of Fire*.

1936 – Present **Pema Chodron** (Canada) is a Buddhist nun. The goal of her teaching is the application of Buddhism to everyday life.

20th Century Mystics—Worldwide
Physics and Mysticism

1879–1955 **Albert Einstein** (Germany, USA) was a deist with a Spinozian concept of God. He said space and time are not absolute but relative. *"The most beautiful and profound emotion we can experience is the mystical."* He was a profound mystic of the intellectual, or jnana yoga, type.

1858–1947 **Max Planck** (Germany) God is an almighty, all-knowing, benevolent God that permeated everything, including physical laws.

1939 – Present **Fritjof Capra** (Austria, USA) wrote *The Tao of Physics*, subtitled *An Exploration of the Parallels Between Modern Physics and Eastern Mysticism*. Physics and mysticism are leading us to the knowledge of reality.

1942 – Present **Stephen Hawking** is a deist whose works show that Einstein's General Theory of Relativity implies space and time have a beginning in the Big Bang and an ending in black holes. The universe has no edge or boundary in imaginary time.

1953–1992 **Michael Coleman Talbot** was the author of several books on the parallels between mysticism and quantum mechanics. He said the physical universe is like a huge hologram.

20th Century English and Irish Mystics

1865–1939 **William Butler Yeats** (Ireland), a poet and dramatist, was awarded the Nobel Prize in Literature for "his always inspired poetry, which in a highly artistic form gives expression to the spirit of a whole nation."

1888–1957 **Ronald Knox** was a theologian, mystery writer, and student of mysticism.

1894–1963 **Aldous Huxley** (England, USA), a true mystic, was the author of *The Perennial Philosophy* and *The Doors of Perception*. He died the same day as John F. Kennedy.

1895–1986 **Wei Wu Wei** (Terence Gray) (England) was a Taoist philosopher and writer with a tremendous influence on mystics.

1896–1985 **Sir Alister Hardy** was a professor at Oxford and a researcher on mysticism. His work continues to this day at the University of Wales.

1898–1963 **C.S. Lewis** was a Christian author and scholar who wrote *The Chronicles of Narnia*. He was a traditional Christian and a mythologist.

1905–1983 **Arthur Koestler** was a journalist, novelist, and social philosopher. Along with Aldous Huxley, he was among the first to experiment with LSD. He wrote about Japanese and Indian mysticism in *The Lotus and the Robot*.

20th Century Mystics—Worldwide

1869–1937 **Rudolf Otto** (Germany) was a professor of theology who researched mysticism.

1874–1917 **Oswald Chambers** (Scotland) was a minister, author, and teacher.

1881–1955 **Pierre Teilhard de Chardin** (France) was a French Jesuit paleontologist who taught spiritual evolution. His writings were condemned by the Catholic Church.

1883–1931 **Kahlil Gibran** (Lebanon) was an artist, poet, and writer best known as the author of *The Prophet*.

1887–1927 **Hazrat Inayat Khan** (India) was born into one of the most musical families in India. Hazrat became immersed in spirituality and adopted the Sufi path, and eventually became head of the International Sufi movement.

1900–1944 **Antoine de Saint-Exupery** (France) is the author of *The Little Prince*.

1900–1990 **Nishitani Keiji** (Japan) said the standpoint of emptiness heals the division in human consciousness.

1903–1981 **Sayyid Muhammad Husain Tabatabai** (Iran) was a Muslim philosopher who said realism is the acceptance of the reality of existence.

1903–1993 **Hans Jonas** (Germany, USA) I was fortunate to be one of Hans Jonas' students. He enjoyed having students over to his house for discussions. He wrote extensively on Gnosticism and is best known for his book *The Imperative of Responsibility*.

1909–1943 **Simone Weil** (France) was a French philosopher, social activist, and mystic. She had a profound mystical experience in 1937 while visiting Assisi in Italy. She was also strongly influenced by the Upanishads and Buddhism.

1910–1997 **Mother Theresa** (Macedonia) was a Catholic Nun and founder of the Missionaries of Charity.

1924–1996 **Idries Shah** (India) was an author in the Sufi tradition on works ranging from psychology and spirituality to travelogues and culture studies.

1929–2003 **Dorothy Solle** (Germany) was a socially-engaged German theologian and writer.

1931–1987 **Anthony de Mello** (India), a Jesuit priest and psychotherapist, is well-known for his books on spirituality.

20th Century Mystics in the United States

1904–1984 **Joseph Campbell** (USA) was a mythologist, professor, writer, and orator best known for his work in the fields of comparative mythology and comparative religion. He was a consultant on the *Star Wars* movies.

1907–1986 **Mircea Eliade** (Romania, USA) was a historian of religion, fiction writer, philosopher, professor at the University of Chicago, and a leading interpreter of mysticism. He saw patterns in different religious experiences. His most influential contribution is his theory of "Eternal Return," one of the most widely accepted ways of understanding the purpose of myth and ritual.

1915–1968 **Thomas Merton** (France, USA) was a Trappist monk of the Abbey of Our Lady of Gethsemane in Kentucky, an acclaimed Catholic spiritual writer, poet, author, and social activist. He was a proponent of inter-religious dialogue and engaged in dialogues with the Dalai Lama, Tich Nhat Hanh, and D.T. Suzuki. His life was cut short when he was electrocuted by a fan while stepping out of his bath on Christmas Day, 1968.

1915–1973 **Alan Watts** (England, USA) was an author and interpreter of Eastern philosophy, mostly Zen Buddhism.

1921–2004 **Wallace Black Elk** was a Native American visionary and the author of *The Sacred Way of the Lakota*.

1925–1991 **Carlos Castaneda** (Brazil, USA) wrote twelve books on the teaching of Don Juan, a Mexican Shaman.

1928–1997 **Robert Adams** was author of *The Silence of the Heart*.

1929–1968 **Martin Luther King, Jr.** was a leader of the American Civil Rights movement, a political activist, and Baptist minister, regarded as a great orator.

1945–2004 **Wayne Teasdale** (USA) was a mystic, monk, teacher, author of books on mysticism, and an advocate of a better understanding between the world's various religions.

Contemporary Hindus, Gurus, and Mystics 1919 – Present

1897–1981 **Ramesh Belsekar** was a student of Maharaja Nisargadatta. Consciousness is all there is.

1920 – Present **Vimala Thakar** teaches balancing inner spiritual development with outward social development.

1926 – Present **Sathya Sai Baba** is a guru, Vedantin, and spiritual leader, known for manifesting of vibhuti (sacred ash).

Contemporary Teachers in the U.S.

1912 – Present **Rabbi Joseph Gelberman** (Hungary, USA) has been for me a "spiritual father." We founded Interfaith Inc. in New York City in 1977 and the New Seminary in 1981.

1919 – Present **Houston Smith** is one of the most outstanding religious studies scholars today. His book *The World's Religions* is a classic.

1923 – Present **Ft. Thomas Keating** is a Cistercian monk and priest and founder of the Centering Prayer Movement.

1931 – Present **John Shelby Spong**, a retired bishop of the Episcopal Diocese of Newark, is a liberal theologian, biblical scholar, religion commentator, and author.

1931 – Present **Bernadette Roberts**, a former nun, is now a post-Christian mystic and author.

1931 – Present **Michael Harner, Ph.D.** is an anthropologist and former colleague. Roger Walsh, once said, "What Yogananda did for Hinduism and D.T. Suzuki did for Zen, Michael Harner has done for shamanism."

1931 – Present **Stanislav Grof** is one of the founders of transpersonal psychology. He did some of the earliest studies on LSD.

1931 – Present **Ram Dass** is a former Harvard Professor who explores psychedelics and Eastern thought.

1937 – Present **Jean Houston, Ph.D.** is a leading figure in the cross-cultural study of spirituality and ritual processes. Influenced by Margaret Mead and Pierre Teilhard de Chardin, she is an author of many books and one of the founders of the Human Potential Movement.

1940 – Present **Dr. Wayne W. Dyer** is a popular American self-help advocate, author, and lecturer.

1942 – Present **Dr. Ken Wapnick** is a prolific author, lecturer, and teacher of *A Course in Miracles*.

1942 – Present **Gangaji** (USA) is a disciple of H.W.L. Poonja (Papaji) dedicated to sharing the mystic path through direct self-inquiry.

1942 – Present **Byron Katie** is an author and teacher. Her works include *I Need Your Love: Is That True?* and *Loving What Is*.

1943 – Present **Neale Donald Walsch** is the author of the series *Conversations with God*.

1944 – Present **A.H. Almaas, Ph.D.** (Kuwait, USA), has developed the Diamond Approach to wisdom. His doctorate is in Reichian Therapy.

1944 – Present **John Davidson** (England) is a scholar at Oxford.

1945 – Present **Jack Kornfield** is an author, Buddhist monk, and co-founder of the Insight Meditation Society. He is the author of *After the Ecstasy, the Laundry*.

1945 – Present **David Spangler** is an author, spiritual philosopher, and a practical mystic. He was instrumental in helping establish Findhorn in northern Scotland.

1949 – Present **Ken Wilbur** is a highly respected author, mystic, American Buddhist, and philosopher.

1948 – Present **Eckhart Tolle** (Germany, Canada) is a contemporary spiritual teacher and author of the best-selling *The Power of Now* and *The New Earth*.

1950 – Present **Lama Surya Das** (USA) is a Lama in the Tibetan Buddhist tradition. He is a respected teacher and spokesperson for Buddhism in the West.

1952 – Present **Marianne Williamson** (USA) is an activist, author, lecturer, founder of the Peace Alliance, teacher of *A Course in Miracles*, and friend.

1952 – Present **Andrew Harvey** (USA) is a poet, author, teacher, and mystic. He sees true spirituality as the divinization of earthly life through spiritual practice.

1952 – Present **Don Miguel Ruiz** (Mexico) was born into a family of healers. His mother was a *curandera* (healer) and his grandfather a *nagual* (shaman). A medical doctor, Ruiz wrote the popular *The Four Agreements*.

1953 – Present **Alex Grey** is an artist specializing in visionary "psychedelic" art.

1955 – Present **Andrew Cohen** (USA) is an American guru who has developed a path of spiritual transformation he calls Evolutionary Enlightenment. He is the publisher of the *What is Enlightenment?* magazine.

The Future of Mysticism and Religion

A survey of the history of philosophy and religion shows that Spirit always seeks freedom and release from tyranny. Laws, dogmas, and creeds made binding block truth. Truth remains constant. What is true becomes clear, as that which is false is seen for what it is. Mystics in each generation seek the truth. They do not seek to force their vision onto others. The path back to God is highly individualized. We all come to God in our own way, in our own time. The study of mysticism and the application of mystical principles bring us closer to that truth and thus to freedom, and where there is freedom there is love—the only thing that is real. At the end of St. John of the Cross' work, he says, "The map ends here." From here on, we have the infinite. We head into the unknown, into silence and a place where there are no words. Beyond self consciousness there is a knowing that transcends this world. Total open mindedness is the way forward. We come at last to nothing and tumble into God.

I've enjoyed this adventure with words. I've learned a lot, and I pray you have as well. Your comments, additions or further simplification is appreciated. Perhaps someday we will meet, look each other in the eye, and smile. If you're ever at a lecture/workshop, please come up and say, "Hi!" I publish a small magazine called Miracles.

Please see: www.miraclesmagazine.org or

jon@miraclesmagazine.org

Love Always and Always Love,

Jon

Bibliography

Foundation for Inner Peace. *A Course in Miracles*. CA: Foundation for Inner Peace, 1975, 1992, 2007.

Abhayananda, S. *History of Mysticism The Unchanging Testament*. Naples, FL: Atma Books, 1987.

Almas, A.H. *Essence With the Elixir of Enlightenment*. York Beach, ME: Samuel Weiser, Inc., 1998.

Lyon, William S. and Wallace, Black Elk. *Black Elk: The Sacred Way of the Lakota*. New York: Harper Collins Publishers, 1991.

Borchert, Bruno. *Mysticism: It's History and Challenge*, York Beach, ME: Samuel Weiser, 1994.

Carmody, Denise Lardner and John Tully Carmody. *Mysticism Holiness East and West*. Oxford University Press, 1996.

Davidson, John. *The Gospel of Jesus: In Search of His Original Teachings*. UK: Element Books, Ltd., 1995.

Eliade, M. "Mysticism." *The Encyclopedia of Religion*. Vol. 10, 245–61. New York: Macmillan, 1987.

Ferguson, John. *An Illustrated Encyclopedia of Mysticism and the Mystery Religions*. New York: Continuum Books, 1977.

Gangaji. *The Diamond in your Pocket: Discovering Your True Radiance*. Boulder, CO: Sounds True, Inc., 2005

Golas, Thaddeus. *The Lazy Man's Guide to Enlightenment*. Redway, CA: Seed Center, 1971, 1972.

Hart, William. *Vipassana Meditation: As Taught by S.N. Goenka*. New York: HarperCollins Publishers, 1987.

Harvey, Andrew. *The Essential Mystics: The Soul's Journey into Truth*. Edison, NJ: BookSales, Inc., 1998.

Isherwood, Christopher. *Ramakrishna and His Disciples*. Hollywood, CA: Vedanta Press, 1980.

James, William. *Varieties of Religious Experience*. Cambridge, MA: Harvard University Press, 1987.

Jung, Carl. *Collected Works*. Princeton, NJ: Princeton University Press, 1979.

Katz, S.T. *Mysticism and Philosophy*. Oxford University Press, 1978.

Kornfield, Jack. *After the Ecstasy, the Laundry: How the Heart Grows Wise on the Spiritual Path*. New York: Bantam Books, 2000.

Livergood, Norman D. *The Perennial Tradition*. Tempe, AZ: Dandelion Books, 2003.

________. *Portals to Higher Consciousness*. Tempe, AZ: Dandelion Books, 2006

Maharshi, R. *The Spiritual Teachings of Ramana Maharaja*. Boston: Shambala Press, 2004.

Maslow, Abraham. *Religion, Values and Peak Experiences*. New York: Penguin Books, 1994.

Merton, Thomas. *The Seven Storey Mountain*. New York: Harvest Books, 1948.

Mc Greal, Ian P. *Great Thinkers of the Eastern World*. New York: HarperResource, 1995

________. *Great Thinkers of the Western World*. New York: Collins, 1992.

Monroe, R.. *Journeys Out of the Body*. New York: Main Street Books, 1992.

Mundy, Jon. *Missouri Mystic*. Unionville, NY: Royal Fireworks, 2004.

Roberts, Bernadette. *The Path to No-Self*. Albany, NY: State University of New York Press, 1991.

Sanford, John A. *Dreams: God's Forgotten Language*. San Francisco: HarperSF, 1989.

Saint Theresa de Avila (translated by Kieran Kavanaugh and Otilio Rodriquez). *Collected Works*. Washington D.C.: Institute of Carmelite Studies, 1976.

Soelle, Dorothy. *The Silent Cry: Mysticism and Resistance*. Minneapolis, MN: Fortress Press, 1997.

Solomon, Robert C and Higgins, Kathleen. *A Short History of Philosophy*. Oxford University Press, 1996.

Suzuki, D.T. *The Zen Doctrine of No-Mind*. York Beach, ME: Weiser Books, 1991.

Talbot, Michael. *Mysticism and the New Physics*. New York: Penguin Books, 1981.

Thoreau, Henry David. *Walden*. Boston: Ticknor and Fields, 1854 (original publication date).

_______, *Letters to a Spiritual Seeker*. New York: W.W. Norton & Co., 2004.

Tolle, Eckhart. *The New Earth: Awakening Your Life's Purpose*. New York: Penguin Group, Inc., 2005.

______. *The Power of Now: A Guide to Spiritual Enlightenment*. Vancouver, Canada: Namaste Publishing, 1997.

Ullman, Robert & Judyth Reichenberg-Ullman. *Mystics, Masters, Saints and Sages: Stories of Enlightenment*. Berkeley, CA: Conari Press, 2001.

Underhill, Evelyn. *Mysticism: A Study in Nature and Development of Spiritual Consciousness*. (Public Domain) 1911, 1921 and 1955.

Vahle, Neal. *Open at the Top: The Life of Ernest Holmes*. Mill Valley, CA: Open View Press, 1993

_______. *The Unity Movement*. Philadelphia: Templeton Foundation Press, 2002

Wapnick, Ken. *Love Does Not Condemn: The World, the Flesh, and the Devil According to Platonism, Christianity, Gnosticism, and 'A Course in Miracles'*. The Foundation for "A Course in Miracles," 1989.

White, John. *What is Enlightenment?: Exploring the Goal of the Spiritual Path*. St. Paul, MN: Paragon House Publishers, 1995.

Wilbur, Ken. *Kosmic Consciousness* (CD). Boulder, CO: Sounds True, 2003

Wood. R. *Understanding Mysticism*. New York: Continuum International Publishing Group, 1981.

Zachner, R.C. *Mysticism Sacred and Profane*. Oxford University Press, 1961.